T0185692

Lecture Notes in Computer Science   10025

Commenced Publication in 1973
Founding and Former Series Editors:
Gerhard Goos, Juris Hartmanis, and Jan van Leeuwen

Sander Münster · Mieke Pfarr-Harfst
Piotr Kuroczyński · Marinos Ioannides (Eds.)

3D Research Challenges in Cultural Heritage II

How to Manage Data and Knowledge
Related to Interpretative Digital 3D Reconstructions
of Cultural Heritage

Springer

Editors
Sander Münster
TU Dresden
Dresden
Germany

Mieke Pfarr-Harfst
TU Darmstadt
Darmstadt
Germany

Piotr Kuroczyński
Herder Institute for Historical Research on
    East Central Europe
Marburg
Germany

Marinos Ioannides
Cyprus University of Technology
Limassol
Cyprus

Cover illustration: The illustration appearing on the cover of this book is the work of Sander Münster. Used with permission.

ISSN 0302-9743   ISSN 1611-3349   (electronic)
Lecture Notes in Computer Science
ISBN 978-3-319-47646-9   ISBN 978-3-319-47647-6   (eBook)
DOI 10.1007/978-3-319-47647-6

Library of Congress Control Number: 2016953629

LNCS Sublibrary: SL3 – Information Systems and Applications, incl. Internet/Web, and HCI

Printed on acid-free paper

This Springer imprint is published by Springer Nature
The registered company is Springer International Publishing AG
The registered company address is: Gewerbestrasse 11, 6330 Cham, Switzerland

Preface

Interpretative digital 3D reconstructions have been extensively used in the context of cultural heritage for almost 30 years especially for rebuilding not physically extant historic artifacts (no longer extant, altered, or never existent). While 3D reconstructions were used and seen as digital substitutes for analog research and presentation methods such as drawings and physical models in the beginning, over the years a unique epistemology of digital 3D reconstruction has evolved. This process is highly driven by the opportunity of digital modelling to support research beyond reconstruction and visualization: by supporting an evaluation of historic sources and their correspondence, a detection of geometric principles in a historic creational process, or the classification and systematization of historic objects with respect to dependencies, similarities, or singularities. Even suppositious objects, like idealistic buildings, based on architectural rules are created using 3D construction technologies. Moreover, digital 3D reconstructions are created within socio technical systems employing various sources of knowledge and created by cross-disciplinary work teams. This raises questions about procedures and strategies for accessing, exchanging, and archiving digital assets along with the underlying knowledge base. Such knowledge has to be defined widely, and deals with query, compilation, harmonization, and contention related to information sources and resulting genetics.

There is a large amount of literature on 3D reconstruction and digital heritage as well as many elaborated concepts for digital libraries and platforms for cultural heritage such as Europeana, DARIAH, and the UNESCO Memory of the World. Closely related are intense research and development efforts for technical tools as well as several methodological questions about procedures and strategies for data management and processing as well as for the organization and representation of related knowledge. But there is a gap between theory and practice: On the one hand many highly elaborated theoretical approaches, principles, and guidelines as well as data schemes and infrastructures are proposed to foster the quality, compatibility, and sustainability of 3D cultural heritage objects. On the other hand, in practice 3D reconstruction projects are often based on unique, and prototypic semantics, workflows, and infrastructures, and are customized for a specific purpose.

A previous volume has focused on insights into ongoing research and future directions in the field of digital heritage preservation; the aim of this volume entitled *How to Manage Data and Knowledge Related to an Interpretative Digital Reconstruction of Cultural Heritage* is to reflect the current state of the art and future perspectives of digital heritage focusing on non-interpretative reconstruction and including and bridging practical and theoretical perspectives, strategies, and approaches. Moreover, comprehensive key challenges are related to knowledge and data handling within a digital reconstruction of not physically extant cultural heritage including aspects of digital object creation, sustainability, accessibility, documentation, presentation, and more general scientific compatibility. A workshop on these topics was organized by the editors of this volume at the International Conference on Cultural Heritage 2014 in Cyprus. Based on the outcomes from this workshop, as well as additionally invited contributions, this volume covers: (a) basic concepts and the current state of the art, (b) grounded strategies, practices, and principles, as well as (c) innovative approaches, concepts, and technologies for data and knowledge management in digital heritage. Overall, the three parts of the book reflect the following challenges.

The first challenge is to gain an overview of the scope of usage scenarios, the current state of infrastructures such as digital libraries, information repositories for an inter-pretative reconstruction of cultural heritage as well as basic concepts and workflows of 3D reconstruction. Moreover, various large-scale cultural phenomena, such as general technology acceptance as well as open data and science, influence the use of digital technology in the context of cultural heritage. Despite various high-ranking publica-tions and charters proposing guidelines and standards as well as many infrastructures and platforms dedicated to 3D reconstruction, there is a low level of acceptance and practical implementation of these extant approaches within a majority of 3D recon-struction projects. Moreover, for these projects there is little information on daily practices and strategies for knowledge and data object management, especially when they are based more on pragmatic decisions and needs and less on academically val-idated input.

The second challenge is to highlight strategies, practices, and principles currently used to ensure the compatibility, reusability, and sustainability of data objects and related knowledge within 3D reconstruction work processes on a day-to-day work basis. A special concern is to obey the variety of data, modelling approaches (i.e., BIM, GIS, VR, CAD), purposes, and output qualities. Cross-disciplinary teamwork brings with it the knowledge of many authors, various sources of information as, well as a high level of tacit knowledge. This causes non-transparency of genetics, which is in contrast to negotiability as an important prerequisite of academic culture. Last but not least, no silver bullet exists on where and how to publish resultant data.

As an overall consequence, challenges for the development of cooperative infras-tructures go beyond the technical development of libraries and platforms as well as joint standards, schemes, or guidelines and include corresponding human- and purpose-related aspects, too. A third challenge is to develop innovative concepts for the exchange, publishing, and management of 3D objects and for inherit knowledge about data, workflows, and semantic structures. This includes not only solutions for data acquisition and modelling but also an information enrichment and documentation including paradata and the exchange, archiving, and managing of 3D models. More-over, the scope covers approaches for visualization and information systems to link 3D objects to other forms of information and make them traceable and accessible on a multimedia level.

We would like to acknowledge the important work done by the reviewers during the double-blind peer review of all the chapters. Moreover, we are very thankful to our editors for their important work on standardizing and enhancing language quality. Last but not least, we would like to thank Claudia Merkle for her support in preparing the final manuscript.

We dedicate this book to the memory of our colleague, good friend and pioneer Dr. Ewald Quak from the Institute of Cybernetics, Tallinn University of Technology, Estonia, who passed away suddenly last year. Ewald was the visioner of this unique series of publication in 2014 and the co-author of the first Volume published by Springer Verlag in 2015.

September 2016

Sander Münster
Mieke Pfarr-Harfst
Piotr Kuroczynski
Marinos Ioannides

Contents

Basic Concepts and a Current State for Data and Knowledge Management for an Interpretative Reconstruction of Cultural Heritage

A Model Classification for Digital 3D Reconstruction in the Context of Humanities Research

Sander Münster[⊠], Wolfgang Hegel, and Cindy Kröber

Media Center, Technische Universität Dresden, 01062 Dresden, Germany
{sander.muenster,cindy.kroeber}@tu-dresden.de,
wolfgang.hegel@uni-wuerzburg.de

Abstract. Digital 3D reconstruction methods have been widely applied to support research and the presentation of historical objects since the 1990s. While technological backgrounds, project opportunities as well as methodological considerations for application are widely discussed in literature, a comprehensive, model classification for digital 3D reconstruction is still lacking. Against this background, this article aims to discuss common approaches to classification of scholarly work. The identification of specific issues and challenges in the context of humanities research is also discussed. A prototype classification scheme for digital reconstruction in humanities research is proposed. It has been applied to and tested in two case studies.

Keywords: Cultural heritage · Information management · Classification model · Digital reconstruction

1 Introduction

According to Merriam-Webster's dictionary, classification is a "systematic arrangement in groups or categories according to established criteria".[1] Classification aims at the creation of a taxonomy as a classification scheme for a certain branch or aspect of information [1]. An ontology combines a taxonomy, as a classification scheme, with the underlying principles of classification. Thereby, an ontology assorts individual items into a specific scheme according to defined rules. What is the purpose of a classification of scholarly work? A classification of scientific activity supports the definition of and distinction between certain scholarly areas and communities. It forms the base for the identification of core objects. For these reasons it is an important prerequisite to head for further research-related tasks, such as the definition of best practice examples; an implementation within academic curricula; the shaping of the scope of conference programs; and to investigate funding and management responsibilities as well as cooperation networks [2]. The main research question here is "in the context of humanities research, how should applications of digital 3D reconstruction methods be structured and classified?".

---

[1] http://www.merriam-webster.com/dictionary/classification. Accessed 31 May 2015.

© Springer International Publishing AG 2016
S. Münster et al. (Eds.): 3D Research Challenges II, LNCS 10025, pp. 3–31, 2016.
DOI: 10.1007/978-3-319-47647-6_1

This chapter focuses on the following:

1. A discussion of common classification approaches to scholarly work;
2. The identification and discussion of specific issues and challenges of humanities research;
3. The concept of a prototype classification scheme for digital reconstruction in the humanities, and
4. its evaluation through applications to selected digital reconstruction projects.

The research methodology is based on the investigation of 2,584 journal articles and conference papers concerning 3D reconstruction of historic objects, employing deductive and inductive methods of content analysis [3] and bibliometrics [4, 5]. Additional outcomes of this investigation include an overview of the scholarly community and related topics [2] as well as characteristics of a typical project [6]. In order to examine project practices and their evolution, a qualitative content analysis of further 26 international publications, concerning digital reconstruction of lost objects, has been carried out. While such publications provide records of past projects, follow up research into four case studies was conducted. It explored 3D reconstruction projects over time in order to examine aspects of visual communication. Moreover, it investigates the evolution of the previously mentioned aspects during a project creation process [7] and led to suggestions for a design of virtual libraries and platforms [8]. A mixed-method approach, including heuristic frameworks and Grounded Theory [9], borrowed from social sciences, served as a paradigm for evaluation. The insights gained are based on theories from organizational and management studies, communication and perception studies, and information science [6].

2 Approaches to the Classification of Scholarly Research

The following section presents general approaches to classification of scholarly work that may support the development of a classification scheme specific to digital 3D reconstruction. Current approaches typically rely on (1) a traditional classification by disciplines that originate in ancient Greece (2) a historiography of a particular school of thought and its transitions, and (3) the scientometrical approach that relies on publication metrics and other measurable indicators.

2.1 Categorization by Academic Disciplines

To categorize generally means "to put (someone or something) into a group of similar people or things".[2] While the already mentioned definition of classification emphasizes a need for criteria, categorization in general does not necessarily rely on a transparent set of criteria, but often on subjective preferences or knowledge. As a consequence,

---

[2] http://www.merriam-webster.com/dictionary/categorize. Accessed 21 Nov 2015.

categorization outcomes can differ greatly between scholars as a number of approaches and categorization schemes can be developed for the same subject.[3]

Classification of scholarly work by discipline or field of inquiry is among most common [c.f. 11]. These are characterized by common methods and theories and have "a particular object of research, [...] [a joint] body of accumulated specialist knowledge, [...] specific terminologies" and "must have some institutional manifestation reference systems, disciplinary ways of thinking, quality criteria, publication habits and bodies" [11, p. 9]. Knorr-Cetina believes that each discipline has its own "epistemic culture" in the sense of different "architectures of empirical approaches, specific constructions of the referent, particular ontologies of instruments, and different social machines" [12, p. 3].

Although disciplines and their boundaries result from social construction processes [13], a number of phenotypic fields can be identified [14]. A basic classification scheme employs the distinction between humanities and science. While humanities – according to Dilthey – try to understand their research object, science aims at its explanation [15]. In a more elaborate classification, the Organisation for Economic Co-operation and Development (OECD) distinguishes between six scientific fields containing about 40 disciplines [16, 17]. Bibliographic classification schemes offer especially sophisticated ways of distinguishing between academic disciplines [18].

2.2 Historiographical Approach

The standard historiographical method is inductive: it looks at the available historic sources, evaluates their reliability, and identifies turning points at which decisive changes to a certain structure can be identified and distinguished from evolutionary processes [c.f. 11, p. 31].

A historiographical approach to academic or scholarly disciplines, on the one hand requires locating the earliest record of a scientific field and identifying periods of continuity, and the development of new branches that eventually emerged into a new separate field, on the other. A field may also disappear or be absorbed by other disciplines. The aim of historiography is therefore to identify the essential disciplinary developments of methods and subjects, and to establish reasons for migration and transgression from one field to another [c.f. 19].

2.3 Scientometrics

Unlike well-established approaches to discrete disciplines the scientometric method is more recent. It was introduced in the 1960 s [20]. A basic approach is to classify scientific work on structural and quantified levels through indicators, for example as patent numbers, project cooperation partners, or co-authorship relationships [c.f. 4, 21].

---

[3] Relevant approaches and principles have been defined by Information Science, see [10].

Beyond the measurement of scientific performance and transition on a macro level – as intended for example by the German Research Council [22] – a data-driven research on scientific structures often focuses on a detection of emerging disciplines on a structural level [23] as well as the investigation and quantification of large-scale phenomena, as for example interdisciplinary cooperation [24].

While a distinction between disciplines relies on a deductive classification scheme, both historiographical and scientometric approaches propose an inductive procedure for a mapping of scholarly community structures and work. A major difference between these latter approaches is their focus either on singularities or aggregated evidence. All three approaches may be of relevance to research discussed here: a distinction between epistemic cultures may support a determination of a scholarly field as well as related research objects, interests and methodological requirements. Both inductive approaches may support the development of a categorization scheme and the identification of relevant aspects.

What are the implications of these three common classification principles for the present discussion? The development of distinguishable categories and variables, similar to the disciplinary distinctions, promises better results in terms of ease of application and comparability of results. Nominal-scaled variables such as "disciplines" – within measurement theory – have limited capabilities for evaluation. In contrast, ordinal- or metric-scaled variables allow further statistical operations to investigate transitions within a field of research, e.g. to evaluate a distribution of reconstructed objects by their locality or date of origin, or of reconstructions by related level of detail (LOD) [c.f. 25, 26]. Both scientometric and historiographical approaches are useful for identifying categories, as well as relevant variables and their values or types.

3   Field of Research

After presenting general approaches to classifying academic research, a definition and mapping of research employing digital 3D reconstruction will be attempted. Such methods have been used in cultural heritage research and presentation in the 1990s and 2000s. In a reconstruction workflow, the main focus of reconstruction projects is on the creation of a virtual 3D model. According to Francesco et al., qualities of 3D models can include [27, p. 231]:

- Geometrical model: acquisition of all dimensions using sensing technologies;
- Manual model: revision of plan/drawing in 2D to obtain 3D without direct measurements;
- Hybrid model: combination of plan in 2D with 3D through measurements by means of an instrument;
- Reconstructed model: reconstruction entirely without measurements.

While the first three approaches describe digitization, the fourth approach focuses on virtual 3D reconstruction. A resulting definition may be:

Digital 3D reconstruction is the creation of a virtual model of historic entities that requires an object-related, human interpretation.[4]

Digital reconstruction does not refer to a specific type of project or object, but denominates a particular technique [7]. It is worth defining and determining what field of research this method of enquiry represents. Digital 3D reconstruction is a method of eHumanities or Digital Humanities, i.e. it makes use of Information Technology (IT) to facilitate humanities research.[5] Research objects derive from material cultural heritage, seen here as a meta-discipline, and raise a number of research questions of interest to Archaeology and the Art History.

3.1 Cultural Heritage

As a meta-discipline, Cultural Heritage Studies involve different sciences and non-scientific disciplines. Research questions derive from the humanities, as well as science and economics. Cultural heritage, being tangible or intangible, invites different approaches.[6]

The European Network of Excellence in Open Cultural Heritage (EPOCH), active between 2004–2008, elaborated an extensive classification of digital cultural heritage. Relying on large-scale pan-European collaboration, the state of the art, the potential for research and development, as well as future research were identified [30]. The outcomes of the EPOCH investigations impacted on European funding programs such as the Framework Programme 7 and Horizon 2020 [31]. Ultimately, the minimization of costs and a good usability are the main objectives.

3.2 Archaeology

Archaeology investigates tangible remains and evidence of human cultures [32, p. XI] in order to generate a realistic representation of what exists now and to closely approximate what may have once been [33]. Often, the physical preservation of the objects is not intended. Thorough documentation and data collection are therefore crucial. Surveying techniques, especially laser scanning [34–36] and image processing [37, 38] as well as photographs and plans are used to record excavations in detail and provide sufficient data for 3D reconstruction of the objects found. Their 3D models support preservation, reconstruction, documentation, research and dissemination of

---

[4] Object-relation stands in contrast to process-related human interpretation which is required, e.g. for algorithm development in context of data-driven acquisition.

[5] A distinction between Digital Humanities and eHumanities is complex. A usual definition determines e(nhanced)Humanities as cooperation between information technologies and Humanities to investigate research questions in the Humanities (c.f. http://www.bmbf.de/foerderungen/21126.php. Accessed 10 Jun 2015) while Digital Humanities means a hybrid discipline, combining computing and humanities methods and approaches [28].

[6] On difficulties concerning the classification and transdisciplinary digital heritage as an 'Agora', which are also relevant to Cultural Heritage, see [29].

cultural heritage [39]. The presentation of research findings and visualization-based reconstructions, some intended for museum education, are closely related to archaeology [40].

3.3 Art History

Art History mainly studies works of art that are part of cultural heritage from the late antiquity to modern age.[7] While these objects themselves are tangible, the Art History is also concerned with tangible and intangible aspects of the work that offer insights into its origin and meaning.[8] This brings in various interdisciplinary connections and - in context of 3D reconstruction - chronological overlaps with objects of Archaeology.

The availability of what is considered a research object played an essential role in defining the Art History as an academic field and establishing its research methods. The development of photography in particular enabled the creation of large, structured collections of print reproductions and gave way to the possibility of comparing images of works in different locations. Methods for investigating genetic and morphologic connections are covered by analyzing style (style critique) and form (formal analysis).[9] Another important range of methods is concerned with the meaning of the works of art (iconography) and systems of meaning (iconology).[10]

Architectural history is particularly relevant to the current study. It is divided into different subfields. Some of the subfields are primarily concerned with the symbolism of visible forms; other mainly study the physical objects and their appearances.

Alongside the study of connections and relationships between certain groups of architectural objects, architectural history involves research into single buildings, based on archeological findings as well as the examination of secondary sources. Models are used for documentation purposes and/or testing the plausibility of historical reconstruction, as well as out of the mere interest of reconstructing lost structures. Making the phases in the construction history, that have not survived, visible again seems to be a way of retrieving them from cultural oblivion.

While two-dimensional digital media have led to new methods and approaches to research and presentation, and remain common, the success of three-dimensional media has been limited. Physical models as research tools have a number of drawbacks in terms of usability and dissemination.

4 Challenges of Scholarly Digital Reconstruction

Gooding's general model concerning the influence of visuals [48] as well as his concept of "professional vision" [49] demonstrate the role of pictures and visualizations in research processes. So far, there is a lack of an academic culture as well related to

---

[7] On the history of the discipline, see [41–44].

[8] On the art term, see [45].

[9] On the critique of style, see [46, pp. 20–32]. On the term style, see [47].

[10] On the methods of iconography and iconology, see [46, pp. 33–49].

visual humanities research. This concerns questions concerning access to and assessment of models, the transparency of authorship, and the connection between the reconstruction process and results as well as its sources. This relates to the question of citation of models and visualization, and their modification by others.

4.1 Model

Three-dimensional digital reconstruction is a representation or translation of either a material cultural object or an intangible cultural phenomenon, into a virtual model. An established explanatory scheme of models is the general model theory. In this context, a model represents a simplified or reduced version of an original. An element of pragmatism denominates a subjective as well as purpose oriented nature of a model [50, p. 131]:

- Feature of reproduction: models represent the originals that come from the world of imagination, from expressions, as well as from physical objects and symbols.
- Feature of reduction: models usually do not include all features of the original but only those considered relevant by the creator or user.
- Feature of pragmatism: models function as a surrogate of the original subjects within a certain time span, for a certain purpose (transactions).[11]

In a general classification according to the time of creation, 3D reconstruction models are "post factum models" [51, p. 335]. Unlike architectural drafts, which are created a priori, these models are created subsequently to the original.

4.1.1 Virtual vs. Physical Models
Unlike virtual 3D reconstruction models, which have been executed since the advent of computer graphics in the 1980s,[12] physical 3D models have been proven useful for representation and communication purposes for centuries [52]. They have proven to be valuable research instruments for conveying knowledge about building history and other architectural information [53]. Although both physical and virtual models share some similar features and scholarly requirements of historical reconstruction, their creation is very different. The technical process of constructing physical model affords separate qualities and functions of the knowledge process [54]. The construction of a physical model results in an artifact whose qualities are similar to a sculpture [52]. Hence, it is more than an intermediate phase in the creation of a thematic, computer-generated visualization.

4.1.2 Intangible Cultural Heritage
Cultural heritage includes tangible and intangible assets alike and aims to safeguard them [55]. Intangible assets are various methods used for artistic expression: music, dance, theater, games, language, story, literature, human behavior, handicrafts, concepts

---

[11] Cited according to [50, pp. 131].

[12] For example: http://3dvisa.cch.kcl.ac.uk/project12.html. Accessed 26 May 2016.

such as architectural style that is only hypothetical. The suitability of 3D reconstruction for preservation and presentation of intangible assets has been a subject of topical research within the community of visualization practice. Different approaches representing cultural activities of the past are carried out by designing avatars of historical characters through motion capture of human actors [56] or a reconstruction based on graph cuts [57] to create dynamic 3D models.

4.1.3   The Role of Models in a Scholarly Reconstruction Process

Models may serve a cognitive process by representing and communicating knowledge [58] as well as a method for "generating [new] knowledge" [59]. Virtual 3D reconstruction models are considered a research and presentation tools. In this context the term "model" has several connotations. Researchers of a historic object conceive various mental models as ideas of the original [c.f. 60]. These notions may be subjective and related to individual experiences. Therefore, the resulting virtual reconstruction 3D model may combine varied individual knowledge.

4.1.4   The Model as an Object

In addition to referencing the original object, its computer model and the knowledge it represents become an item and object of social interaction. This refers to the development of a scholarly discourse related to functions and autonomy of models in science. Kuhn states that models provide analogies to physical or non-physical objects for a certain group of individuals with similar cultural disposition [61]. On the one hand scholarly models rely on individual knowledge, on the other hand, preferences for models may be characterised by disciplinary traditions [62]. Mahr argues that models are detached from the original context [58] and represent a classification system, which may be transferable to other areas of research. With an increasing use of computers and technology in research, simulation techniques provide an opportunity for developing, testing and communicating models.[13] The understanding of complex, abstract data, for example in climate research, benefits greatly from the discourse based on models and their characteristics [64].

4.2   Cross-, Inter- and Multidisciplinary

While "cross-disciplinarity" means the adoption of methods from one discipline by another,[14] "interdisciplinary collaboration" refers to a "collaboration of several disciplines on a [joint] topic or issue" [66, p. 7]. The latter necessitates the development of a multi-disciplinary terminology and common methodologies [67, 68]. Institutionalization of interdisciplinary collaboration ranges from temporary to the creation of new "hybrid" research disciplines [69] such as the digital humanities.

---

[13] On the concept of simulation see [63, pp. 33–41 and 68–69].

[14] One can observe a new trend in the humanities called the "cognitive revolution", which means adapting scientific methods to systematization or formalization of certain phenomena, see [65].

With studies becoming ever more detailed through the invention and adoption of new methods, new disciplines like e.g. Digital Humanities are emerging. It is essential to develop for the latter particular methods and paradigms open to interdisciplinary research questions [11].

Those shifts can be observed in humanities research, especially when the development of digital tools is involved. Since in many cases the research fields overlap, scholarship tends to be defined to some extent by its methods rather than the subject [11]. In particular, digital 3D reconstruction employs various methods borrowed from architectural design, engineering, geo- and computer sciences to deal with humanities research questions. As a consequence, most academic reconstruction projects employ researchers with backgrounds in both humanities and technology or design [70].

4.3 Scholarship

Distinguishing between scholarly and non-scholarly 3D reconstruction involves the principles of objectivity, reliability and validity of scholarly claims [c.f. 71]. Thus, scholarly knowledge is rooted in the ideals of truth, understanding and explanation, transparency, as well as the transferability [72, 73]. The authors' earlier research [7, 8] concluded that a 3D reconstruction process connotes professional vision and experience as tacit knowledge [74], which by definition cannot be introduced into scholarly processes and prevents a comprehensive documentation of a reconstruction.

Three-dimensional reconstructions are usually collaborative, making it necessary to articulate the creator(s) of a model. The individual roles in and contributions to collaborative, scholarly, digital projects should always be provided. Wray even states that joint scholarly publications display decreased quality through the lack of individual responsibility [75]. Other issues are an incomplete listing of contributors within larger research teams as well as the addition of non-contributing people to increase the scientific value of the publications [76]. Both these situations may arise consciously or unintentionally, but they certainly have an influence on the quality of scholarship and its perception. The issue has been known for some time. It questions the accuracy of scholarly literature [77, 78].

Alongside the formerly mentioned issues, other fundamental aspects of scholarly discourses are a falsification of knowledge and its temporary nature. They are based on the main principles of unlimited doubt and trust in the adherence to scientific objectives by fellow scholars [14, 78]. Ensuring the transparent application of the principles and the connection of scholarly knowledge to other disciplines may be achieved through an appropriate discourse. While 3D reconstruction projects are primarily driven by visual perception and imagery, the scholarly discourses in humanities primarily rely on verbal and textual explanations [i.e. 79, p. 233]. Pointing out the insufficiency of these practices Jablonka et al. state, that "inherited limits of archaeology [and 3D reconstruction overall – S.M.] become much more apparent through visualization than through a text" [80].

5 A Preliminary Classification Scheme for Digital Reconstruction in the Humanities

After highlighting several general challenges, the authors would like to propose a preliminary classification scheme for digital reconstruction in humanities research. A related classification matrix distinguishes between (1) the research context in terms of the subject and the historic object and (2) the quality of digital 3D reconstruction. The quality pertains to sources of reconstruction, technologies, the characteristics of resultant computer model, as well as documentation of the reconstruction processes and – if created by an interdisciplinary team [8] – a record of the collaboration between stakeholders (Fig. 1).

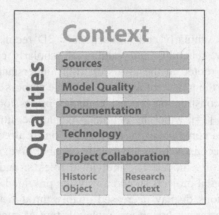

Fig. 1. General structure of a classification scheme for digital reconstruction

5.1 Contexts of Digital Reconstruction

5.1.1 Historic Object

Classification of historic objects is a core subject of historical research in the humanities. As a consequence, many approaches, principles and schemes have been developed within disciplines involved [81]. Digital reconstruction processes require metadata schemes and complex ontologies for classifying historic objects. An object classification generally covers its type and main properties, as well as location [82]. Reconstruction of past stages in the object's development may require a time-based classification.

Type of object (e.g., architectural): There are various context-aware ways to classify types of objects. By means of semantic classification, a church belongs to a certain class of entities (e.g., architectural objects → buildings → churches) [c.f. 7], but could also be classified by other attributes, e.g. by color. Several commonly used hierarchies are available to classify objects, as for example the Art & Architecture Thesaurus (AAT)[15] or the Iconclass classification scheme for arts.[16]

General object properties (e.g. tangible, temporal): Regarding the importance of the existence of an object for a digital reconstruction as proposed in Sect. 4, it is of interest if an object is tangible or intangible. This addresses if the object does no longer exist or it never took physical form and is known solely through plans or concepts. Moreover, the temporality of an object in terms of static (e.g., architecture at a certain date) or dynamic (e.g., dances, mechanical processes) deals with another issue.

Date of origin (year or period): Due to objects undergoing constant transformation a specific date of creation, or start of a particular stage in its creation, may not be possible to establish. A focus of a reconstruction project on a specific time highly depends on a research interest for a specific state.[17] As earlier research confirms, a date of origin is seldom specified beyond a particular period [c.f. 70]. Concurrent times of origin may often be available for the same phase in the object's history [81].

Location or place(s): The precise location of an object may be difficult to establish. A place of origin of a movable object and its subsequent location, or locations, have to be taken into account.[18]

5.1.2   Research Contexts

A record and systematization of the research that went into a digital reconstruction is essential for further investigation [83]. Current approaches are mostly based on historical exemplification – as in the case of the historical method proposed in Sect. 2 – aiming to distinguish several research contexts [e.g. 84]. On a more general level, the process of research and the insights to be gained are widely discussed in sociology and philosophy [i.e. 14, 85–87]. The questions of a purpose and function of individual research, as for example the process of digital 3D reconstruction, requires subject investigation as well. Although there are various other research approaches – such as numeric analysis methods as finite element methods (FEM) or computational fluid dynamics (CFD) – visualization is the most common way to present digital 3D reconstruction. According to Ware, visualization can support research and understanding in five ways [88, cited according to 89, p. V]:

- It may facilitate the cognition of large amounts of data.
- It can promote the perception of unanticipated emergent properties.
- It sometimes highlights problems in data quality.
- It clarifies the relationships between large- and small-scale features.
- It helps one to formulate hypotheses.

---

[15] http://www.getty.edu/research/tools/vocabularies/aat/. Accessed 26 May 2016.

[16] http://www.iconclass.org/. Accessed 26 May 2016.

[17] Further discussed–although dealing with another subject-matter–in [82].

[18] Further discussed in the chapter of Prechtel et al. which is also part of this book.

Taking this generic scheme and several approaches to grounded systematization [83, 84] into consideration, the authors would like to propose a preliminary typology shown in Table 1, which distinguishes between research objects and objectives of relevant research.

Table 1. Research approaches of digital reconstruction

Research approaches	Source	Object	System
Documentation (e.g., compilation and recording of knowledge)	X		
Data quality assessment (e.g., consistency or contingency of sources)	X		
Visualization (e.g., investigation of shape or appearance)		X	
Creative process (e.g., planning or construction)		X	
Conceptualization and contextualization (e.g., typologies, functional segments, archetypical elements, provenance)	X	X	X
Numerical analysis (e.g., structural analysis, lighting)		X	
Hypothetic simulation (e.g., of hypothetic objects deriving from an architectural system)			X

Research object (source, historic object, system): Use of 3D digital reconstruction to research a certain historic object or its parts is common. Three-dimensional reconstruction is also employed to investigate and assess sources. Sometimes not a specific object, but an investigation of schemes and systems is the focus of research, for example, to evaluate the Vitruvian scheme of architectural orders. Against this background, 3D reconstruction methods are often employed to derive archetypes or specific features [90]. The question concerning the "original" being reconstructed is closely related. The "original" can be a certain intention (e.g. of a builder), a specific source, or a historic object.

Research objectives (e.g., documentation, data quality assessment, visualization, process investigation, conceptualization, contextualization, numeric analysis, hypothetical simulations):

- Documentation: In the case of digital 3D reconstruction, the objectives of a virtual model are primarily to assort, store, and compile spatialrelated knowledge [c.f. 91]. For example, the 3D model of the Domus Severiana provided a spatial map and therefore a possibility to geo-reference sources [92].
- Data quality assessment: It is closely related to the contextualization and assessment of the consistency of sources and a focus of research. For example, digital reconstruction of content depicted in drawings or paintings can be used to test perspective features or consistency [c.f. 93].
- Visualization: The most common way to visualize is to formulate a hypothesis of the shape, properties and appearance of a certain historic object. Concerning this

aspect, digital reconstruction allows the non-invasive application and testing of alterations or restoration.[19]

- Process investigation: Another type is the research of historical preparation processes (e.g., planning or construction processes employed by craftsmen).
- Conceptualization: A major question for underlying concepts and intentions, for example, structuring concepts [c.f. 96], refers to functions of certain parts of an object (e.g., rooms, figuration or proportions).[20]
- Contextualization: Other objectives concern the contextualization of objects (e.g., geo-location, relationship to other objects) and the identification of archetypal characteristics. This may refer, for example, to the craftsman's specifications and typologies, as well as a comparison of iconographical concepts. Contextualization may lead to a research interest in sources, specific objects, as well as systems.[21]
- Numerical analysis and simulation: For gaining dynamic data from models there is the possibility of simulating different kinds of forces and processes. Structural analysis is one area of application [c.f. 100], but there is also the possibility of examining the function of certain parts of a building.[22]
- Hypothetical simulations[23]: Different usages are possible without making a reference to concrete historic objects, for example, the exploration of hypothetically possible objects which derive from a certain architectural order and the question for (hypothetical) limits and boundaries of this system [90, 102].

5.2 Quality of Digital Reconstruction

While both historical objects and research contexts are determining factors of a digital 3D reconstruction, another question concerns their quality.

5.2.1 Sources

Types and the quality of sources and their relevance to 3D reconstruction are a prominent subject of scholarly literature [103, 104]. All information input to generate a virtual model can generally be defined as a "source". Every source is essential for the quality of the model and must therefore be evaluated. There are primary sources, which are the originals themselves, but also secondary sources, which can contain additional information. Thus the creators of the reconstruction have to be critical and trained in the respective field to which the source is related. Principles of and approaches to a quality validation of sources are at the core of historical research and widely discussed in

---

[19] For example, removing alterations of statues introduced in the course of an earlier conservation treatment. Discussed in [94]; For the restoration of fragmented objects, see [95].

[20] The approaches followed until now concentrated mainly on analyzing architectural plans. Discussed in [97, 98].

[21] See [99].

[22] For example: Creating simulations of ancient ventilation systems. See [101].

[23] A definition of "simulation": [63].

literature [e.g. 105]. Of the numerous characteristics available to describe the quality of sources, three aspects should be emphasised:

Types of sources (e.g., *original, acquired data, images, texts, "logical sources"*):
Available and accessible primary sources, including the material evidence of the original objects themselves, are the most important base for creation of a digital 3D model. The original structure, or what has survived of it, is often digitized using remote sensing technologies, while never realized or altered objects can be reconstructed through interpretation of secondary sources. As discussed in earlier publications [7, 106], images and plans, as well as panoramas, are the most important to reconstruct this latter type of object. Various other data support digital reconstruction, such as texts and acquired data in the form of digital elevation models or laser scans of adjacent buildings. Analogies to similar objects provide logical implications and help to interpret and extrapolate sources, to bridge information gaps as well as uncertain or contradictive information. Requirements of a system, as for example, the Vitruvian architectural system, would simply rely on inner-model logic.

Inherent knowledge (e.g., *level of accuracy, level of detail, comprehensibility*):
While types of sources distinguish between various sources of data and information included in a reconstruction project on a nominal level, "inherent knowledge" focuses on the quality of information available within these information objects.[24] From a more general point of view, even a secondary source is a "model" of an original. This includes questions of its closeness to an original in terms of a level of accuracy or artistic freedom, as well as for the level of detail and completeness [81]. Moreover, a major criterion for turning information into knowledge (which can be conveyed through a model) is its relevance and (mental) accessibility for a modeler [107].[25] Historical or culturally obscure (in terms of e.g., language, discipline, logics) sources may require specialist historical skills to decipher – hence historians are often part of a modeling team.

5.2.2 Model Quality
A resultant quality of a digital reconstruction can be classified by the geometrical, radiometric and temporal fidelity of the created digital model. In general, for all three aspects a level of accuracy, detail, and coherence may be of relevance for a classification. While this scheme focuses on the quality of a digital model, it has to be taken into consideration that, in current practice, for most digital reconstruction projects only visualizations remain. This points out another criterion of quality, alongside those discussed in Sect. 4.

The geometrical fidelity (accuracy, detail, coherence) in respect to the reconstructed object is related to the question of accuracy as well as the level of detail. Regarding a level of detail (LOD), a digital reconstruction can show only the outer surface of the

---

[24] The distinction between the type of source and inherent knowledge relies on outer and inner source criticism as formal vs. content-based quality [105].

[25] These prerequisites also apply to an automated model creation process, see [108].

original or it can show depth information. For both the question of the numerical accuracy has to be considered.

The radiometric fidelity (properties, property depending accuracy, detail, coherence) in respect to the reconstructed object describes the virtual reproduction of the object's material properties. This concerns information about inherent properties, including physical properties such as colors of a surface or invisible qualities of ultraviolet or infrared wavelength, as well as behavior-related attributes, such as opacity or plasticity, which may be relevant for a numeric simulation [109]. Furthermore, for all simulated properties there is the question of accuracy, detail, and coherence of their virtual representation.

The temporal fidelity (properties, property depending accuracy, detail, coherence): While a static reconstruction of artifacts is still the most popular usage scenario for digital reconstruction, dynamic settings are slowly gaining importance. Similar to the radiometric fidelity, related criteria for the classification of a temporal fidelity, as for example a simulation of transition processes, historic everyday life, or technical workflows, may be properties, accuracy, detail, and coherence.

5.2.3 Documentation

Documentation strategies address the "preservation of knowledge", and are thus linked to transparency and reproducibility. These objectives entail a clarification of "included sources, decisions, workflows, possible misinterpretations and methodology" [110]. On the one hand, this will help project partners with safeguarding and communicating their contribution. On the other hand, such records are intended for external evaluation and discussion of the project's rational and result. While this distinction may appear fuzzy to the end-user, the distinction between the process and the documentation of the outputs is a more appropriate approach.

Documentation of results (reference ontology, application ontology): A widely accepted approach is the documentation of results through metadata. The CIDOC-CRM [111] and CityGML in particular, have – in comparison to other standards – gained wide acceptance as reference ontologies for cultural heritage. The level of adoption (86 references to CIDOC-CRM within the publication stock) still seems low. The quality of implementation in application ontologies is widely heterogeneous [82, 112]. Derived categories for a classification can be the employed reference ontology, as well as the adopted application ontology.[26]

Process documentation (approach): In contrast to result documentation strategies, current approaches to documentation of the creative process are still theoretical [113] or highly prototype [110]. Nevertheless, it is evident that in a majority of projects process documentation occurs by personal notes, communication artifacts, or versioning of states [8]. While these artifacts "document" a workflow and communication history,

---

[26] Further discussed in the chapter of Kuroczynski et al. which is also part of this book.

another question concerns the employed software and algorithms and a documentation of a computational processing.

5.2.4 Technology

A model creation in a digital reconstruction takes place by a more or less human-driven use of computer software. In contrast to digitization processes where a development of technical workflows and tools is one of the topics of focus in the academic discourse, human-driven workflows for digital reconstruction mostly rely on an application of standardized software [70]. Closely connected are questions for certain technological domains and related approaches for a model generation workflow as well as data types for resultant 3D models.

Technological domain (e.g., GIS, VR, CAD, BIM): The common multi-source background of 3D reconstructions touches a variety of technological domains like geo information systems (GIS), virtual reality (VR), computer aided design (CAD), or building information management (BIM) with their own standards. All approaches recommend specific tools and workflows and offer specific benefits – for example information on object volumes (BIM), a highly realistic appearance of surfaces (VR), accurate size measurements (CAD), or large-scale geo-referenced information (GIS).

Model genetics workflow (semi-automated genesis; procedural generators; human-driven modeling approaches): An important distinction is between different grades of automation. Even for interpretative reconstruction workflows, model creation can occur semi-automatically – for example for the semi-automated reconstruction, from historic images, of devastated churches [114]. These semi-automatic approaches make expert knowledge necessary when it comes to judging the reliability and relevance of a certain source for the reconstruction. Another approach for model creation is the use of parametric modeling environments with widely predefined objects. A fully manual approach to reconstruction, entirely based on data and secondary sources, is the third possibility.

Tools (Software): The application of certain software modeling tools greatly influences the modeling approach, exchange formats, prospects for publication and integration, data volume, degree of detail, and the use of different schemes such as CityGML. Customized solutions for an automated modeling, based on photos or laser scan data, may not be as well-known as 3D modeling or GIS software, but a record of software used allows some general estimation and expectations for modeling experts, especially concerning future use of project data.

Geometry data type (Program, Point Cloud, Wireframe-/ Polygon Model, Voxel): The format of datasets used in digital 3D reconstructions affects relevant workflows. Genetic approaches do not rely on storing resultant 3D geometries, but on parameters, and generate a 3D object in real time [115, 116]. In contrast, discrete approaches store all 3D information. Approaches are (A) Point Clouds as a set of points in a defined coordinate system, (B) Wireframe-/ Polygon Models as vertices connected with edges and polygons and (C) Voxels as volume pixels. While geometric data can be widely assorted to one of these archetypes, there is a wide and heterogeneous scope of formats for radiometric or dynamic information.

5.2.5   Project Collaboration

As already pointed out, a major challenge for 3D reconstruction projects results from their configuration as cross-disciplinary collaborative work. Out of the many approaches to categorizing projects, the scope of project and the competences of contributors are important for assessing the quality of a project.

Project scale (e.g., *employees, budget*): Resources, in terms of budget or employees, which are available to particular projects, may provide a clue to estimate the effort spent on research and modeling.

Project dates (starting date – end date): During which time period was the project created?

Involved Competencies (e.g., *humanities, design, technologies*): An important criterion to assess the quality of a 3D reconstruction is to estimate a level of competency and expertise of involved persons. As a limiting fact, individual competencies and skills are usually difficult to measure and disciplinary backgrounds of stakeholders or their certifications provide only weak support.

To summarize the previous paragraphs, Table 2 proposes a preliminary classification scheme.

Table 2. Overview of the preliminary classification scheme

Category	Variable	Characteristics, examples
Sources	Type of source	Original (material) evidence, acquired data, images, texts, "logical source"
	Inherent knowledge	Primary source, secondary source
Model quality	Geometrical fidelity	Accuracy, detail, coherence
	Radiometric fidelity	Properties, properties depending on accuracy, detail, coherence
	Temporal fidelity	Properties, properties depending on accuracy, detail, coherence
Documentation	Result documentation	Reference ontology, application ontology
	Process documentation	Approach
Technology	Technological domain	GIS, VR, CAD, BIM
	Model genetic workflow	Semi-automated genesis, procedural generators, human-driven modeling approach

(Continued)

Table 2. (*Continued*)

Category	Variable	Characteristics, examples
	Tools	software
	Geometry data type	Point cloud, wireframe model, polygon model, voxel model, parametric model (program)
Project cooperation	Project scale	Employees, budget
	Project dates	Start and end date
	Involved competencies	Humanities, design, technologies
Historic object	Type of object	Static artifact, dynamic artifact
	General object properties	Tangibility, temporality
	Date of origin	Year, period
	Location	Place
Research context	Research object	Source, historic object, system
	Research function	Documentation, data quality assessment, visualization, process investigation, conceptualization, contextualization, numeric analysis, hypothetical simulation

6   Application and Evaluation of the Scheme

To evaluate the proposed classification scheme it was applied to two projects, both
have been published [117].

6.1   Project 1: The Ethno-Nature Park "Uch Enmek"

The Altay Mountains boast outstanding cultural heritage. Remains of the once flourishing Scythian culture rank highest among the archaeological heritage found there,
with the most famous being located in the Karakol and Ursul Valley. This has been
reflected in a conservation area termed "Ethno-Nature Park Uch Enmek". Research and
management within a remote, protected area in Siberia suffer from deficiencies which
are, among others, due to a limited access to information technology, disperse data
archiving, and limited access to geo-information. The status quo forms a strong
motivation for the project. Archaeological expertise and data for the project's activities
have been provided through a close collaboration with archaeologists from Ghent
University. The working group led by Jean Bourgeois has been active in the Altay for
some 15 years [118]. Courtesy of the GeoEye Foundation, the Dresden group was
assigned four overlapping IKONOS scenes of the Uch Enmek conservation site,
forming an important data source.

6.2 Project 2: GEPAM: Memorial Landscapes - Dresden and Terezín as Places to Remember the Shoah

The cities of Dresden and Terezín share a tragic history of the persecution of Jewish people during World War II. Memorials in both cities commemorate the victims of the Shoah. The purpose of 3D town models in the GEPAM project is to communicate the variety of documents and information concerning the Shoah and allowing the user to evaluate events in situ. Education concerning the Holocaust complements the process of remembrance. The target structure of the final presentation environment will allow access to documents and records related to the persecution of the Jews within a web-based city model, and shall serve as a virtual memorial. The GEPAM project is financed by the EFRE scheme of the European Union supporting cross-border cooperation between the neighboring countries of the Czech Republic and Germany (Fig. 2).

Fig. 2. Examples of visualization outcomes of the projects Uch Enmek and GEPAM

Table 3. Application of the proposed classification scheme

Category	Ethno-Nature Park "Uch Enmek"	GEPAM Memorial Landscapes
Sources		
Type of sources	Acquired data (satellite images, digital elevation models (DEM)) Excavation plans Contemporary photographs Physical remains	Texts Pictures Photographs Plans Remaining buildings
Inherent knowledge	Primary source with probability of changes: courgan remains Secondary sources: Excavation plans, satellite images	Primary sources: 34 remaining buildings with modifications, 58 lost buildings Secondary historical sources: artistic pictures, photographs, plans Secondary contemporary sources: photographs, plans, texts

(Continued)

Table 3. (*Continued*)

Category	Ethno-Nature Park "Uch Enmek"	GEPAM Memorial Landscapes
Model quality		
Geometrical fidelity	Level of detail (LOD) 2 models and generalized land use	LOD1 of city landscape LOD3 of buildings relevant for the subject
Radiometric fidelity	Generalized color scheme	Generalized color scheme
Temporal fidelity	No temporal changes	Transitions: per year, binary (display/no display)
Documentation		
Process documentation	Textual within thesis	Periodical protocols and changelogs
Results documentation	Not indexed by metadata	XML-metadata: time, author, location for LOD 1 objects according to GIS
Technology		
Technological domain	GIS-based modeling of landscape VR modeling of obstacles, based on acquired data	GIS-based modeling for LOD1 objects VR-modeling for LOD 3 objects
Model genetic workflow	Semi-automated modeling of landscape Human-driven modeling of obstacles	Human-driven modeling of obstacles
Tools	ArcGIS SketchUp Maxon Cinema 4D	ArcGIS SketchUp Maxon Cinema 4D
Geometry data type	Shapefiles Polygon models	Shapefiles Polygon models
Project cooperation		
Project scale	~800 man-hours (modeling and automatization)	~3200 man-hours (modeling only)
Project dates	2007–2014	2012–2014
Involved competencies	Geo scientists, archaeologists, historians	Geo scientists, information scientists, historians, linguists
Historic object		
Original location	Uch Enmek, Russia	Dresden, Germany
Time of origin	~600 A.D.	1935–1945
General object properties	(Partially) no longer extant tangible object	(Partially) no longer extant tangible object
Type of object	Landscape with obstacles	Buildings (3D city model)

(*Continued*)

Table 3. (*Continued*)

Category	Ethno-Nature Park "Uch Enmek"	GEPAM Memorial Landscapes
Research context		
Research function	Visualization Conceptualization of land use (e.g., forest, settlements, courgans)	Documentation of sources and information Visualization Conceptualization of building functions Contextualization (city model) Process investigation (change of use of buildings and devastation due to WWII)

The first application of the proposed scheme, presenting the results for the two different projects in Table 3, was quite convincing in terms of an applicable and easily distinguishable set of categories.

Right away the category Inherent Knowledge proved to be not directly applicable. The definition from Sect. 5 is based on the use and analysis of historical and contemporary sources to assess their closeness to the object and, therefore, their reliability. A distinction between a primary and a secondary source makes more sense since reconstructions are also done for projects with a temporal and cultural absence. Once temporal changes are probable, the reliability of the primary source decreases and has to be combined with secondary sources to obtain more complete information.

A completion of the table is only likely for people very familiar with the project. It cannot be done based solely on publications and project records as some of the aspects might not have been considered worthy of documentation yet. Project outsiders wanting to use the scheme for an overview of reconstructions regarding a certain topic will have difficulties with a complete application. Records of future projects and especially people relying on extensive information within them will benefit from the adaptation of the scheme. Generally, the scheme still needs to be tested on projects involving reconstruction of intangible objects. Broad application within the subject community will provide more information on strengths and weaknesses of the scheme and point out necessary adaptations.

7 Conclusion

At first glance, digital 3D reconstruction in the context of humanities is a melting pot of various disciplinary approaches, methods and contexts. As an example for research activities which cross disciplinary frontiers, it can be hard to determine 3D reconstructions by standard indicators, as for example a joint research object or explanatory approach, but considering the use of a common research method seems promising [11].

While 3D reconstruction processes foster a nomothetic and holistic representation of the past, another more general question is if they are a step back by means of methodology and with regard to modern problem-centered and constructionist approaches of humanities research [c.f. 119]. In particular, the use of digital reconstruction methods – which originate from architectural design, engineering, and geo sciences and rely highly on tools from computing – in humanities is determined by various challenges, as for example the need of simplification by model building, multiple authors, or visual research strategies.

An important challenge for the creation of classification schemes is to make them easily applicable as well as their results comparable to each other. For thus, especially quantifiable categories would be helpful. This relies on two concurring interests: On the one hand, an applicable classification scheme has to provide all variables of relevance to describe a certain object and a comprehensive set of values. On the other hand, an optimal scheme must be generic and slim to make it easily applicable and – against the background that most schemes are rarely applied in practice because of the work-intensive recommendations – to avoid too many unfinished parameters. Thus, the development of the classification scheme which is proposed within this article had to consider the plurality of application scenarios as well as the definition of distinct categories, variables, and characteristics. Even with the amount of nearly 2,500 research papers taken into account, an applicability and robustness of this scheme has to be assessed by further research.

Related to these conflicting interests, we would like to propose a low-level compromise: Our proposed scheme contains some mandatory and widely quantified categories which may be easy to define. A basic set of variables contains the following: Technology: tools and geometry data type; Project cooperation: project scale and date; Historical object: location, time of origin, type of object. Most of the further descriptions (e.g. model qualities, documentation) are optional, not standardized, and qualitative only. We would like to encourage researchers to adopt the scheme according to their needs. Moreover, we would like to invite other researchers to assess, amend, extend, and further develop the proposed core scheme. Finally, its use in further research, e.g., in the development of a disciplinary identity or to guide a methodological assessment and discourse – has yet to be proven.

Acknowledgements. The authors wish to acknowledge the support of Dr. rer. nat. Nikolas Prechtel of the Technische Universität Dresden who provided information on the Ethno-Nature Park "Uch Enmek" project in order to test the proposed classification schema. Furthermore, the authors would like to thank the reviewer of the chapter for providing some suggestions: According to his suggestions, for example, a geometric fidelity could be characterized and distinguished as "simple geometric model", "geometric model with meta-description-elements", "enhanced model", with relationships to further source material or/and time layers, or to express the degree of resolution expressed by numbers.

References

1. Rasch, R.F.R.: The nature of taxonomy. **19**(3), 147–149 (1987)
2. Münster, S., Ioannides, M.: The scientific community of digital heritage in time and space. In: Guidi, G., Scopigno, R., Torres, J.C., Graf, H. (eds.) 2nd International Congress on Digital Heritage 2015, Granada (2015). doi:978-1-5090-0048-7/15
3. Mayring, P.: Qualitative content analysis. Forum Qual. Sozialforschung **1**(2), Article No 20 (2000)
4. Münster, S.: Researching scientific structures via joint authorships – the case of virtual 3D modelling in humanities. In: International Conference on Infrastructures and Cooperation in E-Science and E-Humanities (in print)
5. Moed, H.F., Glänzel, W., Schmoch, U.: Handbook of Quantitative Science and Technology Research: The Use of Publication and Patent Statistics in Studies of S&T Systems. Springer, Berlin (2006)
6. Münster, S.: Interdisziplinäre Kooperation bei der Erstellung geschichtswissenschaftlicher 3D-Rekonstruktionen. Springer, Wiesbaden (2016)
7. Münster, S.: Workflows and the role of images for a virtual 3D reconstruction of no longer extant historic objects. In: Ann Photogramm Remote Sens Spatial Inf Sci II-5/W1 (XXIV International CIPA Symposium), pp. 197–202 (2013)
8. Münster, S., Prechtel, N.: Beyond software. Design implications for virtual libraries and platforms for cultural heritage from practical findings. In: Ioannides, M., Magnenat-Thalmann, N., Fink, E., Žarnić, R., Yen, A.-Y., Quak, E. (eds.) Digital Heritage. Progress in Cultural Heritage: Documentation, Preservation, and Protection. LNCS, vol. 8740, pp. 131–145. Springer, Cham (2014)
9. Kelle, U.: The development of categories different approaches in grounded theory. In: Bryant, A., Charmaz, K. (eds.) The SAGE Handbook of Grounded Theory, pp. 191–213. Thousand Oaks, SAGE (2010)
10. Stock, W., Stock, M.: Handbook of Information Science. De Gruyter Saur, Berlin/Boston (2015)
11. Krishnan, A.: What are academic disciplines. Some observations on the Disciplinarity vs. Interdisciplinarity debate. University of Southampton. National Centre for Research Methods, Southhampton (2009)
12. Knorr-Cetina, K.: Epistemic Cultures. How the Sciences Make Knowledge. Harvard University Press, Cambridge (1999)
13. Weingart, P.: Interdisziplinarität als List der Institutionen. In: Kocka, J. (ed.) Interdisziplinarität. Praxis - Herausforderung - Ideologic. Suhrkamp, Frankfurt a. M., pp. 159–166 (1987)
14. Knorr-Cetina, K.: Die Fabrikation von Erkenntnis. Suhrkamp, Frankfurt a. M. (2002)
15. Dilthey, W.: Der Aufbau der geschichtlichen Welt in den Geisteswissenschaften. Suhrkamp, Frankfurt a. Main (1970)
16. Organisation for Economic Co-operation and Development. Frascati Manual. Proposed Standard Practice for Surveys on Research and Experimental Development. OECD Publications Service, Paris (2002)
17. Organisation for Economic Co-operation and Development. Revised Field of Science and Technology (FOS) Classification in the Frascati Manual. Paris (2007)

18. Semenova, E., Stricker, M.: Eine Ontologie der Wissenschaftsdisziplinen. Entwicklung eines Instrumentariums für die Wissenskommunikation. In: Ball, R. (ed.) Wissenschaftskommunikation der Zukunft, 4. Konferenz der Zentralbibliothek im Forschungszentrum Jülich, 6–8 November 2007, vol Band 18. Reihe Bibliothek/Library edn. Schriften des Forschungszentrums Jülich, Jülich, pp. 61–69 (2007)
19. Bialas, V.: Allgemeine Wissenschaftsgeschichte: Philosophische Orientierungen. Böhlau, Wien (1990)
20. De Solla Price, D.: Little Science - Big Science. Columbia University Press, New York (1963)
21. Glänzel, W., Schubert, A.: A new classification scheme of science fields and subfields designed for scientometric evaluation purposes. Scientometrics 56(3), 357–367 (2003)
22. Wissenschaftsrat. Empfehlungen zu einem Kerndatensatz Forschung. Berlin (2013)
23. Vargas-Quesada, B., Moya-Anegón, F.: Visualizing the structure of science. Springer, Berlin (2007)
24. Abramo, G., D'Angelo, C.A., Di Costa, F.: Identifying interdisciplinarity through the disciplinary classification of coauthors of scientific publications. J. Am. Soc. Inf. Sci. Technol. 63(11), 2206–2222 (2012). doi:10.1002/asi.22647
25. Biljecki, I.F.: The concept of level of detail in 3D city models, vol. 62. GISt Report. TU Delft, Delft (2013)
26. Luebke, D.P.: Level of Detail for 3D Graphics. The Morgan Kaufmann Series in Computer Graphics and Geometric Modeling, 1st edn. Morgan Kaufmann Publishers, Boston (2003)
27. De Francesco, G., D'Andrea, A.: Standards and guidelines for quality digital cultural three-dimensional content creation. In: Ioannides, M., Addison, A., Georgopoulos, A., Kalisperis, L. (eds.) Digital Heritage: Proceedings of the 14th International Conference on Virtual Systems and Multimedia. Project Papers, pp. 229–233. Archaeolingua, Budapest (2008)
28. eHumanities CCf. Digitale Geisteswissenschaften. Köln (2011)
29. Ch'ng, E., Gaffney, V., Chapman, H.: Visual Heritage in the Digital Age. Springer, London (2013)
30. Arnold, D., Geser, G.: EPOCH Research Agenda – Final report. Brighton (2008)
31. European Commission. Survey and outcomes of cultural heritage research projects supported in the context of EU environmental research programmes. In: From 5th to 7th Framework Programme. European Commission, Brussels (2011)
32. Renfrew, C., Bahn, P.: Archaeology. The Key Concepts. Routledge, New York (2005)
33. Rua, H., Alvito, P.: Living the past: 3D models, virtual reality and game engines as tools for supporting archaeology and the reconstruction of cultural heritage – the case-study of the Roman villa of Casal de Freiria. J. Archaeol. Sci. 38(12), 3296–3308 (2011). doi:10.1016/j.jas.2011.07.015
34. Christofori, E., Bierwagen, J.: Recording cultural heritage using terrestrial laserscanning – dealing with the system, the huge datasets they create and ways to extract the necessary deliverables you can work with. Int. Arch. Photogrammetry Remote Sens. Spat. Inf. Sci. 1(2), 183–188 (2013)
35. Clini, P., Nespeca, R., Bernetti, A.: All-in-one laser scanning methods for surveying, representing and sharing information on archaeology. Via Flaminia and the Furlo tunnel complex. Int. Arch. Photogrammetry Remote Sens. Spat. Inf. Sci
36. Lasaponara, R., Coluzzi, R., Masini, N.: Flights into the past: full-waveform airborne laser scanning data for archaeological investigation. J. Archaeol. Sci. 38, 2061–2070 (2011)
37. Brutto, M.L., Meli, P.: Computer vision tools for 3D modelling in archaeology. In: Ioannides, M. (ed.) Progress in Cultural Heritage Preservation – EUROMED 2012, pp. 1–6 (2012)

38. Martin-Beaumont, N., Nony, N., Deshayes, B., Pierrot-Deseilligny, M., Luca, L.D.: Photographer-friendly work-flows for image-based modelling of heritage artefacts. In: International Archives of the Photogrammetry, Remote Sensing and Spatial Information Sciences XL-5/W2, 2013, XXIV International CIPA Symposium, 2–6 September 2013, Strasbourg, pp. 421–424 (2013)

39. Bruno, F., Bruno, S., De Sensi, G., Luchi, M.-L., Mancuso, S., Muzzupappa, M.: From 3D reconstruction to virtual reality: a complete methodology for digital archaeological exhibition. J. Cult. Heritage 11(1), 42–49 (2010). doi:10.1016/j.culher.2009.02.006

40. Carrozzino, M., Bergamasco, M.: Beyond virtual museums: experiencing immersive virtual reality in real museums. J. Cult. Heritage 11(4), 452–458 (2010). doi:10.1016/j.culher. 2010.04.001

41. Dilly, H.: Kunstgeschichte als Institution. Studien zur Geschichte einer Disziplin. Frankfurt a.M (1979)

42. Locher, H.: Kunstgeschichte als historische Theorie der Kunst 1750–1950, München (2001)

43. Ratzeburg, W.: Mediendiskussion im 19. Jahrhundert. Wie die Kunstgeschichte ihre wissenschaftliche Grundlage in der Fotografie fand. Kritische Berichte 30(1), 22–39 (2002)

44. Rößler, J.: Kunstgeschichte als Realpolitik. In: Bałus, W. (ed.) Die Etablierung des Faches Kunstgeschichte in Deutschland, Polen und Mitteleuropa, Warszawa, pp. 61–85 (2010)

45. Locher, H.: Kunstbegriff und Kunstgeschichte – Schlosser, Gombrich, Warburg. In: Bałus, W. (ed.) Die Etablierung des Faches Kunstgeschichte in Deutschland, Polen und Mitteleuropa, Warszawa, pp. 391–410 (2010)

46. Seippel, R.-P.: Architektur und Interpretation. Methoden und Ansätze der Kunstgeschichte in ihrer Bedeutung für die Architekturinterpretation, Essen (1989)

47. Suckale, R.: Stilgeschichte. Kunsthistorische Arbeitsblätter 11, 17–26 (2001)

48. Gooding, D.C.: Visualizing scientific inference. Top. Cogn. Sci. 2(1), 15–35 (2010). doi:10.1111/j.1756-8765.2009.01048.x

49. Goodwin, C.: Professional vision. Am. Anthropologist 96(3), 606–633 (1994)

50. Stachowiak, H.: Allgemeine Modelltheorie. Springer, Wien (1973)

51. Wilton-Ely, J.: Architectural model. In: n.b. (ed.) The Dictionary of Art, Bd. 2. London [u. a.], pp. 335–338 (1996)

52. De Chadarevian, S., Hopwood, N.: Models - The Third Dimension of Science. Stanford University Press, Stanford (2004)

53. Carpo, M.: Architecture in the Age of Printing. Orality, Writing, Typography, and Printed Images in the History of Architectural Theory. Cambridge University Press, Cambridge (2001)

54. Kurz, M.: Die Modellmethodik im Formfindungsprozess am Beispiel des Automobildesigns. Baden-Baden (2008)

55. Vecco, M.: A definition of cultural heritage: from the tangible to the intangible. J. Cult. Heritage 11(3), 321–324 (2010). doi:10.1016/j.culher.2010.01.006

56. Yang, C., Sun, S., Xu, C.: Recovery of cultural activity for digital safeguarding of intangible cultural heritage*. In: IEEE Proceedings of the 6th World Congress on Intelligent Control and Automation, 21–23 June 2006, Dalian, China, pp. 10337–10341. IEEE (2006)

57. Hisatomi, K., Tomiyama, K., Katayama, M., Iwadate, Y.: Method of 3D reconstruction using graph cuts, and its application to preserving intangible cultural heritage. In: IEEE 12th International Conference on Computer Vision Workshops, ICCV Workshops, pp. 923–930 (2009)

58. Mahr, B.: Das Wissen im Modell. Technische Universität, Fakultät IV, Berlin (2004)

59. Stephan, P.E.: Denken am modell. In: Bürdek, B.E. (ed.) Der digitale Wahn, Frankfurt a. M., pp. 109–129 (2001)
60. Niccolucci, F.: Setting standards for 3D visualization of cultural heritage in Europe and beyond. In: Bentkowska-Kafel, A., Denard, H., Baker, D. (eds.) Paradata and Transparency in Virtual Heritage, pp. 23–36. Ashgate, Burlington (2012)
61. Kuhn, T.S.: Die Entstehung des Neuen. Suhrkamp, Frankfurt a. M. (1978)
62. Köhler, T.: Die Konstruktion des Selbst in der computervermittelten Kommunikation. VS Verlag für Sozialwissenschaften, Wiesbaden (2003)
63. Hinterwaldner, I.: Das systemische Bild. Ikonizität im Rahmen computerbasierter Echtzeitsimulationen. eikones, München (2010)
64. Lenhard, J.: (Im Druck) Designing an image. Functions of imagery in simulation modeling (Arbeitstitel). In: Ammon, S., Hinterwaldner, I. (eds.) Bildlichkeit im Zeitalter der Modellierung
65. Honing, H.: On the growing role of observation, formalization and experimental method in musicology. Empirical Musicology Rev. 1(1), 3 (2006)
66. Schophaus, M., Dienel, H.-L., von Braun, C.-F.: Von Brücken und Einbahnstraßen. Aufgaben für das Kooperationsmanagement interdisziplinärer Forschung (Discussion paper Nr. 08/03). Berlin (2003)
67. Gibbons, M.: The New Production of Knowledge. The Dynamics of Science and Research in Contemporary Societies. SAGE, London (1994)
68. Münster, S.: Interdisziplinäre Kooperation bei der Erstellung virtueller geschichtswissenschaftlicher 3D-Rekonstruktionen. In: Stelzer, R. (ed.) ENTWERFEN ENTWICKELN ERLEBEN 2014. Beiträge zur virtuellen Produktentwicklung und Konstruktionstechnik, pp. 299–312. TUD Press, Dresden (2014)
69. Klein, J.T.: A conceptual vocabulary of interdisciplinary science. In: Weingart, P., Stehr, N. (eds.) Practising Interdisciplinarity, pp. 3–24. University of Toronto Press, Toronto (2000)
70. Münster, S., Köhler, T., Hoppe, S.: 3D modeling technologies as tools for the reconstruction and visualization of historic items in humanities. A literature-based survey. In: Traviglia, A. (ed.) Across Space and Time. Papers from the 41st Conference on Computer Applications and Quantitative Methods in Archaeology, Perth, 25–28 March 2013, pp. 430–441. Amsterdam University Press, Amsterdam (2015)
71. Peterßen, W.H.: Wissenschaftliches Arbeiten. nicht leicht, aber erlernbar. München (1987)
72. Meinsen, S.: Konstruktivistisches Wissensmanagement. Weinheim (2003)
73. Baumgartner, P.: Der Hintergrund des Wissens. Vorarbeiten zu einer Kritik der programmierbaren Vernunft. Kärntner Druck- und Verlagsgesellschaft, Klagenfurt (1993)
74. Polanyi, M.: The tacit dimension, 18th edn (2009). University of Chicago Press, Chicago (1966)
75. Wray, K.B.: Scientific authorship in the age of collaborative research. Stud. Hist. Philos. Sci. 37(3), 505–514 (2006). doi:10.1016/j.shpsa.2005.07.011
76. Osborne, J.W., Holland, A.: What is authorship, and what should it be? A survey of prominent guidelines for determining authorship in scientific publications. Pract. Assess. Res. Eval. 14(15), 1–19 (2009)
77. Biagioli, M.: Rights or rewards? Changing frameworks of scientific authorship. J. Coll. Univ. Law 27(1), 83–108 (2000)
78. Deutsche Forschungsgemeinschaft. Vorschläge zur Sicherung guter wissenschaftlicher Praxis. Empfehlungen der Kommission "Selbstkontrolle in der Wissenschaft" (Denkschrift). Wiley-VCH, Weinheim (1998)
79. Goetz, H.-W.: Proseminar Geschichte. Mittelalter, vol. 1719. Ulmer, Stuttgart (1993)

80. Jablonka, P., Kirchner, S., Serangeli, J.: Troia VR. A virtual reality model of troy and the troad. In: Proceedings of Computer Applications in Archaeology (CAA) 2002, 2003, pp. 13–20 (2002)

81. Howell, M., Prevenier, W.: Werkstatt des Historikers Eine Einführung in die historischen Methoden. Köln (2004)

82. Ronzino, P., Amico, N., Niccolucci, F.: Assessment and comparison of metadata schemas for architectural heritage. In: XXIII CIPA Symposium – Proceedings (2011)

83. Pfarr-Harfst, M.: Virtual scientific models. In: Ng, K., Bowen, J.P., McDaid, S. (eds.) Electronic Visualisation and the Arts, London, pp. 157–163 (2013)

84. Günther, H.: Kritische Computer-Visualisierung in der kunsthistorischen Lehre. In: Frings, M. (ed.) Der Modelle Tugend. CAD und die neuen Räume der Kunstgeschichte. Weimar, pp. 111–122 (2001)

85. Fleck, L.: Entstehung und Entwicklung einer wissenschaftlichen Tatsache. Einführung in die Lehre vom Denkstil und Denkkollektiv. Suhrkamp, Frankfurt a. M (1980)

86. Peirce, C.S.: Collected Papers of Charles Sanders Peirce, vol. 1, besucht am, 10 January 2014 (1931)

87. Latour, B., Woolgar, S.: Laboratory Life. The Construction of Scientific Facts. Princeton University Press, Princeton (1986)

88. Ware, C.: Information Visualization: Perception for Design. The Morgan Kaufmann Series in Interactive Technologies, vol. 22. Morgan Kaufman, San Francisco (2004)

89. Frischer, B., Dakouri-Hild, A.: Beyond Illustration: 2D and 3D Digital Technologies as Tools for Discovery in Archaeology. BAR International Series, vol. 1805. Archaeopress, Oxford (2008)

90. Ling, Z., Ruoming, S., Keqin, Z.: Rule-based 3D modeling for chinese traditional architecture. In: Remondino, F., El-Hakim, S. (eds.) 3D-ARCH 2007, Zürich (2007)

91. Sachse, P.: Idea materialis. Entwurfsdenken und Darstellungshandeln. über die allmähliche Verfertigung der Gedanken beim Skizzieren und Modellieren. Logos-Verl., Berlin (2002)

92. Wulf, U., Riedel, A.: Investigating buildings three-dimensionally. The "Domus Severiana" on the palatine. In: Haselberger, L., Humphrey, J., Abernathy, D.: (eds.) Imaging Ancient Rome: Documentation, Visualization, Imagination: Proceedings of the 3rd Williams Symposium on Classical Architecture, Rome, 20–23 May 2004, pp. 221–233. Journal of Roman Archaeology, Portsmouth (2006)

93. Carrozzino, M., Evangelista, C., Brondi, R., Tecchia, F., Bergamasco, M.: Virtual reconstruction of paintings as a tool for research and learning. J. Cult. Heritage 15, 308–312 (2014)

94. Fontana, R., Greco, M., Materazzi, M., Pampaloni, E., Pezzati, L., Rocchini, C., Scopigno, R.: Three-dimensional modelling of statues: the Minerva of Arezzo. J. Cult. Heritage 3(4), 325–331. doi:10.1016/s1296-2074(02)01242-6

95. Arbace, L., Sonnino, E., Callieri, M., Dellepiane, M., Fabbri, M., Iaccarino Idelson, A., Scopigno, R.: Innovative uses of 3D digital technologies to assist the restoration of a fragmented terracotta statue. J. Cult. Heritage 14(4), 332–345 (2013). doi:http://dx.doi.org/10.1016/j.culher.2012.06.008. Accessed 27 July 2016

96. Saft, S., Kaliske, M.: Computational approach towards structural investigations for the restoration of historical keyboard instruments. J. Cult. Heritage 135, 165–174 (2012)

97. Wiemer, W.: Harmonie und Maß – Ergebnisse der Proportionsanalysen der Abteikirche Ebrach. In: Archaeology in Architecture: Studies in Honor of Cecli L. Striker, Mainz, pp. 199–216 (2005)

98. Masini, N., Fonseca, C.D., Geraldi, E., Sabino, G.: An algorithm for computing the original units of measure of medieval architecture. J. Cult. Heritage 5(1), 7–15. doi:http://dx.doi.org/10.1016/j.culher.2002.12.001. Accessed 28 July 2016

99. Kohle, H.: Digitale Bildwissenschaft. Glückstadt (2013)
100. Mele, E., De Luca, A., Giordano, A.: Modelling and analysis of a basilica under earthquake loading. J. Cult. Heritage **4**(4), 355–367 (2003). doi:http://dx.doi.org/10.1016/j.culher. 2003.03.002. Accessed 27 July 2016
101. Balocco, C., Grazzini, G.: Numerical simulation of ancient natural ventilation systems of historical buildings. A case study in Palermo. J. Cult. Heritage **10**(2), 313–318 (2009). doi: http://dx.doi.org/10.1016/j.culher.2008.03.008. Accessed 28 July 2016
102. Havemann, S., Wagener, O.: Castles and their landscape – a case study towards parametric historic reconstruction. In: Hoppe, S., Breitling, S., Fitzner, S. (eds.) Virtual Palaces II: Lost Palaces and Their Afterlife, Virtual Reconstruction Between Science and Media, Proceedings of the European Science Foundation Research Networking Programme PALATIUM Meeting at Munich, 13–15 April 2012 (2016)
103. Hermon, S.: Reasoning in 3D. A critical appraisal of the role of 3D modelling and virtual reconstructions in archaeology. In: Frischer, B. (ed.) Beyond Illustration: 2D and 3D Digital Technologies as Tools for Discovery in Archaeology, vol. 1805, pp. 36–45. Tempus Reparatum, Oxford (2008)
104. Remondino, F., El-Hakim, S., Girardi, S., Rizzi, A., Benedetti, S., Gonzo, L.: 3D virtual reconstruction and visualization of complex architectures - the 3D-ARCH project. In: Remondino, F., El-Hakim, S., Gonzo, L. (eds.) 3D-ARCH 2009, Zürich (2009)
105. Munslow, A.: The Routledge Companion to Historical Studies. Routledge, New York (2006)
106. Münster, S., Jahn, P.-H., Wacker, M.: Von Plan- und Bildquellen zum virtuellen Gebäudemodell. Zur Bedeutung der Bildlichkeit für die digitale 3D-Rekonstruktion historischer Architektur. In: Ammon, S., Hinterwaldner, I. (eds.) Bildlichkeit im Zeitalter der Modellierung. Operative Artefakte in Entwurfsprozessen der Architektur und des Ingenieurwesens. eikones. Wilhelm Fink Verlag, München (in print)
107. Hasler Roumois, U.: Studienbuch Wissensmanagement. Grundlagen der Wissensarbeit in Wirtschafts-, Non-Profit- und Public-Organisationen. vol. 2954, 2., *berarb. und erw. Aufl.. edn. Orell Füssli, Zürich (2010)
108. Schumann, H., Müller, W.: Visualisierung. Grundlagen und allgemeine Methoden. Springer, Berlin (2000)
109. Reers, J.: The properties of materials and their everyday uses. In: Reers, J. (ed.) That's Chemistry! abpi, pp. 11–24 (2000)
110. Pfarr-Harfst, M.: Documentation system for digital reconstructions. Reference to the Mausoleum of the Tang-Dynastie at Zhaoling, in Shaanxi Province, China. In: 16th International Conference on "Cultural Heritage and New Technologies" Vienna, Wien, pp. 648–658 (2011)
111. Doerr, M.: The CIDOC CRM – an ontological approach to semantic interoperability of metadata. AI Mag. **24**(3) (2003)
112. Felicetti, A., Lorenzini, M.: Metadata and tools for integration and preservation of cultural heritage 3D information. In: XXIII CIPA Symposium – Proceedings (2011)
113. Hermon, S., Nikodem, J., Perlingieri, C.: Deconstructing the VR - data transparency, quantified uncertainty and reliability of 3D models. In: Arnold, D., Ioannides, M., Niccolucci, F., Mania, K. (eds.) 7th International Symposium on Virtual Reality, Archaeology and Cultural Heritage (VAST 2006), pp. 123–129. Eurographics Association, Nicosia (2006)
114. Stojakovic, V., Tepavcevic, B.: Optimal methods for 3D modeling of devastated architectural objects. In: Remondino, F., El-Hakim, S., Gonzo, L. (eds.) 3D-ARCH 2009, Zürich (2009)
115. Havemann, S., Fellner, D.W.: Generative parametric design of gothic window tracery. In: VAST 2004: The 5th International Symposium on Virtual Reality, Archaeology and Cultural Heritage. Eurographics Association, Brussels (2004)

116. Garagnani, S., Manferdini, A.M.: Parametric accuracy: building information modeling process applied to the cultural heritage preservation. In: 3DARCH 2013 (2013)
117. Prechtel, N., Münster, S., Kröber, C., Schubert, C., Sebastian, S.: Presenting cultural heritage landscapes - from GIS via 3D models to interactive presentation frameworks. In: ISPRS Annals of the Photogrammetry, Remote Sensing and Spatial Information Sciences XL-5/W2 (XXIV International CIPA Symposium), pp. 253–258 (2013)
118. Bourgeois, J., De Wulf, A., Goosens, R., Gheyle, W.: Saving the frozen Scythian tombs of the Altai Mountains (Central Asia). World Archaeol. 39, 458–474 (2007)
119. Wengenroth, U.: Was ist Technikgeschichte? (1998)

Typical Workflows, Documentation Approaches and Principles of 3D Digital Reconstruction of Cultural Heritage

Mieke Pfarr-Harfst[✉]

Technische Universität Darmstadt, Digital Design, Darmstadt, Germany
pfarr@dg.tu-darmstadt.de

Abstract. Three-dimensional, scholarly computer models are part of digital cultural heritage. As such, they should be considered as a medium of communication and put under the scrutiny of academic research. Starting by outlining the background to the Author's research, specific topics such as typologies of three-dimensional models, their use in scholarship and relevant work processes are considered in detail. Based on current studies and investigation of working processes, a definition of typology terms and guidelines are discussed.

Keywords: Cultural heritage · Digital reconstruction · Workflows · Guidelines · Working process

1 Background

Three-dimensional (3D) computer models have been used as a medium of communication in the area of cultural heritage research and knowledge transfer since 1980s. Despite the initial strong resistance within the mainstream academia [1] this method of representation has been widely established in popular science, e.g. in the context of exhibitions.

It is possible to communicate knowledge available about a cultural heritage object, raise awareness of it and generate a new knowledge, by means of three-dimensional models. This, in turn, may in part become a component of the scholarly process. The models themselves become the conveyers of information, and part of digital cultural heritage [2], a source for scholarship and means of information transfer. Knowledge itself is always connected to a medium and representation [3, p. 6]. If one considers the models to be bearers of knowledge, they are then, in the interaction with speech and written language, another form of expression, a digital medium for representing knowledge.

Space, in its entire complexity, constitutes a research theme that is central to build cultural heritage. The interaction of space shaping elements, their rhythm, design and organization, as well as their appearance, depends on the individual perception of space and can often be only experienced, and understood, in near-realistic three-dimensionality. Research into cultural heritage objects and their spatial positioning also play a significant role. Here as well, the process of modelling the digital object stimulates a discovery of knowledge.

S. Münster et al. (Eds.): 3D Research Challenges II, LNCS 10025, pp. 32–46, 2016.
DOI: 10.1007/978-3-319-47647-6_2

The workflow that results in the computer model is a great opportunity for studying architectural design and other characteristics of a building, the architectural language of an architect and the inclusion of his concept in the urban plan, or other scheme, in more detail [1, pp. 133–145].

This learning process, at the end of which one acquires new knowledge, is for the most part an incidental by-product of the many visualization projects for use in museums and exhibitions [4, pp. 13–22]. Three-dimensional models are purposely being used for gaining knowledge of built or object-related cultural heritage. Cultural heritage researchers increasingly recognize the potential of scholarly methods of visualization.

The areas of application and scope of three-dimensional computer models have become far more complex and multi-faceted, also within the history of art, than were conceivable at the inception of 3D digital visualizations. Alongside educational use, two additional areas of application have been established: the examination and preservation of cultural heritage. Due to technological developments within these three areas, the range of applications of three-dimensional models of cultural heritage have become diverse. Application areas and potential use generally overlap because, in an ideal scenario, a digital model or dataset may serve various applications and output formats.

Diversity of possible applications presupposes the heterogeneity of methodologies and workflows available. A fundamental approach and rudimentary research are required, depending on how information about a model, and new knowledge it may generate, are dealt with in the future.

2   Correlation Model

The workflow and methodology relate directly to chosen application, its characteristics and potentiality that can be juxtaposed in a correlation model (Fig. 1). In this way, structuring of what appears impenetrable may be achieved. The correlation starts with the characteristics of three-dimensional models from which potentials can be generated. These potential use can be transferred to the possibilities of technical applications as well as three application fields. These areas of application – research, communication of knowledge and preservation – can be traced back to recognized principles of CH visualizations.

Digital three-dimensional models display three characteristics: products of digital technology, three-dimensionality and graphics.

A dataset consists of a sequence of numbers that can be fragmented and reassembled without damage. This opens up many possibilities for application of data.

Three-dimensionality makes it possible to experience spatial interrelationships within the entire complexity. Thus it refers to space as a question central to the discussion of architectural heritage. So the contextualization of object and space becomes comprehensible.

The language of images is universal and requires no encoding to be understood. This is in contrast to blueprints and architectural plans, which are subject to normed encoding and are thus not readable to everyone.

The three characteristics of three-dimensional computer models of cultural heritage, identified above, offer a range of possibilities to:

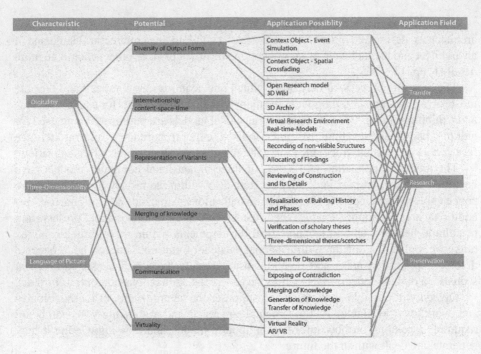

Fig. 1. Correlation model

- Diversity of formats of output
- Clarify complex interrelationships of content and space
- Represent variants
- Combine and verify existing knowledge and generate new knowledge
- Communicate and transfer knowledge
- Experience virtuality

2.1 Diversity of Output Formats

Many different output formats are possible for a digital dataset, such as renderings, simulations, film sequences, web-based applications, haptic models, 3D PDFs, Virtual Reality (VR) and Augmented Reality (AR) applications. These output formats have supported knowledge transfer for many years. The output format may be chosen to suit the requirements of particular scholarly questions, which offers many research opportunities. Examples of possible output formats include:

- **Simulations** put events into the context of their built surroundings;
- **Crossfading** of 3D models with images can clarify spatial relationships, also *in situ*;
- **Models accessible in real time** make the space, object and concept perceptible;
- **3D Wiki** provides a basis for an open research model that may be revised and updated;
- **3D PDF,** coupled with a database, may constitute a 3D archive, contributing primarily to the preservation of cultural heritage.

Owing to ongoing and rapid technological advances, further applications are being developed.

2.2 Clarification of Complex Spatial and/or Temporal Relationships

The potential of computer models of cultural heritage for clarification of complex spatial and/or temporal relationships is based on three-dimensional and graphic characteristics of the models.

By means of these characteristics, structures, that have not survived or were never built, can be visualized and understood, thus contributing to enhanced understanding of the broader context. A further application may also be possible through interlinking of different data. Thus, it is possible to investigate and verify construction details and principles, or the relationships, between the object and its space. The investigation and superimposition of different phases in the construction history, as well as the inclusion of temporal data may be possible.

2.3 Representation of Versions

Owing to the digital nature of media employed to create the virtual space, different versions of design or building phases may be represented within a single architectural computer model. Three-dimensional propositions or sketches may be created to support cognitive processes and facilitate systematic scholarly verification of existing assumptions about the subject of representation. Different design solutions may be juxtaposed. The model may thus serve as a medium of scholarly discourse and contribute to discovery of new knowledge.

2.4 Fusion, Generation, and Verification

Scholarly three-dimensional models rest upon fundamental knowledge that is generated from sources of varying nature, origin and authorship. An opportunity therefore arises to fuse and verify the existing knowledge, generate and communicate new knowledge. The associated research process involves consolidation of earlier findings, the creation of a basis for further research, generation of new knowledge and the preservation of knowledge about cultural heritage. Over and above that, this knowledge can be processed through the transfer of the dataset in appropriate output formats for transfer in a popular-scientific manner.

2.5 Virtuality

The digital and graphic nature of three-dimensional computer models brings further opportunities for the research process: communication, interaction and intuitive interaction within virtuality. Precisely such models have been developed e.g. for design production since year [5]. Communication, interaction and intuition are becoming important research components of these models. Devices such as tablets and smartphones are directly based on such functionalities. For research applications, these technical developments may mean communication, including a meeting of the involved parties in virtual space, in which one can touch spatial elements and discuss questions and solutions.

The characteristics of computer models and a wide range of their applications to scholarship, outlined above, do not pretend to be exhaustive. Further research is being undertaken. The preliminary correlation model (Fig. 1), presented here, displays a considerable complexity. It demonstrates the heterogeneity of three-dimensional computer models used in cultural heritage studies alongside relevant workflows and methodologies.

3   Interdisciplinarity

Owing to the interdisciplinary nature of most research projects in this area, the heterogeneity and complexity should be emphasized. Research into cultural heritage involves not only disciplines traditionally preoccupied with reconstruction of the past, such as the history of art and archaeology, but also borrows methods of architecture and computer science. The scholarly role is generally taken on by art and architectural historians and archaeologists, while the architects deal with the creation of models and technical information systems. The composition of the interdisciplinary team is becoming ever more complex and varies according to given research questions. In addition to the theses disciplines that pioneered digital architectural reconstruction, the following can be included: computer graphics, geodesy, artists, historians – to mention only a few. One may however ask, what are the advantages and the effect of these 3D models on the technical development and the scholarly methodology chosen for the investigation?

In order to establish the long-term standards and guidelines for a workflow and methodology, the influence of other factors, such as a situation given, the project goal, the project partners – i.e. the project context – must all be considered. In addition to the aspect of workflow and methodology there are so many challenges to fundamental scientific theory. It should be possible, subject to further research, to construct a model of disciplinary contribution that considers the participation of the individual disciplines within the given context of a project, as in the correlation model. Alongside the dependency on disciplinary participation and the said context is directly connected to the question of common working methodology for these models of disciplinary contribution.

4   Models as Sources of Information

If models may be understood as sources of information, it may be useful to categorize this information. Thus, the following types of information can be identified [3]:

- information contained within models
- information about models
- information that may be derived from models.

The information contained within models is primarily the information gathered and generated therein as a result of information acquisition from sources, the process of generating and the project context. The information about models concerns the context of the given project and its background. information from models can be gained through combining the information contained within and about models.

The information in and about the models could be lost if an individual person, who generated these models is not involved in the project or the process of generating anymore [3]. Thus, the information contained within models is subject to a codification that can be deciphered through secondary information that may be assumed from models. If one takes Mahr's concept of knowledge – mentioned above - and applies it to a three-dimensional model considered as a source of information, the model should be of something and for something.

A three-dimensional computer model of built cultural heritage is a model of a built structure or an object. From the point of view of the general public it is important whether this object or building still exists or not. Yet not only the model, but also its spatial, historical, social contexts and the associated secondary, even tertiary information are components that must be taken into account in any case. However, the model should also reflect various other factors that impact upon its development [6].

The principle of a "model for something" is far more complex. The computer-generated model can itself become a model for further research. In order to further substantiate Mahr's concept of knowledge, the understanding of the model as representation of something, while at the same time illustrating something, must be directly included in the correlation model. This confirms the complexity of the field.

According to the UNESCO definition of cultural heritage, all knowledge that computer models impart constitutes cultural heritage [2].

5   Loss of Information

The lack of standards and guidelines is like "missing rules of the game for the community" [3, p. 7]. In the process of knowledge acquisition and methodology the lack of common guidelines is directly connected to the loss of information within, about and from the models. The heterogeneity and complexity of the field includes a series of paradigms that favor the loss of knowledge. A further factor contributing to the loss of knowledge has most certainly been in recent years the technological development and the subsequent proliferation of models. Owing to the availability of open-source software for three-dimensional applications, a non-academic user community has expanded. One can observe a noticeable increase of non-professional models and the associated problems.

According to the website of the online archive Google 3D warehouse, there are "millions of 3D models" [7] in a wide range of categories. Three-dimensional computer models of built cultural heritage can be found there mainly under the designation "reconstruction". However, to be considered a reconstruction in the academic sense, they lack a documented verification of sources and a record of the creation process. At the time of writing the archive lists 402 models in the category "Castles of the World" and 237 models of "Churches"; a search for "Town" yields approx. 700 visualization projects [7]. This proliferation of models, paired with the overall heterogeneity of the field and the unhindered access to information, forebodes the far-reaching consequences for the quality of three-dimensional models of cultural heritage and their scholarly and pedagogical values. Here we are facing the democratization of information and the ever increasing volume of unverified information. The universal language of images is a decisive factor in the dissemination of potentially incorrect information. Pictures lodge in our minds and are more rapidly absorbed than texts. Thus, no "model can do without a system of order to qualify as knowledge" [3, p. 7]. This idea of Mahr can be directly applied to three-dimensional models. The information contained in models and the associated digital cultural heritage, as well as the loss of control over the quality of information conveyed has already become reality. Although 15 years ago there was an initial theoretical debate concerning this topic, as summarized in Frings's "Der Modelle Tugend", these efforts seem to have been in vain or negated [1]. Three-dimensional models of cultural heritage have a life of their own. A scholarly theory is lacking.

A study of the subject, which investigates 452 digital reconstructions and three-dimensional models, should be noted. It is striking that very few studies deal with theoretical questions of universal interest, but rather with technical implementation and production [8]. This lack of theoretical framework affects all scholarly levels in the field of CH visualizations. Rudimentary issues currently affecting research have been identified through a survey of the members of the working group "Digital Reconstructions" which has been established in Germany in 2013. The issues range from a definition of a theoretical frameworks and system of documentation to scholarly structures for methodologies and localization of 3D models [9].

In 1995 Koob published the paper, "Architectura Virtualis", in which he noted the lack of: a guiding theory and generally accepted principles, generally accepted principles that could be coupled with appropriate systems of documentation and archiving:

- "Wir forschen und arbeiten an der neuen Technik, dokumentieren unser Wissen mit der alten Technik". [We are investigating and working with new technology, but document our knowledge with old technology]. [10, p. 19]
- "Wir betreten ein neues Territorium und haben noch keine Regeln." [We are entering a new territory, but do not yet have any rules]. [10, p. 21]

Despite more than twenty years of applying three-dimensional computer models to the study of cultural heritage, Koob's observations are still valid. This is also based on the fact that further development of technology has had precedence over rudimentary research, in recent years in particular. Most research projects are either technology oriented or based on a special research question, but not really universal. Researchers concentrate on a concrete problem that is generally irrelevant to other questions. A superordinate, universally accepted theoretical approach is generally lacking. However, both levels, the theoretical and user-oriented, are indispensable for establishment of three-dimensional computer models in the three areas of application – preservation, transfer of knowledge and research. The reasons for the absence of such basic principles can be found, among other motives, in the lack of recognition of this research method.

6 Documentation, Sustainability and Preservation of Information

The scholarly use of digital models and development of relevant methodologies necessitates a scholarly approach, transferability and sustainability of data. For several years, scholarly papers and research projects have been focusing on archiving, documentation and sustainability of three-dimensional computer models. Theoretical work must be distinguished from projects that address specific questions. Sustainable preservation of three-dimensional models should distinguish between possible loss of technical functionality of software and/or hardware, and the loss of content. Each model is created using a certain technical system and depends on its requirements. When the technical system stops working, data may be lost. The notorious obsolescence of three-dimensional models of the first generation poses the problem of data that are no longer readable. Had the models been stored in a different manner, the knowledge about the digitally reconstructed buildings and structures would not have been lost alongside the data. This represents a loss of content. The lack of documentation strategies and standards results in the loss of knowledge represented by the models and the knowledge about the models. This subsequently hinders passing the knowledge on; therefore, knowledge cannot be reused in later research.

The development of suitable documentation systems and strategies must be undertaken on both the theoretical and applied levels. Implementation must always respect the interaction between theory and practice. The theoretical scholarly approaches to digital reconstruction involve a definition of possible basic components of a documentation system. Four parts must be covered and integrated in such a documentation system in order to preserve the knowledge represented by the models in a sustainable manner. The four part documentation [11, pp. 83 ff.] should cover the background, its sources and contexts, as well as record the processes involved. The four part documentation should derive directly from the defined principles of scholarly documentation. It should be structured, reproducible, transparent, sustainable, editable, true, complete and clearly presented.

The first part should concern the background to the reconstruction i.e. the basic information about the project, including the contributors, the start date, the technical system used, the project rationale, aims and objectives that have direct influence on the results.

The second part should document the cultural, historical and architectural contexts of the building and its objects to be reconstructed.

The third part should concern the documentation structure of reconstruction project- The documentation structure must be adjusted individually to the conditions of each research project. This is also applicable to three-dimensional computer models. Each project has its own system of order, terminology and structures that affect documentation and must be controlled.

The fourth part of documentation should concern evaluation and should demonstrate direct connection between the sources, processes and the model. The four part documentation fulfils the documentation requirement of an explicit allocation of object to document. Here the simplest form is the source or method catalogs for the individual objects, structures and buildings. The allocation of a source to objects takes place in a tabular source catalogs. In the method catalogs the object is linked to a process and source. The process steps, as well as the interim results, are shown by means of a simple input-output representation. These tabular catalogues are entered and linked to a simple datum archive that has been defined in part three.

Bearing in mind that data are individual to a given project, which steps in the development of a 3D model should be archived. This question should be carefully considered in order to avoid an unnecessary overload of data. Milestones in the development of models may serve as reference values of basic decisions made in the course of modeling process. In recent years numerous pilot projects [12–14], with various aims and approaches were realized and solutions these certain projects developed. The pilot projects are being only mentioned here; their evaluation in terms of sustainability, applicability and validity, is yet to be carried out.

It will be necessary in the future to bring the theory closer to practice and enhance user-friendly applications. The goal is to design a documentation system that requires minimum effort to generate maximum knowledge that can be sustained and preserved.

7 Study of Workflows, Principles and Typologies

It has been argued above that, the development process of three-dimensional models is generally associated with generation of new knowledge. The application of these models to research into cultural heritage, as virtual research environments (VREs), has increased during the past decade. The general use of the models as VREs has long been established e.g. in aircraft industry, and recognized as a development tool [5]. In order to employ VREs in basic, object-oriented investigations into cultural heritage adequate methodological principles are necessary. Here, however, studies and evaluations related to status quo of existing workflows of VREs in CH are required. Within the scope of research conducted by the Action "Colour and Space in Cultural Heritage" (COSCH) [15], the workflows of various research projects were investigated at three leading academic institutions. The result was a definition of a workflow and of methodological principles and typology of three-dimensional visualization of cultural heritage. Twenty-five research projects conducted in the 2000s and 2010s were investigated. The study was conducted by the Author in 2015 at the following institutions participating in the COSCH Action:

- Digital Design Unit, Technische Universität Darmstadt (formerly: Information and Communication in Architecture)
- Department of Digital Humanities, King's College London
- Centre for Humanities, University College London
- Department of Computer Science, University of Sarajevo.

The outcomes of workshops held bilaterally with colleagues from these institutions were included in the study.

The following research questions guided the investigation:

- Are there any similarities between different methods and workflows?
- What are the similarities (definition) and differences (definition)?

- What are the reasons for the identified differences and similarities of the 3D modeling work?
- Are there any dependencies between the properties and scope of workflows, capacity, and possible applications?
- Is it possible to identify some general phases of a workflow and define key concepts?

The investigation involved:

- Part I: analysis, evaluation and comparison of different projects of the three institutions
- Part II: workshops and discussions with research staff at the three institutions.

The various conditions of the 3D-modeling process were an essential part of the investigation (part I). Initially, the conditions were defined as a basis for the systematic and objective investigation of the projects.

In the meetings (part II) typical visualization techniques were discussed (3D modeling, laser scanning, photogrammetry, 3D imaging, BIM), as well as different workflows and the problem of how knowledge may be evidenced.

The investigation of the 25 research projects was based on the defined objective criteria:

- Project background
- Project [organisational/historical/other] context schedule of work
- Contributors
- Aims and objectives of the project (research, transfer of knowledge, preservation)
- Application field(s)
- Application/preservation format
- Area of possible application
- Type of 3D visualization method(s)
- Technical system
- Visualisation methods and the workflow
- Outcomes

These criteria have been identified in the course of earlier research by the Author and through a review of literature [16]. Establishing these criteria is essential for ensuring visualisation-based research is as reliable as possible and for the results of respective projects to be comparable.

To design a proper documentation system or assure scholarly content of desired quality, fundamental questions need to be addressed first.

These questions pertain to the following:

- Workflows
- Typologies of 3D visualization
- Capacity of 3D scholarly visualization
- Possible application fields.

Based on the Author's investigation, it was possible to define the working process as an input-output design. Comparing different workflows of the projects conducted in Sarajevo, London and Darmstadt a similarity of the respective workflows was observed.

It was possible to identify four broad phases: preparation, collection, processing, finishing (Fig. 2).

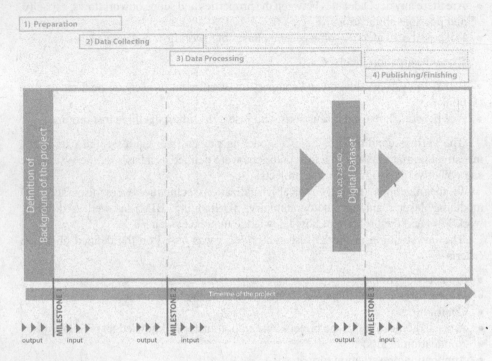

Fig. 2. Workflow and milestones

For a project to reach completion, all criteria identified above - aims and objectives, human and financial resources, work plan and provision of technical infrastructure, etc. - should be addresses during the preparation phase. The output of this phase is the input for the next phase, and defines the method of and technology for collecting the data.

The input of the "data processing" phase is based on the results of "data collection" and the chosen method. During the "data processing" phase the collected data may be used in different ways, depending on the objectives and the aim of the project. The result of "data processing" is a digital dataset (2D or 3D), which subsequently becomes the basis for the "finishing" phase and the final result of the workflow. The different application fields and possibilities of use offer a great scope for processing the digital dataset.

During and between these phases there is a principle of input-output. The background of the project generates the framework for the project and its workflows.

At the beginning of a project some milestones should be defined to manage the project effectively.

8   Principles of a Workflow

The discussed study of the Author is the basis for first principles and guidelines for working processes and methodology. In the future, recognized guidelines [17] will be indispensable for ensuring scholarly quality of the models and to alleviate the loss of knowledge. Similar technical rules have long been established, and generally accepted, in architectural practice. In connection with quality assurance, Mahr refers to "rules of conduct in the community" into which project context and working process are incorporated [3]. The following initial methodological guidelines have been compiled through experience and theoretical considerations:

- Choosing the technical system
- The process of creation of a three-dimensional computer model depends on the aims and objectives of the project. These, in turn, influence the choice of hardware and software, depending on the type of representation required and the type of associated media.
- Determination of LODs (level of detail) of the model
- The research results and desired scholarly objective refer to the structures of the model. A detailed digital reconstruction of the building is often not possible. The design of the model structures and the required level of detail facilitate the workflow and archiving.
- Terminology
- Data exchange during a research process, data entry into databases and the structured documentation of a digital dataset and results are only possible through a suitable vocabulary for describing 3D, scholarly models. This topic is directly linked to challenges related to documentation strategies.
- Classification of and structuring the sources
- The 3D-model, the working process and the underlying resources must be divided into meaningful classes specific to a given project. Only then the catalogs of sources and methods can be compiled
- Recording the milestones
- As described above, in the section on documentation, keeping a record of significant steps in the production of models is absolutely necessary for the transparency of the decision-making process and workflows. A suitable filing system (file structure or database) supported by principles of classification, model structuring and referencing process is a further guideline. This provides a basis for the verification of technical and scholarly standards and sustainability of 3D-models.
- Documentation of the working process in a uniform system
- The progress of work should be recorded (alongside the model status) according to the milestone principle. The introduction of a simple mask (Fig. 2) subsequent to the input-output procedure fulfils scholarly criteria.

After the above-mentioned guidelines or principles have been implemented, all data can be contained in a repository, consisting of sources, description of the workflow and the model. The structure of the repository should be adapted to the given project.

There is no claim to completeness of the guidelines presented above. They have rather been conceived to stimulate a discussion of future directions. Adherence to these basic principles is expected to help with archiving, sustaining and reviewing of data, without complicated technical systems. The latter would require staff and financial resources. Before an adequate documentation system becomes available, the first step proposed here is expected to counteract the loss of technical and subject-related knowledge that is already present and growing.

9   Typology, Localization and Definition

The initial objective of the present book was to examine how one should deal with data and knowledge represented through three-dimensional computer models. Knowledge implies a search for universally recognized rules. The lack of a theoretical basis for producing three-dimensional models of cultural heritage is an issue that arises alongside questions concerning their documentation and archiving. These include questions of typology, conceptual definition of basics and ultimately localization in the research environment. The range of possible applications available for these models (considered as a research tool and method of preservation of cultural history, as well as a medium of knowledge) have increased significantly. This expansion clearly makes it difficult to see such 3D models as tools of a particular academic discipline. Research funders still regard the 3D model only as a visualization method, but not as a research method or archiving tool. Those applying for grants and grant awarding bodies both face a problem of allocating the projects to the appropriate grant program. For this purpose, a theoretical-superordinate approach with the goal of extracting typologies and generally valid definitions is necessary; these are found directly at the intersection of methodology and workflow as research process.

As mentioned above, the applications of three-dimensional models of cultural heritage are many. Eight different typologies have been defined so far (Fig. 3).

- **Type A**: Images, renderings or films resulting from a 3D dataset; original film or image as an object in itself
- **Type B**: 3D images or panoramic photos as a 2,5D visualization
- **Type C**: 3D data resulting from photogrammetry

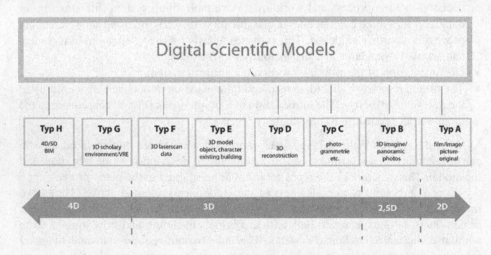

Fig. 3. Typologies of CH visualizations

- **Type D**: 3D reconstruction of a no longer existing building or object
- **Type E**: 3D model of an existing building or object; 3D model of character as an avatar
- **Type F**: 3D data resulting from laser scanning as a method of preservation and recording method
- **Type G**: Virtual research environments or 3D scholarly environments
- **Type H**: Building Information Modeling (BIM) and Heritage BIM

The identification of eight types of cultural heritage visualizations represents work in progress. Further investigation is needed to verify this preliminary typology and enhance it with further types, as well as to define all types, based on earlier research and publications.

The question of typology is directly related to the question of a superordinate terminology. The listing of typologies once again shows the heterogeneity of the entire subject area, which goes far beyond pure reconstruction with 3D tools. This again refers to the relationship between applications and potentials, and again digital reconstruction is only a portion of the application spectrum. A possible superordinate concept therefore could be "digital scientific models". In the context of this discussion, digital scientific models could be defined, in a universally valid way, as computer-aided models of historic buildings, structures or construction elements, which collect, merge, summarize and visualize subject-related knowledge. These processes result in new knowledge. The models communicate past research and open the subject to future research. As such they are an innovative and sustainable tool for investigation, communication and preservation of building culture.

Such a neutral formulation does justice to the heterogeneity and complexity of the entire field. It includes all possible application and considers the information represented in the models.

10   Conclusion

However, the heterogeneity and complexity of this subject area requires fundamental research. Communities of practice may first agree upon guidelines based on well-grounded theoretical research. The questions of order structures, methodological guidelines, or even required technical standards of workflows may only be addressed through collaborative research. All three aspects of work – theory, pilot projects and applications – are important and must continuously interact.

Acknowledgements. The authors gratefully acknowledge the support of the European Cooperation in Science and Technology, the COST Action TD1201 "Colour and Space in Cultural Heritage" (www.cosch.info).

References

1. Frings, M. (ed.): Der Modelle Tugend. CAD und die neuen Räume der Kunstgeschichte, Weimar (2001)

2. UNESCO: Charter on the Preservation of Digital Heritage, Records of the General Conference, Paris, 29 September to 17 October 2003
3. Mahr, B.: Das Wissen im Modell, Berlin (2004)
4. Hermon, S.: Scientific Method, Chaîne Opératoire and Visualization - 3D Modelling as a Research Tool in Archaeology. In: Bentkowska-Kafel, A., Denard, H., Baker, D. (eds.) Paradata and Transparency in Virtual Heritage, Ashgate, Farnham (2012)
5. http://www.lufthansa-technik.com/de/virtual-cabin-fitcheck. Accessed 22 June 2015
6. Bentkowska-Kafel, A., Denard, H., Baker, D. (eds.): Paradata and Transparency in Virtual Heritage. Ashgate, Farnham (2012)
7. https://3dwarehouse.sketchup.com/index.html. Accessed 07 June 2016
8. Münster, S.: Entstehungs-und Verwendungskontexte von 3DCAD-Modellen in den Geschichtswissenschaften. In: Meissner, K., Engelien, M. (eds.) Virtual Enterprises, Communities and Social Networks, Dresden (2011)
9. http://www.digitale-rekonstruktion.info/1-arbeitstreffen-am-21-11-2014. Accessed 22 June 2015
10. Koob, M.: Architectura Virtualis. Projekt Weltkulturerbe. Lecture notes, Technische Universität Darmstadt, Darmstadt (1995)
11. Pfarr, M.: Dokumentationsystem für Digitale Rekonstruktionen am Beispiel der Grabanlage Zhaoling, Provinz Shaanxi, China. Technische Universität Darmstadt (2010)
12. http://www.probado.de/. Accessed 25 July 2016
13. http://www.3d-coform.eu/. Accessed 25 July 2016
14. https://www.herder-institut.de/forschung-projekte/laufende-projekte/digitale-3d-rekonstruktionen-in-virtuellen-forschungsumgebungen.html. Accessed 25 July 2016
15. http://cosch.info. Accessed 22 June 2015
16. Münster, S.: Interdisziplinäre Kooperation bei der Erstellung virtueller geschichtswissenschaftlicher 3D-Rekonstruktionen. Diss. Technische Universität Dresden (2014)
17. https://de.wikipedia.org/wiki/Anerkannte_Regeln_der_Technik. Accessed 27 July 2016

Digital Reconstruction in Historical Research and Its Implications for Virtual Research Environments

Juliane Stiller[1]([✉]) and Dirk Wintergrün[2]

[1] Berlin School of Library and Information Science, Humboldt-Universität zu Berlin,
Dorotheenstr. 26, 10117 Berlin, Germany
juliane.stiller@ibi.hu-berlin.de
[2] Max Planck Institute for the History of Science Berlin, Boltzmannstr. 22,
14195 Berlin, Germany
dwinter@mpiwg-berlin.mpg.de

Abstract. This articles deals with (digital) reconstruction in historical research and reflects on the use of digital methods within the research cycle. For historians, reconstructions of varying degree, detail and focus are an invaluable research tool. We argue that different stages of reconstruction result in different reconstructed objects, outlining the implications in terms of publication, citation practices and the research cycle. The paper contends that these aspects need to be reflected in virtual research environments. The process of reconstruction needs to become transparent revealing the parameters of the different stages that resulted in the reconstructed product.

Keywords: Digital reconstruction · Historical research · Virtual research environments · Digital humanities · Digital methods · Publications · Research life cycle

1 Introduction

The term *reconstruction* has various meanings and connotations in the humanities. It covers a wide range of processes from the reconstruction of arguments in a historical debate, via the reconstruction of contexts and conditions of research, up to the reconstruction of artifacts. An appropriate reflection on all these aspects goes far beyond the scope of this chapter. Therefore, we will restrict ourselves to the technical and conceptual challenges for the (digital) humanities presented by reconstruction in historical research. Our aim is to highlight the impact on digital research processes which either result in reconstruction or use reconstructions as source. We focus on two aspects: (a) the process of digitally recording and publishing reconstructions of physical objects and (b) the actual digital reconstruction – two sides of one coin with different implications.

Regardless of specific domains, we classify three levels of reconstruction: the reconstruction of the visual representation of an object, of its historical context, and finally of an object in use. Creators of digital infrastructures, tools and methods need to consider

© Springer International Publishing AG 2016
S. Münster et al. (Eds.): 3D Research Challenges II, LNCS 10025, pp. 47–61, 2016.
DOI: 10.1007/978-3-319-47647-6_3

how these levels of reconstruction work together. Each one of these levels bears its challenges – most of them not limited to digital environments.

At all levels, the central challenge is to record the degree of completeness and detail required to justify the historical correctness of the reconstruction. This fosters an environment in which the reconstruction process can be retraced and repeated. This issue is well understood in the natural and life sciences, although it is not completely solved.[1] New standards for data and metadata help in meeting the challenge, as does the integration of technical innovations like new display technologies.

Digital methods will not solve every problem in the reconstruction process and the resulting product but they can make many ambiguities and insecurities more visible, transparent and quantifiable. For example, with regard to publishing reconstructions, digital methods present opportunities for creating a new type of scholarly publication. This qualitative shift towards combined data publication and publications of other research outcomes is discussed in the first section below highlighting the parallels between preservation and reconstruction and their impact on publication practices. We will further identify gaps and issues which need to be addressed by all stakeholders in virtual research environments. In Sects. 3 and 4, we will debate the different stages of reconstruction resulting in different types of research objects. Section 5 explores the relationship between models and reconstruction. In Sect. 6, the theoretical assumptions will be transferred to different use cases, highlighting the wide range of applications for historical research. Section 7 identifies the impact of reconstructions on the research process, concluding with consequences for virtual research environments in Sect. 8.

2   Preservation, Reconstruction and Publication

An important aspect of reconstruction is its close relationship to preservation. Heritage institutions such as libraries, archives, and museums, which are dedicated to providing access to cultural heritage material on a long-term basis, have to take this into account. For several decades, digitization campaigns aimed at making library items more accessible while preserving the objects for future use. To preserve at least one copy in case of a disaster hitting the physical object,[2] public and private bodies have financed digitization.[3] When digitization was introduced to libraries on a large scale, questions about the economic and long-term access aspects of digitization strategies arose. Stiller [3]

---

[1] One approach to this is the use of electronic laboratory notebooks; see Rubacha et al. [1].

[2] This is not only an issue in war zones. Other disasters cause irretrievable loss of cultural heritage material, e.g., the collapse of the Historical Archive of the City of Cologne in 2009.

[3] The EC-funded project ENUMERATE is currently running its third survey on digitization practices in cultural heritage in the EU, see http://pro.europeana.eu/enumerate/. Accessed 26 July 2016. The results of the previous two surveys suggest that museums progressed the most in digitizing their collections (24 % of analogue heritage collections were digitally reproduced) whereas archives and libraries (11 % and 12 %) lag behind. As the report states, these numbers should be interpreted with caution as the institution size was not weighted in the average [2, p. 21].

distinguished between three types of digitization in libraries. The first aims to broaden access to the resources, referencing them to make them retrievable online. These digital additions to the physical original object often cannot be considered a reconstruction, as characteristic features might be missing. Examples include digital objects found in aggregation portals such as Europeana,[4] which references digital objects with a thumbnail. The second type is the digital surrogate which is a reconstruction that could be the basis for historical research without consulting the original resource. The scope and level of detail of the reconstruction is often difficult to determine. Of course no object is an exact digital copy of its physical counterpart. The material of an object that bears some historical significance can hardly be reproduced in digital environments yet. The last type of digitization strategy deploys technology to add information to the digitized object, for example through Reflectance Transformation Imaging (RTI), which allows historians to investigate how brushes were used [3].

All these digitization strategies ease decision making for cultural institutions in terms of costs, broader access, awareness and preservation. If the digital representation of an object delivers the same information a scholar could retrieve by consulting the original, this saves the physical object from more damaging handling. The scholar needs to be clear about how the reconstruction was created and which parameters were used. Accuracy in terms of both content and material is a major concern, in case the original object is ever lost.

The publication process is closely related to preservation and reconstruction processes. Every scholarly publication about an artifact asks readers to reconstruct the original objects in their minds. The more information one can add to the replication, the more ambiguities are avoided. This not only strengthens the argument but will lead to a reconstruction that replaces the textual description.

All three processes determine the research cycle, methods, and results, influencing how research objects can be used and re-used. The question is not simply what and how one will publish but also leads to the question of how much the digital reconstruction and preservation impact scholarly publication practices today, and how they can be steered.

3 Stages of Reconstruction

Historians use the term *reconstruction* to mean different things, as illustrated by the following selection of examples. We introduce a classification of terms, which is useful in providing digital tools to support reconstruction processes. We want to emphasize again that we have a very broad understanding of the concept *object*, applicable not only to material objects but also to experimental and investigative procedures.

There are different stages of reconstruction ranging from purely preserving an object in its physical form to the full scientific reconstruction of knowledge acquisition. These

---

[4] http://www.europeana.eu/. Accessed 26 July 2016.

stages are often not clearly distinguished, but revealing their characteristics helps to create more transparent virtual environments.

3.1 Reconstructing the Object

The most obvious form of reconstruction is the digital representation of a physical object. Artifacts are scanned or photographed, either to make them digitally accessible as such, or to reconstruct a surrogate for the historical source. The level of reconstruction depends on the research questions and which part of the object carries the informative value. For example, a digital copy of a library book loses none of its information if the text is the research object [4, p. 33], whereas a museum object is uniquely defined by its meaning and its interpretation, both of which are almost impossible to digitize. Especially in library digitization campaigns, the objects are considered to be "frozen" as none of their characteristics change over the course of time – the object is complete and whole by itself. Yet a significant amount of information on the materiality of the object is lost. From the historian's perspective, traces of usage and materiality are highly relevant carriers of information about the context of an object.

3.2 Understanding and Reconstructing Contexts of Objects

It is crucial to reconstruct all the information which uniquely identifies the object and makes it valuable for research. While reconstructing the context of an object and the circumstances in which it was created, the problem of clarifying the scope of reconstruction comes to the fore. Archives and museums do more than simply keep documents; they also preserve their provenience and original order. Reconstructing archives in digital environments is an enormous challenge as "the identifiable object of interest in the archive is a complex body of interrelated, unique materials" [5] determined by its context. If this issue is not addressed, researchers are in danger to narrow research on objects only to their digitally reproducible qualities.

3.3 Reconstructing Historical Contexts and (Social) Networks

The mainly material context described above can be broadened to the historical context of an object, that is, the circumstances which surround its creation and use. What are sufficient criteria for completeness of this type of reconstruction process? Thematically arranged digital libraries and virtual research environments belong to this category. Good examples of projects with a long history of context reconstruction include ECHO[5], the Virtual Laboratory (VL)[6] or the ColorConText[7] at the Max Planck Institute for the History of Science (MPIWG).

---

[5] http://echo.mpiwg-berlin.mpg.de/home. Accessed 26 July 2016.
[6] http://vlp.mpiwg-berlin.mpg.de/index_html. Accessed 26 July 2016.
[7] https://arb.mpiwg-berlin.mpg.de/. Accessed 26 July 2016.

In general, this category includes the reconstruction of living conditions of social groups.[8] Detailing social network reconstruction would go beyond our scope but we are able to provide two examples here: the reconstruction of working conditions in a laboratory and the reconstruction of discovery processes.

3.4 Bridging the Approaches

Digital methods open up a range of unheard-of possibilities. Whole historic sites, their inhabitants and movement paths are brought to life in virtual reality. As the digital reconstruction of context appears so convincing and plausible, it often raises the question of authenticity and historical accuracy, especially in terms of sociological relations. It is difficult for the viewer to judge these parameters, so the risk of historical inauthenticity is real. To avoid accusations of inaccuracy, the process of reconstruction has to be transparent disclosing all the information that leads to the digital representation. In this regard, the development of complex reconstructions is very similar if not equal to a complex research cycle. Combining reconstruction with a theoretical model of the research cycle may make it easier to distinguish hypotheses from reality.

4   The Reconstructed Object

The role of digitization in preserving, archiving, and access to cultural heritage objects has been widely discussed, especially in library and information science [7–9]. Cultural heritage institutions are the driving force in this debate. Their large digitization projects do not only aim to make objects more accessible but also to create a "digital backup". If this endeavor is taken seriously, we need to know how much information about a material object has to be digitally available to reconstruct it if it is irretrievably lost. Obviously, the answer to this question is constantly changing along with the constraints and technical capabilities for replicating, storing, viewing and reconstructing. The "replicator" from Star Trek: Enterprise[9] will never be realizable. It will always only be possible to achieve a partial reconstruction. The amount of information required to reconstruct an object's functionality and form can serve as a guideline. Of course this amount is determined by the research questions. Also, form and function are not necessarily connected. The functionality of an object can be well understood and fully reconstructed without in-depth knowledge of its materiality, and vice versa.[10]

---

[8] Analysis of social networks is one increasingly popular method of historical research in this category, e.g., [6]. Maybe the best overview over this topic can be found at http://historical-networkresearch.org/. Accessed 26 July 2016.. Attached to this is a Zotero group https://www.zotero.org/groups/historical_network_research which compiles most of the relevant literature. Accessed 26 July 2016.

[9] https://en.wikipedia.org/wiki/Replicator_%28Star_Trek%29. Accessed 26 July 2016.

[10] One example is the reconstruction of the camera obscura, see [10]. The reconstruction of the creative process of drawing in a manuscript [11]. The University of Oldenburg was at the forefront of reconstructing experiments as part of historical research. See the work of Hans Otto Sibum.

In the following, we will describe the different results of reconstruction ranging from the representation of the object in its physical form to the reconstruction of its use and functionality. The aim is to achieve a more systematic view of the problem of reconstruction in relation to preservation, laying the groundwork for answering the question of what and how to store. We see this classification as analytical tool to systematize constraints and demands, and an instrument for the digital humanist to foster a common understanding.

4.1   The Reduced Object

The overwhelming majority of digitization projects reduce the material object to a two dimensional immaterial object by photographic replication. This is true for museums, libraries, and also increasingly now for archives. We do not want to belittle the importance of these endeavors in any way; they are a significant step in the right direction. Projects like Europeana and Archival Portal Europe[11] broaden access to cultural heritage material from various providers.

Significant progress has been made in describing the content of objects. The Text Encoding Initiative[12] (TEI), has created a standard for encoding textual information which is more or less universally accepted for exchanging and archiving textual content. The standards for describing the overall structure of a text with METS/MODS[13] are also highly developed. The same is true of standards for both metadata and for the data itself; archival and presentation formats have been well defined.

The problem of reducing the information value of objects is also discussed in the humanities. For example, Buzetti and Rehbein [12] discuss the problem of representation of text in editions; the fluidity of a text is not fully acknowledged in its materiality. They argue that the problem of static printed text editions, which cannot answer the diverse questions researchers might pose, can be overcome with digital editions. Traces of usage, which in most cases are not directly expressible as additions to the text, are often overlooked in the process of creating digital editions. TEI allows for the description of underlines, manual deletions, and so on, but is limited in terms of describing traces of usage and its impact on the object, for example a fingerprint.

4.2   The Resting Object

Larger technical and conceptual problems have to be solved for resting material objects. Again there are two sides: the metadata and the data itself. This distinction can be blurred. For example, is data resulting from a spectrometric analysis metadata or data describing a given object? Museums are developing standards for describing the history of an object. For example CIDOC CRM[14] makes it possible to describe the journey of a museum object from the outside world to a museum or archive (be it virtual or real).

---

[11] https://www.archivesportaleurope.net. Accessed 26 July 2016.
[12] http://www.tei-c.org/index.xml. Accessed 26 July 2016.
[13] http://www.loc.gov/standards/mods/. Accessed 26 July 2016.
[14] http://www.cidoc-crm.org/. Accessed 26 July 2016.

With this standard, the process of (re)-naming, moving from one place to another, or relevant events in the lifecycle of an object can be described.

Discussing the object itself, however – not only its shape but its materiality – means leaving the safe harbor of standardization. Various imaging processing methods have been developed to represent an object's outer shape and visual structure. Photographic methods ranging from 3D scanning to CT are already used in the humanities.[15] In addition, the materiality of the object is researched and data based on the results of material sciences is collected, for example in art history or archeology.[16] We are still nowhere near a standard for describing and storing all this data to make them available on a long-term basis. We propose an Object Encoding Initiative (OEI) as a logical extension of TEI. In such an initiative, the perspective of potential users has to be incorporated in addition to the provider's view.

4.3 The Object in Action

Finally, we are adding another layer of complexity when we are talking about *objects in action*. Action means reconstructing the production process of the object as well as its use. The object in action adds another dimension to the problem of reconstruction: time.

Although services like Vimeo[17] or YouTube[18] have made it significantly easier to publish movies and animations, how to do this in a scholarly publication remains an open question. The moving images could be linked to background information or parts of the moving object could be annotated so a viewer can understand and trace the production process of the reconstruction in every detail. Reasonable progress has been made in publishing annotated films online, such as projects in Heidelberg[19] and Nijwegen,[20] but this is still a niche.

Adding sensory information about touch, smell or taste to the reconstruction is an almost impossible endeavor. A recent workshop at the MPIWG[21] discussed the reconstruction of paint making on the basis of historical artists' recipe books and the analysis of paintings. This is a striking example of interdisciplinary collaboration between art historians, general historians, conservators, chemists and physicists, all working together to reconstruct a historical process. It also shows the complexity of documenting the process of reconstruction and its outcomes. For example, sensory impressions like judging the consistency by touching or the success of a reaction by the smell, which are

---

[15] E.g., for statues http://www.iflscience.com/technology/ct-scans-reveal-mummy-inside-statue. Accessed 26 July 2016, and the "Ancient Lives" exhibition at the British Museum http://www.britishmuseum.org/whats_on/past_exhibitions/2014/ancient_lives.aspx. Accessed 26 July 2016.

[16] Material data and scholarly analysis also need to be combined in other contexts, e.g., ink analysis to date the writing on a manuscript, e.g. [11].

[17] https://vimeo.com/. Accessed 26 July 2016.

[18] https://www.youtube.com/. Accessed 26 July 2016.

[19] http://kjc-sv006.kjc.uni-heidelberg.de:8083/home. Accessed 26 July 2016.

[20] https://tla.mpi.nl/tools/tla-tools/elan/. Accessed 26 July 2016.

[21] https://drupal.mpiwg-berlin.mpg.de/workshops/node/63. Accessed 26 July 2016.

documented in the historical recipe, need to be part of the reconstruction process.[22] This requires convergence of the digital documentation techniques used by the different disciplines, including the scientist's electronic laboratory book and the detailed visual representation of the outcome supported by visual artists.[23]

4.4 Challenges of Reconstruction

The major problem of reconstruction is the level of completeness and detail. These questions arise when thinking about the reconstruction of objects: How much detail is needed to answer the research question? How does one ensure that the reconstruction corresponds to the historical object? Where can detail be lost without influencing the results? Another challenge is that the digital reproduction might be perfect, but the end user device might not be suitable for display (e.g. the screen might be too small or incorrectly calibrated). This becomes even more crucial when the reconstruction is used as the primary source. What level of accuracy is required to ensure good scholarly practice? Dalbello [13, p. 494] elaborates this point in the realm of digital editions:

"Because texts are generated and constructed over time and tradition, they are constantly developed and mutated, and an archive supporting textual studies should represent that historical cumulative generation – involving authors, editors, typographers, book designers, and publishing agents, all those who are constructing the materiality of literary text. Therefore, a meaningful scholarly archive stages documents to preserve the context of their creation and materiality accompanying literary creation."

The problem of completeness concerns all levels of reconstruction and all research objects in all disciplines. Where can one draw the line? How does one determine how well the reconstruction is presenting the object, its context and its network? One solution is to reveal and show the workflows and parameters which resulted in the reconstruction.

5 Models and Reconstruction[24]

Reconstruction as a historical method is closely linked to the concept of a *model*. Although the term has been used in various contexts in science and the history of science, it is impossible to find a concise definition. Models are involved in all historical periods and stages of scientific work, from problem setting to teaching and popularization. Their meaning varies from models as abstraction and simplification to models as copies that are intended to be as close as possible to the original. Models can be material objects, theoretical concepts or cognitive structures for knowledge organization. De Chadarevian and Hopwood [15] investigated the potential of working and researching the use of 3D

---

[22] For online representations of color recipes, see the "Colour Context" database: http://web.philo.ulg.ac.be/transitions/colour-context-2/ and the database of medieval and early modern art technology recipes by Doris Oltrogge: http://db.re.fh-koeln.de/ICSFH/forschung/rezepte.aspx. Accessed 26 July 2016.

[23] This insight is not new. The collaboration of artists and scholars in print has been a topic of historical research for decades.

[24] The longer version of this section can be found in [14].

models for the history of science. In their introduction, they outline the establishment of a research program focusing on scientific practice and the ways in which scientific knowledge is conceptualized and communicated. The research program resulted in two-dimensional (2D) representations becoming a subject in the history and philosophy of science, constituting a "science around visual languages and working objects" (p. 2). Three-dimensional models remained neglected. As Jordanova [16] points out in her commentary, this was encouraged by academic practice in the humanities, where textual representation was the primary language of scholarly communication. Two-dimensional models in the form of graphical representation were only used as illustrations of otherwise textually communicated analysis. This traditional division narrowed the scope of research, neglecting both non-textual representations and practical knowledge. Griesemer defines 1D and 2D models models as "1D linguistic or symbolic expressions" as part of logical empiricism, and "2D, non-linguistic, pictorial, diagrammatic, and graphical displays" [17, p. 433]. Three-dimensional models have very diverse uses, including mathematics, anatomy and molecular biology, all of which directly aid the understanding of abstract concepts and otherwise physically inaccessible objects. Material models can be used for learning by assembling and reassembling constituent elements, which is often not possible with the real object. The whole body and all the senses are involved in learning through exploration. Thus the principles required to understand how the model functions are more easily accessible than the principles governing the complex real object. The model allows the principle of knowing-by-making to be extended to the end user.

6 Use Cases and Examples of Reconstructions in Historical Sciences

To demonstrate the variety of reconstructions in research into the history of science, this section presents some use cases in digital environments and their effects on research questions and methods. These examples from our own field cannot represent all possible use cases but they illustrate the challenges faced in reconstruction. Thus they complement the more detailed strategies explored elsewhere in this volume.

The presented projects take different approaches to historical reconstruction. They aim to aggregate material and create a knowledge base which can be used for discovering new connections within the digitized material, fostering scholarly exchange through collaboration and using technology to answer specific research questions. Renn understands these connections as harbingers of the "Epistemic Web: a Web optimized for the representation of human knowledge and its global processing" [18, p. 10].

The Virtual Laboratory (VL of physiology)[25] is a platform initiated by a project hosted at MPIWG and initially supported by the Volkswagen Foundation. The platform aggregates resources on "the experimentalization of life".[26] The digitized resources are available in various formats, cross-referenced and augmented by a collaborative space where researchers can share their collections publicly. The navigational structure of the

---

[25] http://vlp.mpiwg-berlin.mpg.de/. Accessed 26 July 2016.
[26] http://vlp.mpiwg-berlin.mpg.de/about/goals.html. Accessed 26 July 2016.

materials and the possibility to pivot browse through the collection was envisioned to generate new research questions and insights [19]. From the beginning, this project was designed to be more than a comprehensive digital library (although when it started in 1996, this was already an ambitious project). It was intended to be a virtual environment which recreates and reconstructs researchers' access to sources and materials in a 19th century laboratory, augmented by their connections to colleagues and affiliations. The aim was to understand the conditions under which decisions were made in the lab. The reconstruction process itself is done by essays published in the lab and linked to the material in the VL. Its design and continuous adaption was driven by the interests of the researchers involved in the project.

As early as 1998, Peter Damerow and Robert Englund envisaged that a digital library was needed for research into the origins of writings and calculations.[27] This could bring together the fragmented collections of cuneiform writing on clay tablets held by museums spread around the world. They wanted to gather collections of high quality images and transcriptions of the calculations written on the tablets in computer readable forms. The goal was not only to collect and combine existing sources but to create an infrastructure for reconstructing the empirical contexts in which writing and calculation could have emerged. Similarly, the Archimedes project[28] created a digital research library for the history of early modern mechanics.

In their groundbreaking work, Paolo Galluzzi and his team at the Museo Galileo physically and virtually reconstructed the instruments and experiments used at the time of Galileo Galilei and Leonardo Da Vinci.[29] Their work shows how detailed historical research and reconstruction methods lead to a deep understanding of the knowledge structures behind early modern mechanics, combining scholarly and practical knowledge. It demonstrates the power of the virtual exhibition as a tool for communicating scholarly research results by setting reconstruction in a wider context. This strategy was also taken up in creating the virtual exhibition[30] about Albert Einstein's discoveries and their context which complemented the physical exhibition at the Kronprinzenpalais (Crown Prince's Palace, Berlin) [23]. The infrastructure is designed to be continuously extended by researchers, also after the end of the physical exhibition, to show new insights into the history of modern physics.[31]

All these projects aim to provide a historical research basis contextualizing the different objects with cross-links and digital references. This approach provides scholars with the opportunity to review, search, and work on a corpus of objects that represent a certain research field. It allows them to quickly get an overview and use the material

---

[27] http://cdli.ucla.edu/. Accessed 26 July 2016. For the context of counting and calculation methods in reconstruction, see [20], and for a brief history of computer aided reconstruction see http://damerow.mpiwg.de/doku.php/obituary. The history of this early digital humanities project still has to be written.

[28] http://archimedes2.mpiwg-berlin.mpg.de/archimedes_templates. Accessed 26 July 2016.

[29] see [21] and the website of the museum http://www.museogalileo.it/en/index.html, for the wider context. Accessed 26 July 2016, please refer to [22].

[30] http://einstein-virtuell.mpiwg-berlin.mpg.de/VEA/SC879771616_en.html. Accessed 26 July 2016.

[31] http://virtualspaces.sourceforge.net/. Accessed 26 July 2016.

online from their desk. The level of reconstruction in these digital libraries is diverse. The decision whether the digital object is sufficient depends on the research question.

A completely different approach to reconstruction was taken by Gerd Graßhoff und Michael May in 2003 in their work on the urea cycle [24]. They developed an epistemic model that could be implemented as a computer program. So they were able to computationally reconstruct the process that took place in the laboratory of Hans Krebs and Kurt Henseleit. The outcome of this reconstruction was a full simulation of the scientific discovery process.

The extensive field of computer-aided archeology can only briefly be mentioned. Digital reconstruction often supports scientific discovery when the original research object is no longer complete. This is particularly important for archeologists, who rely on reconstructions and models to support scientific discovery [25]. Graßhoff and Berndt [26] reconstructed the design principles which guided the portico columns of the Pantheon in Rome. To achieve this, they not only accurately measured the properties of the site, but also reconstructed the knowledge base that was needed to come up with the given design principles at the time. Saldaña [27] presents a framework for creating 3D models used in archeological research that lets the researcher determine rules for selecting information and contexts for the modeling process and its iteration. The goal of this procedural modeling approach is a 3D model whose creation can be reproduced by tracing the underlying sources and information.

The above examples show that there are promising and successful developments in historical research. These cases exploit technologies to reconstruct historical information which can be used to make relations between historical objects more evident. They also show the ongoing challenges to date: projects are still isolated and only loosely connected to outside contexts. To change this, reconstruction could be embedded more directly into the environments which scholars are using, enabling seamless integration. The next section explores how reconstructions fit into the research life cycle and can be products of such a cycle.

7 Reconstruction and the Research Life Cycle

Research life cycles can be designed to clarify the humanist's research process and to enable infrastructure stakeholders to better adapt their services to the needs of scholarship. They act as blueprints to better support the processes of creating reconstructions.

Cluster 1, the work package for accompanying research within DARIAH-DE,[32] developed a model of the research life cycle looking at the research activities, their immediate output and their results as a form of knowledge generation [28]. This life cycle was based on the activities and primitives developed by Unsworth [29], Hennicke et al. [30] and TaDiRAH.[33] Each activity within the research cycle produces output in form of data that is the basis for the next activity. For example, exploration and discovery will yield an aggregation of sources, articles and data. This output will be used in the

---

[32] https://de.dariah.eu/. Accessed 26 July 2016.
[33] https://github.com/Tadirah/TaDiRAH. Accessed 26 July 2016.

next activity – sampling and aggregating the research corpus. Some of the output of each research step will generate new knowledge that should be preserved and referenced. The corpus of sources might mark the beginning of the research process, and the publication often marks the end. Both these products of knowledge could be shared with other researchers and the public.

It is clear that such a life cycle can only be a simplification of the actual research process in the humanities. Often activities do not follow one another like pearls on a string; instead a mixture of processes can run simultaneously. Nevertheless, it is essential to understand the research activities and their products to better support and reproduce them in a digital environment. Seamless integration of all activities and their products in the research cycle without gaps in data processing and management is the goal of digital research infrastructures. These cycles are not static models but frameworks that focus on the needs of scholars. They can help to identify tools and services for the various tasks of their work.

Theoretical cycles can serve as indicators for reconstructing knowledge processes in digital environments. Knowledge production is enabled not only by the different levels of reconstruction of the research objects but also by reconstructing the foundations of research. Making reconstructions re-usable for other scholars necessitates coherent reconstruction of the research process that generated the results. The prerequisite is that all results should be useable in other contexts so that they can be revised and improved. To achieve this, each knowledge product generated in the research process and its inter- pretation needs to be preserved and referenced. The reconstruction of digital research practices has wide-ranging consequences for the publication process in the humanities and for the development of virtual research environments.

8   Consequences of Reconstruction for Virtual Research Environments

Virtual research environments that aim to support the full research cycle need function- alities which adhere to the standards and expectations of their users. One has to distin- guish between the needs and requirements researchers have regarding (1) the use of digital tools and services and (2) research practices in the different disciplines. Within DARIAH-DE, Stiller et al. [31] aggregated requirements and needs from researchers in the arts and humanities. General requirements applying to digital tools and services include thorough documentation and technical stability [32]. Important requirements for the humanities include research specific requests for long term accessibility of the research data [33]. Requirements concerning the practices of historical research are rare. Boonstra et al. [34] point out that historical information science needs to solve four problems which are directly related to the development of virtual research environments. Historical sources need to be connected to interpretations, they are defined by relation- ships with other resources, historians need tools that can take changes of time and space into account, and there is a lack of presentation techniques and tools in digital history.

The consequences of digital reconstruction for research practices need to be consid- ered when developing research environments. The discovery and aggregation of sources is the first step in the research cycle. In a digital environment, it is characterized by the change of sources used. More and more digitized material is becoming the source of research. Hitchcock [35] points out that digitized material is used as primary source for further work, but often not quoted in publications. This makes the research process increasingly less transparent as workflows or research methods cannot be criticized based on these uncited sources. Hitchcock further elaborates that corpora are constructed online using search engines, so it is not evident how the documents are compiled, blurring the methodology used with the conclusions reached [35]. Even if search strategies are documents, it is not possible to reproduce the results because of the continuous changes in the underlying data. Classical search tools at least track different versions, so that researchers can trace the results of other scholars. To adhere to scientific standards, simply referencing the search engine or website and the specific time of use is not enough, although this is often recommended in the standard rules for quoting websites. We need better web archives and workflows for referencing the objects within them in a sustainable way.

One way of adapting research practices to the conditions of using digital resources is by integrating them into research environments, for example by offering stable and citable references for each product of the research process. History as a discipline has to think about further ways of handling digital sources, especially if these are historical reconstructions. The reconstruction of material, whether as a source or a result, needs to be transparent and traceable.

In particular, if the reconstruction is the result of the research, appropriate publication practices need to be supported by the virtual research environment. The source data must be separable from the interpretation. Standards for the historical critique of sources (in German "Quellenkritik") in digital environments have to be developed. It should be possible to re-use the resulting publication by embedding it into a larger or different context. For this, the structure of publications needs to be preserved in an editable format, which means that fixed formats like PDF are no longer suitable. Emerging technologies and practices such as Linked Data can help to connect different perspectives and contexts and to make relations more visible.

Ideally, every reconstruction should be handled as a research process whose result is the given reconstructed research object. Only if the reconstruction itself adheres to scientific standards such as validity, reliability and utility, it can be evaluated and assessed by scholars using it as a source for further studies. There is still a lack of standards and tools for granular reference to multidimensional objects online. Links to and from supporting sources are required in order to comply with scholarly standards. Only the embedding of several contexts makes the digital reconstruction valuable and adds information. To achieve this, standards must not only target reconstruction but also reflect upon it from different perspectives such as preservation and publication. One step in this direction would be a TEI for objects as described above. Driven by examples, an Object Encoding Initiative (OEI) should propose a standard format to determine how data and metadata can be attached to an object, how this data should be stored and preserved on a long-term basis. These measures would make reconstructions more transparent and comparable, bringing us one step closer to meaningful data publication in the humanities.

Acknowledgements. We would like to thank Klaus Thoden from the Max Planck Institute for the History of Science for giving feedback on this article.

URLs quoted: The nature of this article made it necessary to quote a number of websites. We last checked all the links while finishing this article in July 2016. We chose URLs that we believe are stable enough to serve as examples for this article for a reasonable amount of time. We are in doubt about the sustainability of these references but think this only reiterates the importance of establishing a sustainable infrastructure for the (Digital) Humanities.

References

1. Rubacha, M., Rattan, A.K., Hosselet, S.C.: A review of electronic laboratory notebooks available in the market today. J. Lab. Autom. **16**, 90–98 (2011)
2. Stroeker, N., Vogels, R.: Survey Report on Digitisation in European Cultural Heritage Institutions 2014. ENUMERATE Thematic Network (2014)
3. Stiller, J.: Auf dem Wege zur digitalen Bibliothek: Digitalisierungsstrategien und ihre Konsequenzen. VDM Verlag (2008)
4. Buckland, M.K.: Information and Information Systems. ABC-CLIO (1991)
5. Pitti, D.V.: Encoded archival description: an introduction and overview. D-LIB Mag. **5**(11), November 1999. http://www.dlib.org/dlib/november99/11pitti.html. Accessed 27 July 2016
6. Lemercier, C.: Formale Methoden der Netzwerkanalyse in den Geschichtswissenschaften:warum und wie? Österreichische Zeitschrift für Geschichtswissenschaft **23**, 16–41 (2012)
7. Rieger, O.Y.: Preservation in the age of large-scale digitization. A White Paper. CLIR Publication 141 (2008). https://www.clir.org/pubs/reports/reports/pub141/pub141.pdf. Accessed 27 July 2016
8. Lopatin, L.: Library digitization projects, issues and guidelines: a survey of the literature. Libr. Hi Tech. **24**, 273–289 (2006)
9. Hughes, L.M.: Digitizing Collections: Strategic Issues for the Information Manager. Facet Publishing, Abingdon (2004)
10. Lefèvre, W.: Inside the camera obscura: optics and art under the spell of the projected image. Preprint 333. Max-Planck-Institut für Wissenschaftsgeschichte (2007). https://www.mpiwg-berlin.mpg.de/Preprints/P333.PDF. Accessed 27 July 2016
11. Renn, J., Damerow, P., Rieger, S., Giulini, D.: Hunting the white elephant: when and how did galileo discover the law of fall? Sci. Context **13**, 299–419 (2000)
12. Buzzetti, D., Rehbein, M.: Textual fluidity and digital editions. In: Proceedings of the International Workshop on Text Variety in the Witnesses of Medieval Texts, pp. 14–39 (1998)
13. Dalbello, M.: A genealogy of digital humanities. J. Doc. **67**, 480–506 (2011)
14. Wintergrün, D.: Book review. In: de Chadarevian, S., Hopwood, N. (eds) Models: The Third Dimension of Science, vol. 9, pp. 363–366. Stanford University Press, Stanford (2004). Visual Communication (2010)
15. De Chadarevian, S., Hopwood, N.: Models: The Third Dimension of Science. Stanford University Press, Stanford (2004)
16. Jordanova, L.: Material models as visual culture. In: Models: The Third Dimension of Science, pp. 443–452. Stanford University Press (2004)
17. Griesemer, J.: Three-dimensional models in philosophical perspective. In: Models: The Third Dimension of Science, pp. 433–442. Stanford University Press (2004)
18. Renn, J.: Beyond editions: historical sources in the digital age. In: Internationalität und Interdisziplinarität der Editionswissenschaft, pp. 9–28. De Gruyter (2014)

19. Schmidgen, H., Dierig, S., Kantel, J.: The Virtual Laboratory for Physiology. Preprint 140. Max-Planck-Institut für Wissenschaftsgeschichte (2000). https://www.mpiwg-berlin. mpg.de/Preprints/P140.PDF
20. Nissen, H.J., Damerow, P., Englund, R.K.: Archaic Bookkeeping: Early Writing and Techniques of Economic Administration in the Ancient Near East. University of Chicago Press (1993)
21. Galluzzi, P.: The career of a technologist. In: Leonardo da Vinci: Engineer and Architect, pp. 41–109. Montreal: Montreal Museum of Fine Arts (1987)
22. Valleriani, M.: Galileo Engineer. Springer, Dordrecht (2010)
23. Renn, J.: Albert Einstein - Chief Engineer of the Universe. Wiley, Hoboken (2005)
24. Graßhoff, G., May, M.: Hans Krebs' and Kurt Hanseleit's laboratory notebooks and their discovery of the urea cycle - reconstructed with computer models. In: Reworking the Bench: Research Notebooks in the History of Science, pp. 269–294. Klüwer (2003)
25. Olsen, S., Brickman, A., Cai, Y.: Discovery by reconstruction: exploring digital archeology. In: SIGCHI Workshop (Ambient Intelligence for Scientific Discovery (AISD)) (2004)
26. Graßhoff, G., Berndt, C.: Decoding the pantheon columns. Archit. Hist. 2, 18 (2014)
27. Saldaña, M.: An integrated approach to the procedural modeling of ancient cities and buildings. Digit. Scholarsh. Hum. (2015). http://dx.doi.org/10.1093/llc/fqv013. Accessed 27 July 2016
28. Leganovic, O., Schmitt, V., Stiller, J., Thoden, K., Wintergrün, D.: Anforderungen undBedürfnisse von Geisteswissenschaftlern an einen digital gestützten Forschungsprozess. In:DHd2015 - Book of Abstracts - Poster (2015)
29. Unsworth, J.: Scholarly primitives: what methods do humanities researchers have in common, and how might our tools reflect this. In: Humanities Computing, Formal Methods, Experimental Practice Symposium, pp. 5–100 (2000)
30. Hennicke, S., Gradmann, S., Dill, K., Tschumpel, G., Thoden, K., Morbindoni, C., Pichler, A.: Research Report on DH Scholarly Primitives. Digitized Manuscripts to Europeana
31. Stiller, J., Thoden, K., Leganovic, O. Heise, C., Höckendorff, M., Gnadt, T.: Nutzungsverhalten in den Digital Humanities. DARIAH-DE (2014)
32. Warwick, C., Terras, M., Galina, I., Huntington, P., Pappa, M.: Evaluating Digital Humanities Resources: The LAIRAH Project Checklist and the Internet Shakespeare Editions Project (2007)
33. Rutner, J., Schonfeld, R.C.: Supporting the changing research practices of historians. Final Report from ITHAKA S+R (2012)
34. Boonstra, O., Breure, L., Doorn, P.: Past, Present and Future of Historical Information Science. KNAW-DANS (2006). http://www.dans.knaw.nl/nl/over/organisatie-beleid/ publicaties/DANSpastpresentfuturehistoricalinformationscienceUK.pdf. Accessed 27 July 2016
35. Hitchcock, T.: Confronting the digital: or how academic history writing lost the plot. Cult. Soc. Hist. 10, 9–23 (2013)

Digital Research Infrastructures: DARIAH

Mirjam Blümm[✉] and Stefan Schmunk

Research and Development Department, Göttingen State and University Library,
Papendiek 14, 37073 Göttingen, Germany
{bluemm,schmunk}@sub.uni-goettingen.de

Abstract. DARIAH-DE, the German national contribution to DARIAH-EU – a European initiative, initiated by the European Strategy Forum on Research Infrastructures (ESFRI), which aims to enhance and support digitally-enabled research and teaching across the arts and humanities – develops and maintains a digital research infrastructure for the Arts and Humanities. This research infrastructure consists of four components: teaching, research, research data and technical modules. DARIAH-DE addresses current research questions and methods, integrates them into the digital research infrastructure, and is in particular research driven. The topic of "digital reconstruction" will be one of the most important new topics of DARIAH-DE and it will be one of the challenges to integrate tools and cover research-lifecycles of these specific communitiy.

Keywords: Digital humanities · e-humanities · Research infrastructure · Research data management

1 Introduction

Digital humanities (DH) opens up new perspectives, not only for computer scientists and "conventional" humanists working on linguistics or literature, but also for researchers from neighboring fields such as cultural heritage preservation, architecture, and art. By comprising a large number of digital practices and applications, DH enables collaboration across different disciplines which had previously seemed incompatible. This changes traditional methods and makes it possible to develop new approaches.

The direct result of this is an urgent need for an infrastructure to facilitate teaching and research. While computing centers can easily supply technical resources like virtual machines, storage, hosting of databases and so on, there are further requirements such as easy access to digitized resources, methods and tools to analyze and interpret the information gathered. Research data must be managed, curated and preserved long-term in order to make it reusable – in short, supporting the entire research (data) lifecycle. The European project DARIAH [1] tries to meet this demand in a reliable and sustainable way.

2 Towards a European Research Infrastructure

The Digital Research Infrastructure for the Arts and Humanities (DARIAH) aims to enhance and support digitally-enabled research and teaching across the arts and

© Springer International Publishing AG 2016
S. Münster et al. (Eds.): 3D Research Challenges II, LNCS 10025, pp. 62–73, 2016.
DOI: 10.1007/978-3-319-47647-6_4

humanities. DARIAH is developing and operating an infrastructure to support infor-mation and communication research practices and assist researchers using ICT-enabled methods to analyze and interpret digital resources.

DARIAH emerged as a research infrastructure on the ESFRI [2] Roadmap in 2006. It was one of 48 projects, of which only five came from the social sciences and human-ities and only two are based directly in the humanities – the other is CLARIN [3]. The European Strategy Forum on Research Infrastructures (ESFRI), was established as "a strategic instrument to develop the scientific integration of Europe and to strengthen its international outreach." [2] Every ESFRI project can register as a European organization with a legal entity, called a European Research Infrastructure Consortium (ERIC) [4].

DARIAH has been an ERIC since August 2014 with fifteen founding members: Austria, Belgium, Croatia, Cyprus, Denmark, France (the host country), Germany, Greece, Ireland, Italy, Luxembourg, Malta, The Netherlands, Serbia, and Slovenia [5]. The initial standard membership period is five years. The vision is, however, that DARIAH will run for 20 years, if not longer.

DARIAH operates through its European-wide network of Virtual Competency Centres (VCCs), which are cross-disciplinary, multi-institutional, and international. Each VCC is based on a specific area of expertise [6]:

- **VCC e-Infrastructure** is establishing a shared technology platform for arts and humanities research.
- **VCC Research and Education Liaison** is exposing and sharing researchers' knowl-edge, methodologies, and expertise.
- **VCC Scholarly Content Management** is facilitating the exposure, sharing, and sustainability of scholarly content (research data).
- **VCC Advocacy, Impact and Outreach** is interfacing with key influencers in and for the arts and humanities.

Each DARIAH member appoints a National Coordinator to manage national DARIAH activities and prepare in-kind contributions. DARIAH is an integrating activity, bringing together the state-of-the-art digital arts and humanities activities of its member countries.

3   DARIAH-DE

DARIAH-DE [7] is the German national contribution to DARIAH-EU. It supports digi-tally-enabled research in the arts and humanities, focusing on the following disciplines: Archaeology, art history, epigraphy, history, Jewish studies, musicology, philology, philosophy, and theology. DARIAH-DE is a joint research project consisting of 20 partner institutions: Seven universities, four computing centers, four discipline-specific research institutions, two libraries, one academy of sciences and humanities, one commercial partner, and one non-governmental organization.

The project is funded by the German Federal Ministry of Education and Research (BMBF) [8] for a period of five years. In the first phase of the project (03/2011–02/2014), the focus of DARIAH-DE was on developing the digital research infrastructure shown in Fig. 1.

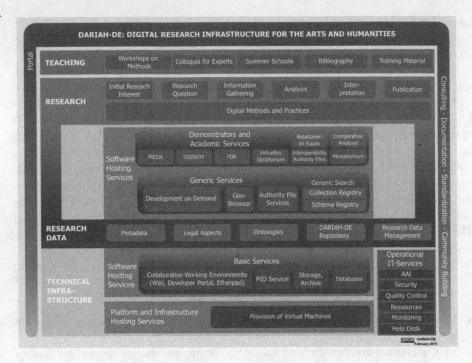

Fig. 1. The DARIAH-DE research infrastructure

The DARIAH-DE Research Infrastructure is divided into four main components:

- **Teaching and research**: Organizes seminars and workshops geared towards researchers at all levels to establish DH use and methods in academic disciplines and coordinates national and international curricular developments in the field of DH.
- **Research**: Promotes research on and development of DH methods and practices as well as the development of and access to academic services (text analysis, spatial and temporal visualization, annotation, etc.).
- **Research data**: Offers diverse options for dealing with research data and data management (assembling and describing research data collections, licensing and legal aspects, recommendation and development of standards, best practices in dealing with metadata and research data, etc.).
- **Technical infrastructure**: Offers infrastructure and software components, tools and services for DH research projects, researchers, and developers (collaborative working environments, storage services, virtual machines, Persistent Identifier [PID] Service, Monitoring, Authentication and Authorization Infrastructure [AAI], etc.).

This structure rather closely mirrors the European VCC structure described above. For the second project phase (03/2014–02/2016), DARIAH-DE was reorganized, bearing in mind that DARIAH was preparing to change its status as a project to become an organization. To this end, DARIAH-DE abandoned the traditional work-package structure and replaced this with thematic clusters, each of which works on a specific research topic (see Fig. 2).

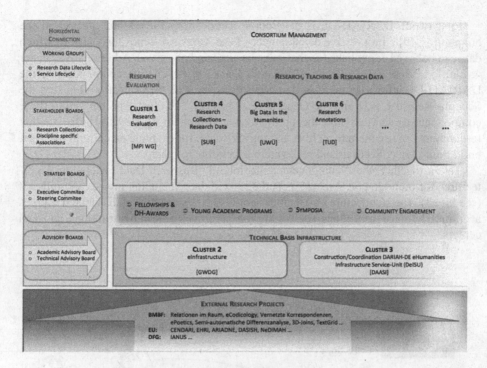

Fig. 2. DARIAH-DE II structure

The clusters collaborate closely: Clusters 2 and 3 work on maintaining the technical infrastructure and developing an infrastructure service unit. Clusters 4, 5, and 6 concentrate on research, teaching, and research data by addressing current research questions and methods and integrating them into the digital research infrastructure. Cluster 1 evaluates the research infrastructure, for example in terms of usability and user acceptance. Several working groups and boards facilitate communication, not only between clusters but also with the DH community. DARIAH-DE is also involved in a number of initiatives on different levels, from exchanging methods to using the entire infrastructure. At present about 30 external joint research projects and many individual researchers use DARIAH-DE, and more requests for cooperation are under way.

The framework is open to integrating new topics, so new clusters may be established if necessary. A seventh cluster concerning pattern recognition is currently in the planning stage.

4 Options for Data Management in Digital Reconstructions of Cultural Heritage

Initial thoughts about proposing a thematic cluster on 3D reconstruction have not been pursued yet, but DARIAH-DE already offers a range of options for working with data relating to digital reconstructions.

First of all, DARIAH-DE is developing a repository for research data from the humanities, [9] a progressive development of the TextGrid Repository, [10] in which data can be saved or published so that it can be cited and preserved. Additionally, Cluster 4, entitled "Research Collections/Research Data", is developing components of the DARIAH-DE infrastructure related to collections, such as the Collection Registry, the Schema Registry, [11] and the Generic Search. [12] The cluster is integrating these components as services into the productive environment of DARIAH-DE, so that researchers can use them to archive and retrieve data, for example on cultural heritage, build their own collections and make them accessible to others.

Taken together, these components constitute a "Research Data Federation Architecture" for bibliographical metadata and digitized data, including images and full text (see Fig. 3). The architecture also includes collection descriptions of distributed sources at cultural heritage institutions, such as libraries, archives, research institutions, and data centers.

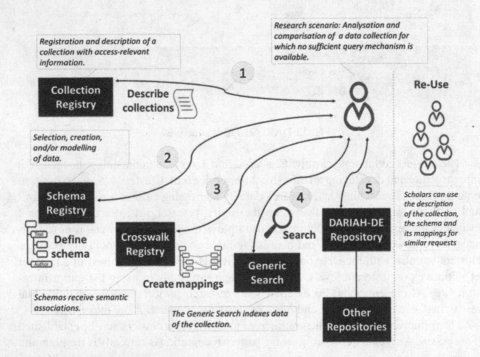

Fig. 3. DARIAH-DE II Federation Architecture (The Schema Registry, the Crosswalk Registry, and the Generic Search are developed by Andreas Henrich and Tobias Gradl from the Chair of Media Informatics at the University of Bamberg.)

The following figure illustrates the tools and services for searching within distributed sources/data within DARIAH-DE:

The Collection Registry is a service for registering collections of research data – described with different metadata schemes – including their machine-readable interfaces so this information can be made available via the Generic Search. Collections from different distributed sources such as libraries, museums, archives, and Internet sources can be added. It is sufficient that descriptions and interfaces are passed to the Collection Registry.

The Schema Registry stores different metadata schemes for use by the Crosswalk Registry and the Generic Search. Both the schemas and the underlying algorithms can be generated with the Crosswalk Registry, as shown in Fig. 4. The Schema Registry is a GUI (graphical user interface) based tool that allows users to map the connections between different schemas themselves. For this purpose, only graphical links between the output schema and the target schema have to be created. The appropriate crosswalks created using this method form the basis for the search tools integrated in the infrastructure integrated. Researchers in the arts, humanities, and social sciences can use this method to map different metadata standards stored in the Schema Registry, which does not demand a high level of ICT expertise. This mapping allows automated translation from one data schema to another, so scholars can use just this one tool to search data from different collections.

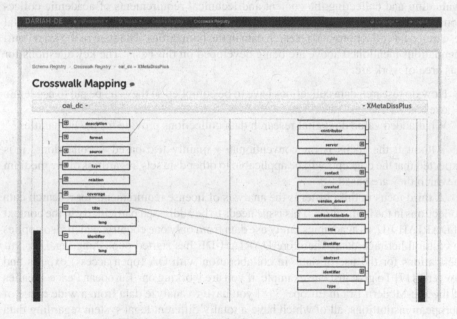

Fig. 4. The DARIAH-DE crosswalk registry

The Generic Search provides a front end for the data registered in the Collection Registry. Generic Search can search the registries and third party sources. This tool allows the user to search in heterogeneous data sets, such as data from ZVDD, [13] HathiTrust, [14] or other repositories. This is particularly useful as research data of various provenances and in different formats can be combined within this tool, making it flexible for user-specific and individual research perspectives.

The DARIAH-DE Repository [15] makes it possible to archive data of any kind in a sustainable and persistent manner. Both the data describing the collection and the research data itself can be indexed and found by Generic Search. For sustainable referencing of data and collection descriptions, the EPIC PID Service [16] can be used.

This combination of different tools and services creates new options for data management in the digital reconstruction of cultural heritage. Some services allow the user to link data stored by different data providers. Other services of the DARIAH-DE tool-kit make data and schemas that are described with different metadata interoperable, without changing the original schemas. DARIAH-DE has created an interoperable Federation Architecture for storing and managing research data, including 3D data of digital reconstruction. Each service enables access to heterogeneous data sources of various provenances. This facilitates new methods of analyzing existing distributed data collections in a unified way.

Cluster 4, entitled "Research Collections/Research Data", supports academics and research projects in building digital research data collections with recommendations and guidelines. To this end, research data collections created by external research projects and/or facilities in recent years can be analyzed, evaluated, and described. This includes evaluating and collecting the content and technical requirements of academic collections, culminating in the conception of a theory and process-led model to describe digital research data collections and research data in the humanities. The state of the art recommendations mentioned above are being developed on this basis. The key questions for this area of work are:

- How do research data collections have to be compiled so they can be put to academic use?
- What added value do digital research data collections provide for the humanities?

Although the focus is on conventional – mainly text-based – collections, it is expected that the concepts will be applicable to other data sets, regardless of the medium in which they are based.

A third focus in this cluster is the analysis of license requirements for research data collections in the humanities. This issue needs to be addressed particularly in the context of DARIAH-EU, as academics rarely use data from only one country, which also applies to cultural heritage data. Therefore DARIAH-DE has started publishing legal recommendations for the use of data, in collaboration with OA (open access) experts and lawyers. [17] To give just one example, if you are working on "European Peace Treaties of the Pre-Modern Era in Europe" [18] you have to analyze data from a wide range of European institutions, all of which have a totally different legal system regarding data use and reuse. The situation becomes even more complex if you are planning to publish the data online. One aim of a research infrastructure is to make access to (digitized) data possible.

It is characteristic of DH research that members of different institutions – often in different countries – work together. Collaborative writing and documentation tools are therefore vital in project management. DARIAH-DE provides collaborative tools such as a wiki system or Etherpad [19]. The developer portal provides additional tools and services for developers including GreenHopper/Jira Agile, SVN, Jenkins, and JIRA/

Chili (see Fig. 5). Access is very simple, since DARIAH-DE has developed an authentication and authorization infrastructure, based on Shibboleth (SAML) [20]. Authenticated users can access services and certified content regardless of their location.

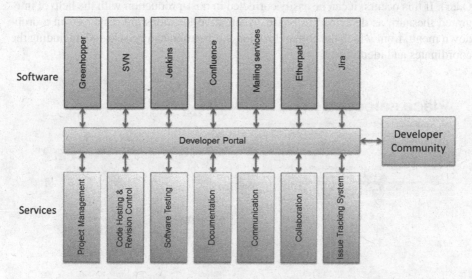

Fig. 5. Overview of the current service catalogue on the DARIAH-DE Developer Portal [19].

For data visualization, DARIAH-DE offers the Geo-Browser service. This can be used to analyze space-time relationships in (humanities) data. The Geo-Browser [21] consists of two correlating components: a frame for data visualization and a Datasheet Editor for easy data entry. It is also possible to ingest data in standardized formats (KML, csv etc.) via interfaces. DARIAH-DE started developing the Geo-Browser in 2011 based on the developments of europeana4D [22] and GeoTemCo, [22] and the tool is still being improved. The Datasheet Editor was added in 2011–2012.

The Datasheet Editor [23] offers two different options to prepare data for visualization. Either existing csv tables can be imported and subsequently enriched, or time and space data can be entered directly via a chart. Generally, the records are transferred directly to the DARIAH-DE storage, secured and managed there, regardless of their origin.

Direct data entry is very simple. Only information about place and time is required. Then automatic geo-location and geo-referencing (identifying the latitude and longitude) is done using the Getty Thesaurus of Geographic Names (TGN) [24], open GeoNames (OGN) [25] and/or OpenStreetMap (OSM) [26]. This is a semi-automatic method, which saves time for identifying. Additionally, the place is enriched with information about latitude and longitude and the corresponding unique identifiers of the used vocabularies. Data which has been enriched with geo-coordinates in the Datasheet Editor can be downloaded in a KML format and visualized and also analyzed in other applications. Data visualization within the Datasheet Editor allows the user to directly control the maps used in the Geo-Browser. This is needed because place names are not unique, and geo-references not directly human-readable – especially if you are working with a large amount of data – so you can check it on a visual level easily. Places may be assigned incorrectly by automatic geo-referencing, such as identical place names in different countries or regions (e.g. Paris/Texas and Paris/France; Frankfurt/Main and Frankfurt/Oder). If this occurs, it can be easily corrected in post-production with the help of integrated thesauri, as described in Fig. 6. Alternative locations are displayed in a drop-down menu, from which the correct location information can be selected, including the coordinates and identifier.

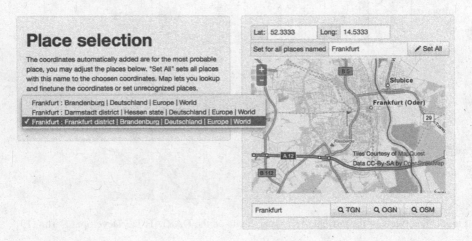

Fig. 6. Place selection options

The map module is another useful feature. If places cannot be found in the thesauri or identified by geo-referencing, the appropriate latitude and longitude can be set by a marker on the map. This applies, for example, to villages and towns that have disappeared during the late Middle Ages. Thus the Datasheet Editor can also be used as a tool for professional scholarly issues. Unknown or inhabited places, such as archaeological sites or historic monuments, can be manually geo-referenced, e.g. the coordinates of the Limes Arabicus.

The Geo-Browser combines three correlating elements: a map, a timeline and documentation of the visualized data set. The maps can be chosen interactively from contemporary ones and those showing historical borders. There is also the option of integrating your own geo-referenced maps. The standard map material of the Geo-Browser covers a period of over two millennia, so a map corresponding to the period of the data can be chosen. Data sets from the early 20th century, for example, can be displayed on maps representing states and borders on the eve of the First World War.

In order to structure multiple individual locations or the corresponding amount of data, individual data is accumulated in regional clusters according to density and quantity, as shown in Fig. 7.

Fig. 7. Accumulation of geo-referenced data. On selecting a cluster of data, the temporal dimension is shown in the correlating timeline.

Unfortunately, 3D data cannot be visualized with the Geo-Browser, but the service can be used to correlate the spatial and temporal information related to 3D data sets. This enables further analysis, especially new types of electronic access and contextualization of such forms of data.

The Geo-Browser is an example of how the components of a research infrastructure for the humanities and cultural studies can be used to develop sustainable modular services. It is not difficult to create a service-oriented architecture with eneric usable components.

5 Summary and Outlook

Over the past few years, rapid changes in research methods and practices in the humanities have led to an increased demand for an appropriate infrastructure to facilitate DH research. DARIAH is a European attempt to meet that demand, but it has its limits. Digital research infrastructures like DARIAH – despite their aims to support the digital humanities as a whole – have to focus on the general, basic or most wanted features. Emerging requirements from new fields, such as digital reconstruction and work with 3D objects, are not yet covered in a specific and satisfying way.

DARIAH focuses on text-based tools and services, as text is the basis for many literary and linguistic analyses. Nevertheless, it includes components that are ready to use and support cultural heritage preservation and digital reconstruction.

On the level of technical infrastructure, a variety of generic components can be used to develop specific tools and services in the field of 3D visualization and analytics. These include not only storage and PID services, including monitoring services to check virtual machines and technical components, but also the authentication and AAI provided by DARIAH-DE. Especially with the AAI, a decentralized user administration can be set up to manage a roles and rights system. A number of digital tools can also support both development and collaboration.

DARIAH-DE offers a variety of services for long-term preservation and interoperable reuse of research data. It is not yet clear which metadata and data formats are most feasible and useful. As a rather young sub-discipline in humanities and cultural studies, 3D visualization can take advantage of recent developments in the more text-based subjects. Building on these results from other disciplines can certainly make system-independent storage and reuse of 3D data possible in the longer term.

A variety of existing components can be put to interdisciplinary use and adapted to a variety of visualization processes. It would be desirable to share developments made for specific projects with other projects and researchers. For example, 3D tools for research and teaching could be implemented in the DARIAH infrastructure and made available to for everyone.

Perhaps the very strength of digital research infrastructures like DARIAH lies in its accessibility and interoperability. Rather than attempting to support every conceivable need of every possible research question and discipline, DARIAH is open to integrating tools and services for the benefit of all researchers. In the light of this, a new cluster working on digital reconstruction and 3D objects would be very welcome within the DARIAH research infrastructure.

References

1. https://dariah.eu. Accessed 14 June 2016
2. http://ec.europa.eu/research/infrastructures/index_en.cfm?pg=esfri. Accessed 14 June 2016
3. http://www.clarin.eu/. Accessed 14 June 2016
4. http://ec.europa.eu/research/infrastructures/index_en.cfm?pg=eric. Accessed 14 June 2016
5. http://dhd-blog.org/?p=3899. Accessed 14 June 2016
6. http://dariah.eu/activities.html. Accessed 14 June 2016

7. https://de.dariah.eu/. Accessed 14 June 2016
8. http://www.bmbf.de/en/index.php. Accessed 14 June 2016
9. https://de.dariah.eu/repository. Accessed 14 June 2016
10. http://www.textgridrep.de. Accessed 14 June 2016
11. https://de.dariah.eu/schema-registry. Accessed 14 June 2016
12. https://de.dariah.eu/generische-suche. Accessed 14 June 2016
13. http://www.zvdd.de/startseite/. Accessed 14 June 2016
14. http://www.hathitrust.org. Accessed 14 June 2016
15. Das TextGrid und DARIAH-DE Repositorium. Nutzung von geistes- und kulturwissenschaftlichen Forschungsdaten. http://gams.uni-graz.at/o:dhd2015.v.024. Accessed 14 June 2016
16. https://de.dariah.eu/pid-service; http://www.pidconsortium.eu. Accessed 14 June 2016
17. Klimpel, P., Weitzmann, J.H.: Forschen in der digitalen Welt. Juristische Handreichung für die Geisteswissenschaften. DARIAH-DE Working Papers Nr. 12. Göttingen: DARIAH-DE, 2015. URN: urn:nbn:de:gbv:7-dariah-2015-5-0. Accessed 14 June 2016
18. http://www.ieg-friedensvertraege.de/likecms.php?function=set_lang&lang=en. Accessed 14 June 2016
19. https://de.dariah.eu/developer-portal. Accessed 14 June 2016
20. https://shibboleth.net/. Accessed 14 June 2016
21. https://dev2.dariah.eu/wiki/pages/vi.ewpage.action?pageId=30376748. Accessed 14 June 2016
22. http://wp1187670.server-he.de/e4d/. Accessed 14 June 2016
23. http://www.informatik.uni-leipzig.de:8080/geotemco. Accessed 14 June 2016
24. https://geobrowser.de.dariah.eu/edit/. Accessed 14 June 2016
25. http://www.getty.edu/research/tools/vocabularies/tgn/. Accessed 14 June 2016
26. http://www.geonames.org. Accessed 14 June 2016

Grounded Practices, Principles and Strategies for Data and Knowledge Management

Rapid Prototyping in the Context of Cultural Heritage and Museum Displays

Buildings, Cities, Landscapes, Illuminated Models

Marc Grellert[✉]

Faculty of Architecture, Technische Universität Darmstadt, Digital Design Unit
and Architectura Virtualis GmbH, cooperation partner of the Technische
Universität Darmstadt, Darmstadt, Germany
grellert@architectura-virtualis.de

Abstract. The Digital Design Unit at the Darmstadt Technical University has
been producing virtual reconstructions since the beginning of the 1990s.
Advances in industrial prototyping and rapid prototyping led to the desire to
develop new kinds of exhibits by using the 3D printing technology to convert
the digital datasets into haptic models. Among the advantages of the new
technology is the fact that it tends to be markedly cheaper than traditional model
production. Moreover, it can be used to achieve extremely intricate detailing and
to produce relatively inexpensive duplicates. It allows for assessment and correction of the virtual dataset before printing – as well as for easy updating and
reprinting – and thus for great accuracy. The technology has given rise to novel
forms of museum exhibits with fresh aesthetic qualities and to new ways of
conveying information through projections and the selective illumination of the
models.

Keywords: Rapid prototyping · Virtual model · Virtual reconstruction ·
Museum

1 Introduction

The Digital Design Unit of the Architecture Faculty at the Technische Universität
Darmstadt and Architectura Virtualis, cooperation partner of the Darmstadt University,
have been producing digital exhibits for museums for more than twenty years.[1] The
department started out with virtual reconstructions[2] of buildings and cities that no
longer exist or that have undergone substantial change. Among these were the papal
palace in the Vatican, the Moscow Kremlin, the palaces of Berlin and Dresden as well
as sacred buildings such as the Basilica of Saint Peter in Rome and Khmer temples in

---

[1] See the Internet pages of the Digital Design Unit at the TU Darmstadt, Department of Architecture
and of the Architectura Virtualis GmbH, cooperation partner of the TU Darmstadt: www.dg.archi
tektur.tu-darmstadt.de/dg/forschung_dg/digitale_rekonstruktionen/projekte.de.jsp, www.architectura-
virtualis.de. Both Accessed 26 July 2016.

[2] On virtual reconstructions, see [1].

© Springer International Publishing AG 2016
S. Münster et al. (Eds.): 3D Research Challenges II, LNCS 10025, pp. 77–118, 2016.
DOI: 10.1007/978-3-319-47647-6_5

Cambodia. Particular importance attaches to the visualisation of destroyed German synagogues[3], a project that was initiated by the author at the department in 1994 and that is still ongoing. The most recent virtual reconstructions developed in Darmstadt focus on the architectural history of Florence Cathedral (2013) and on the Aramaic/Assyrian palace complex in Tell Halaf in Syria (2014). All of these projects were developed for exhibitions in Germany and abroad. Further to virtual reconstructions, the work for museums also comprises:

- The production of animated maps which track complex historic events that unfolded across time and space, for example, the Migration Period.
- The development of special digital installations and the conceptualisation and provision of the entire digital media package for the exhibition.
- The production of haptic models from threedimensional digital datasets (rapid prototyping) - or, to put it simply: the printing of virtual models.

Over the course of the last ten years, the production of haptic models in particular has been playing an increasingly important role in the work of Architectura Virtualis in Darmstadt. As a result, we can now build on a large and diverse body of rapid prototyping projects. Rapid prototyping describes a group of techniques that allow for the "overnight" fabrication of haptic objects from digital datasets. Originally developed for the production of industrial prototypes, these techniques are now being increasingly applied to the preparation of museum exhibits. The development of rapid prototyping made us wonder whether and to what extent we might be able to translate our virtual models into physical ones and thus be able to make the best of both kinds of models. For a long time, virtual and physical models were seen as mutually exclusive, for reasons of both cost and principle. Patrons used to commission either a virtual model or a haptic one, but not both. This situation has since changed fundamentally. In addition to virtual reconstructions, over the last couple of years the Darmstadt workshops have produced numerous physical models of buildings, cities and landscapes for exhibitions. Drawing on many years' experience, I propose to present a few fundamental thoughts on rapid prototyping models in exhibitions and to break them down into four categories:

1. Applications
2. Materials and manufacturing techniques
3. Advantages
4. Examples

2 Applications

The applications of rapid prototyping can be divided into three subsets: mono, parallel and hybrid. *Mono* designates a physical exhibit (a three-dimensional model) that is based on a digital model which is not exhibited. Mono tends to be used when rapid

---

[3] On the synagogue project, see [1, pp. 285–356].

prototyping offers particular advantages over traditional model-building techniques. Among others, these advantages include reduced cost, greater scope for detailing or the possibility of checking the accuracy of the model on the computer model and of being able to ascertain that it complies with the latest state of knowledge.

Parallel denotes a parallel presentation of virtual and haptic models in an exhibition, for example a film with virtual reconstructions complementing a haptic model based on the dataset. Parallel applications such as this cater to the commissioning institution's desire to combine the advantages of both physical and virtual models within the one and the same exhibition. To highlight the enormous potential of parallel applications, the following paragraphs briefly summarize the advantages of the two forms of display.

Speaking about virtual reconstructions, it is impossible to overstress the computer model's ability to present the appearance of architecture – lost or extant – especially when one wants to shed light on the complex relationship between a building's external and internal space and its urban setting. There is no traditional architectural model – short of a full-size reconstruction – that can match the accuracy of detail, realistic surfaces and atmospheric lighting achievable in a digital model. Moreover, the digital model can clarify spatial relationships by taking the viewer on a virtual tour, allowing them to experience the building as though they were moving through it. These advantages are most pronounced in the digital reconstruction of interior spaces.

Further to this, digital models offer other, new possibilities of experiencing architecture. Of particular interest are the presentation of variants and different time periods, dynamic simulations and access to buildings that are not open to the public. Variants and different time periods can be presented more clearly and vividly in computer models than in traditional forms of reconstruction, because digital models allow for the layering of images, seamlessly dissolving from one historical aspect to the next. Traditional architecture reconstructions, especially if they are to visualize a sequence of historical stages, take up a fair amount of space. Computer models, on the other hand, can visualize any number of variants or construction phases on one and the same display or screen without running out of space and, crucially, without taking up space that could more profitably be devoted to other exhibits. Another key advantage of digital models is their ability to simulate technical or physical processes in motion. Last, but by no means least, thanks to their capacity for visualizing interiors in minute detail, digital models offer the public a glimpse of buildings they do not usually have access to. This can be of significance, especially in the context of the cultural heritage debate.

In parallel displays the advantages of digital models listed above can be combined with those of traditional ones. Like traditional architectural models in exhibitions, rapid prototyping models have a unique aesthetic appeal. They allow visitors to view the exhibit as, when and for how long they choose. The presentation of virtual reconstructions, on the other hand, may be subject to a fixed schedule of screening times that not all visitors will want or be able to abide by. Moreover, the time it takes to watch the animation tends to be considerably longer than that invested into looking at a physical model. At the same time, it has to be kept in mind, that one of the great advantages of haptic models lies in their immediacy and in the speed with which the visitor can grasp the shape and structure of the building.

The advantages listed above clearly show that it does not make sense to favour one form of model over the other as a matter of principle. Both have specific advantages and uses within exhibitions. Their parallel combination allows for the greatest possible clarity and vividness and makes for an interesting change of medium for the viewer.

Analysis of the different advantages of virtual and haptic models in parallel applications led us to explore the potential of their direct combination in one, so to speak, *hybrid* exhibit. This works best in models of cities and landscapes. Because the haptic models are based on digital datasets, it is possible to create exact, digitally mapped overlay projections. Thus individual buildings in a city model can be picked out by means of a projector, while a corresponding screen takes the visitor on a virtual tour of their interior.

With hybrid exhibits, we can differentiate between those that involve a projection onto the haptic model and a second projection onto a wall, panel or screen and those which work with a single projection onto the model and that present all additional information on a designated space on the model's base plate. The projection of texts, images and animations onto the model creates a new kind of exhibit with a fresh aesthetic appeal and novel ways of conveying information. Another advantage of hybrid models is the ease with which they can be updated. An exhibit at the Frankfurt Historical Museum which presents the development of the city since Roman times was updated only ten days after the discovery of remains of a medieval port. The location of the port was identified in the model and the projection was revised to include the new information, images and a virtual representation of the port. In each of the applications – mono, parallel and hybrid – different materials and production techniques can be used, which I propose to outline here based on our own practice and experience.

3 Materials and Production Techniques

First of all, it has to be kept in mind that there is a wide range of materials and production techniques to suit any given task; and the technology is advancing rapidly.[4] In terms of techniques, we differentiate between additive and subtractive processes. An object produced in an additive process (also known as generative process) is built up in successive layers. This allows for complex forms and undercutting. The process is commonly referred to as 3D printing, for example plaster-based 3D printing. Conversely, subtractive techniques, for example the milling of a landscape, do not allow for complex forms with hollow spaces and undercutting. Furthermore, we can differentiate between objects produced entirely in a rapid prototyping process and those in which rapid prototyping was used to complement more traditional manual techniques such as the joining or painting of components.

Any consideration of using rapid prototyping to produce a model for an exhibition should be preceded by the following questions: What should the model look like and should it be touchable? Generally speaking, not all processes allow for larger objects to be manufactured in one piece. This raises a number of questions: Is it acceptable to

---

[4] See also [2]. The catalogue is written in German and English.

have visible seam lines? What resolution and what degree of detailing are required? The choice of materials and techniques depends on the answers to these questions. The materials range from gypsum plaster, sand, plastic – painted or unpainted – to ceramic and metal. It is important to consider the long-term behavior of the materials used. Discoloration and shrinkage are just two of many possible problems. Large complex models are often made using several different techniques. Flat components like the walls in the model of the Staufen Tower for the Frankfurt Historical Museum, for example, are milled, while highly detailed small components like the tracery of the windows are 3D printed. The different components were then assembled and painted. The larger the model, the more likely it is that it is made in a combination of techniques, or that it is assembled from individual components, which requires extra finishing touches. Despite the increasing automation of technical processes, these exhibition models are made by highly skilled specialists and always require a certain amount of professional finishing by the model builder. But the industry is moving fast. For one, there is a great deal of hype surrounding DIY 3D printers for home use. The quality of their output, however, is not yet good enough to be of use in a museum context. It is not worth investing here, unless one wants to get into the technology and gain some experience without huge financial outlay. With regard to exhibition use, it is worth keeping an eye on the market and to look out for new materials and/or material properties. One such intriguing new development is metal printing, where we are beginning to see the first viable and affordable processes. The technology, however, is not yet as fully developed as that of plaster printing, but the results we achieved in a model of St. Peter's were very promising (see examples: 5.3.1). Brand new technologies are glass printing, which is in the first steps of development at MIT [3], and Carbon3D printing, which "creates objects from the top down, in one continuous motion. It's faster and eliminates the layering that can result in weak, jagged objects. ... Carbon3D can print up to 100 times faster than leading 3-D and stereolithographic printers" [4].

4   Advantages

Compared with traditional model-making techniques, rapid prototyping has a number of distinct advantages. The rapid development of the technology means that these advantages will become even more significant and that we should expect to see further useful applications. At the moment we can discern the following advantages:

4.1   Cost

Many projects have shown that rapid prototyping models are cheaper to manufacture than traditional handmade ones. Two variables need to be considered: detailing and size. First of all, it should be noted that the cost of rapid prototyping models consists of the cost of developing the virtual model plus that of actually printing it out. There may be additional costs for finishing touches such as paintwork, smoothing over the lateral aspects of the model or the addition of stabilizing, constructive elements. With regard to printing costs, it makes little difference whether the building is depicted in minute detail or just as a simple cube. The cost is calculated on the basis of machine running time and the volume of material used. Thus the smaller the model – even if highly detailed – the cheaper the print. In contrast, small models built in the traditional manner can be more expensive because it is difficult and time-consuming to produce intricate architectural elements on a tiny scale. In other words, for larger models it may be financially advantageous to opt for traditional manufacturing techniques, since the cost of rapid prototyping rises exponentially (by a factor of 3) with the size of the model. Ultimately, 90 % of the personnel costs of rapid prototyping models is the cost of preparing the virtual model. The more identical or similar architectural elements there are, and the more detailed they are, the more it makes financial sense to use rapid prototyping technology. Here the elements can simply be copied from the virtual model, whereas they have to be individually produced in traditional handmade models.

4.2 Detailing

Rapid prototyping allows for an extremely high degree of detailing – even in very small models. The accuracy of the detailing depends on the accuracy of the machine's resolution and on the material used. In plaster-printing, for example, it is possible to fashion self-supporting flying roofs with a thickness of a mere 0.3 mm. Elements such as these are, of course, extremely delicate and touch-sensitive when they are executed in plaster. But even elements as thin as that can be quite sturdy when they are executed in other materials, for example in plastic.

4.3 Duplicates

Rapid prototyping processes are of particular interest in the production of duplicates or multiples. Once the virtual model is complete, all that is left to pay for is the automated reproduction. Depending on the job in hand, the machine costs come to somewhere between 20 and 70 % of the total cost. If we accept that rapid prototyping models are, on the whole, cheaper to produce than traditional handmade models, then the economies of scale mean that duplicates can be made at a much lower cost per unit. What is more, duplication does not impinge on the freedom of executing the model in different materials or sizes. If the change of size does not jeopardize stability, it can be achieved by simply scaling the virtual model up or down.

4.4 Touchability

Rapid prototyping technology allows museums to exhibit models without having to entomb them in protective showcases. In the event of damage, a replacement can be made at relatively little expense from the original virtual dataset stored on the computer. This option is of particular interest for objects that can be produced at low cost. Display cases can also be dispensed with for relatively abstract large-scale plaster models and for models made of more robust materials such as plastic or metal. More complex models, which can easily cost a five-figure sum in Euros even if they are entirely 3D printed, should not be displayed unprotected. Here barriers provide a simple solution. Display cases offer greater safety, but they can sap models of their immediacy and direct appeal.

4.5 Pre-production Review in the Computer – Scientific Soundness 1

Thanks to the fact that virtual models can be thoroughly checked and evaluated before printing, rapid prototyping offers academics and model makers new ways of working and collaborating. Images of the virtual model can be sent to scientific advisers for evaluation, revision and correction. Unlike with traditional model-building, all necessary amendments can be made in the virtual dataset without damaging the substance of a physical model. It is not until every last detail has been checked, double-checked and approved that the haptic model is produced.

4.6 Updating – Scientific Soundness 2

Rapid prototyping models can be updated with relative ease when new information emerges that needs to be incorporated. This applies above all to models of cities. When the state of knowledge changes, the affected sections can be updated in the virtual model, 3D printed and inserted into the haptic model to replace the outdated ones. Naturally, this only works if the model was designed to allow for such updates, and the buildings can be detached from the base plate.

4.7 Illuminations

Since rapid prototyping models are based on digital data sets, it is relatively easy to achieve illuminations with exactly mapped overlays which give rise to new forms of models of great aesthetic appeal.

5 Examples

In the final chapter I would like to present and illustrate a selection of projects in greater detail. The individual case notes are preceded by a table listing the title of the exhibition/model, the commissioning institution/location and the date of completion (Table 1). For ease of reference, the specific advantages and qualities exemplified by each model are recorded under the heading "Special feature". The remaining rubrics provide information about the type of model (mono, parallel, hybrid), geographic span (world, Europe, section of Europe, region, city, city section, building) and as to whether or not the model features projections (P) and/or screens (S) and, if so, how many. The table is arranged by the reach of the model's geographic span, beginning with a globe-girdling landscape model and ending with models of individual buildings.

Table 1. Examples

	Kind of model	Special feature	Type	Span	P/S
5.1	Landscape models				
5.1.1	Roots of Humanity Rheinisches LandesMuseum, Bonn On permanent display since 2006	Map animation	Mono	World	P
5.1.2	Political Borders in Europe Deutsches Historisches Museum, Berlin On permanent display since 2006	Interactive	Mono	Europe	P
5.1.3	Via Claudia Augusta Museum der Stadt Füssen Bayerische Landesausstellung Temporary exhibition 2010	Mill-cut path with LEDs	Mono	Part of Europe	–
5.1.4	War in the Ploegsteert Region Centre d'interprétation, Ploegsteert (Belgium) On permanent display since 2013	Size, interactive language selection	Hybrid	Region	P/P
5.2	City models				
5.2.1	Model of the city of Munich Landeshauptstadt München Temporary exhibition 2008	Large scale	Mono	City	–
5.2.2	Model of the Frankfurt Judengasse Jüdisches Museum Frankfurt On permanent display 2009–2014	Model on map	Parallel	City section	–

(*Continued*)

Table 1. (*Continued*)

	Kind of model	Special feature	Type	Span	P/S
5.2.3	Fortifications of Florence, Michelangelo Rheinisches LandesMuseum, Bonn Temporary exhibition 2007	Small, aesthetically appealing and inexpensive exhibit	Parallel	City section	–
5.2.4	The Dresden palace precinct (1678) Staatliche Kunstsammlungen Dresden, Grünes Gewölbe Completion 2011 To go on permanent display after refurbishment of the exhibition space	Scientific soundness	Parallel	City section	–
5.2.5	Olympic grounds, Berlin Deutsches Historisches Museum, Berlin On permanent display since 2006	Color coding provides information on the period the existing buildings were built	Parallel	City section	–
5.2.6	Frankfurt and the Staufen Period Historisches Museum Frankfurt On permanent display since 2012	Projection onto the model with a window on the model for secondary information	Hybrid	City	P
5.2.7	Urban development of Hildesheim Temporary exhibition Roemer und Pelizaeus Museum Hildesheim, 2015 On permanent display since in 2015 Besucherzentrum Welterbe, Tempelhaus Hildesheim	Model of the terrain and buildings printed in one	Hybrid	City	P/S

(*Continued*)

Table 1. (*Continued*)

	Kind of model	Special feature	Type	Span	P/S
5.2.8	Torgau during the Reformation Schloss Hartenfels, Torgau Temporary exhibition 2015 On permanent display since 2015	Virtual simulation of the exhibit in the exhibition	Hybrid	City	P/S
5.2.9	The Foundation of Medieval Cities Deutsches Historisches Museum, Berlin On permanent display since 2006	Special design, display case	Hybrid	City	P/P
5.2.10	Flossenbürg Concentration Camp Flossenbürg memorial site On permanent display since 2007 Deutsches Historisches Museum, Berlin On permanent display 2009–2014	Duplicate for a second museum	Hybrid	City section	P/P
5.3	Buildings				
5.3.1	Saint Peter's Basilica, Rome Research models 2005–2013 TU Darmstadt, Digital Design Unit	Metal print	Mono		–
5.3.2	Hochzeitsturm, Darmstadt Outdoor model on the Mathildenhöhe hill since 2011	Outdoor model, cast bronze based on a plaster-printed model	Mono		–
5.3.3	Bell tower in the Moscow Kremlin State Historical and Cultural Museum Moscow Kremlin 2006	Color	Parallel		–

(*Continued*)

Table 1. (*Continued*)

	Kind of model	Special feature	Type	Span	P/S
5.3.4	Imperial palace, Frankfurt Archäologisches Museum Frankfurt On permanent display since 2008	Relatively abstract model Natural appearance of plaster-printed models	Parallel		–
5.3.5	Staufen Tower, Frankfurt Historisches Museum Frankfurt On permanent display since 2012	Combination of different technologies, 3D Viewers	Hybrid		–

5.1   Landscape Models

5.1.1   Roots of Humanity

Project: Roots of Humanity
Special feature: Map animation
Location: Rheinisches LandesMuseum, Bonn
Type: Mono
Span: World
Use of media: Projection onto the model
Completion: 2006, permanent exhibition

Made for the exhibition *Roots of Humanity* at the Rheinisches LandesMuseum in Bonn in 2006, the three-dimensional landscape model illustrates the evolution and spread of mankind. The model presents the continents of Europe, Africa, Asia and Australia and shows their topography in threedimensional relief. The evolution and spread of the different species of primates, pre-humans and humans is projected onto the model in chronological order as a continuous animation.

The animation begins 9.5 million years ago and clearly shows that Africa was the origin of each of the hominid populations that peopled the world – with the exception of the Neanderthals. The relief also shows the impact of topographical features such as mountain ranges and oceans on migration and expansion patterns.

The relief model (Fig. 1) is based on a computer model and was mill-cut into a block of synthetic material. The exhibit is part of the permanent exhibition of the Rheinisches LandesMuseum.

The animation (Fig. 2) is also on display at the Deutsches Historisches Museum in Berlin, the Swedish Museum of Natural History in Stockholm and the Museum für Vor- und Frühgeschichte Berlin.

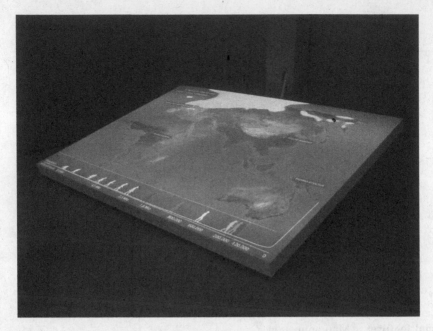

Fig. 1. Roots of Humanity, exhibit for the Rheinisches LandesMuseum, Bonn (© Architectura Virtualis GmbH)

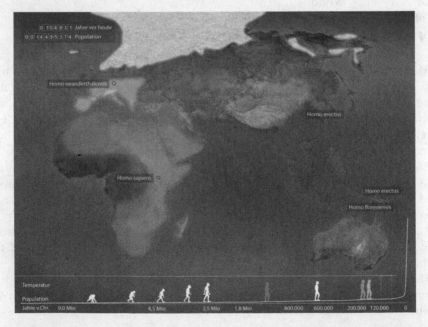

Fig. 2. Roots of Humanity, still from the animation (© Architectura Virtualis GmbH)

5.1.2 Political Borders in Europe

Project:	Political Borders in Europe
Special features:	Interactivity, large model
Location:	Deutsches Historisches Museum, Berlin
Type:	Mono
Span:	Europe
Scale:	1:1,000,000
Use of media:	Projection onto the model
Completion:	2006, permanent exhibition

This model, developed for the opening of the permanent exhibition at the Deutsches Historisches Museum in Berlin in 2006 and displayed in the entrance area, shows the history of borders and territories in Europe (Fig. 3). A landscape model on the floor, 4 × 3 m in size, shows the topography of Europe. A projection is mapped onto the model, picking out the political borders at 30 different points in time. Shown in chronological sequence, these dates quickly convey a comprehensive idea of the development of the political territories in Europe from antiquity to the present. It becomes apparent that many of Germany's neighbors had far more stable borders than Germany, and that Germany with its countless principalities constituted an exception over a long period of time.

The landscape model was mill-cut into polyurethane foam (Uriol 650) on the basis of a computer model developed earlier. The model was delivered in two parts on rollers and assembled on site. Touch panels allow visitors to navigate to specific periods, stop the animation or go back in time (Fig. 4).

Fig. 3. Political Borders in Europe, Exhibit for the Deutsches Historisches Museum, Berlin (© Architectura Virtualis GmbH)

Fig. 4. Political Borders in Europe, Touch panel (© Architectura Virtualis GmbH)

The exhibit has since been moved from the foyer to the first floor, where it serves as the opening exhibit of the permanent exhibition. No longer displayed on the floor, it is now installed vertically.

5.1.3 Via Claudia Augusta

Project:	Via Claudia Augusta
Special feature:	Mill-cut path with LEDs
Location:	Museum der Stadt Füssen
Type:	Mono
Span:	Section of Europe
Scale:	1:33,000
Use of media:	LEDs
Completion:	2010, temporary exhibition

The model of the Via Claudia Augusta, one of the key Roman trade routes between southern Germany and northern Italy, was made for the Bayerische Landesausstellung 2010, which focused on the relationship between Bavaria and Italy. The Via Claudia Augusta connected Augsburg and Füssen in Bavaria with Trento in the Adige river valley and the coastal town of Altino near modern-day Treviso and Venice.

A mill-cut channel filled with red synthetic resin visualized the course of the Roman road. LEDs on the underside of the landscape model illuminated the translucent resin (Figs. 5 and 6). The model was commissioned by the Haus für Bayerische Geschichte Augsburg.

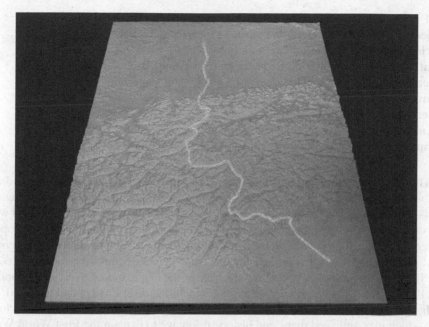

Fig. 5. Via Claudia Augusta, model with LED-lit path (© Architectura Virtualis GmbH)

Fig. 6. Via Claudia Augusta, model with LED-lit path (© Architectura Virtualis GmbH)

5.1.4　The Great War in the Ploegsteert Region

Project:　　　　　　The Great War in the Ploegsteert Region (West Flanders)
Special features:　Large model, multilingual
Location:　　　　　Centre d'interprétation, Ploegsteert (Belgium)
Type:　　　　　　　Hybrid
Span:　　　　　　　Region
Scale:　　　　　　 1:8,760
Use of media:　　 Projection onto the model and the wall
Completion:　　　 2013, permanent exhibition

The Centre d'interprétation, Ploegsteert (Plugstreet) in Belgium commissioned an exhibit to explain the course of the war in the region. An animation of the frontlines of 1914–1918 is projected onto a landscape model of the Ploegsteert region. The model was mill-cut into polyurethane foam (Uriol 540) on the basis of a computer model developed earlier. The mapped projection on the model of the terrain is complemented by a second synchronous projection of texts and images onto the wall behind the model (Figs. 7 and 8). Pushbuttons are integrated into the base of the haptic model to allow visitors to start the animation in one of four languages (French, Flemish, English and German).

In addition to that, Architectura Virtualis created an eighteen-minute introductory film, which uses animated maps and historical footage to explain the First World War, and an interactive five-meter multi touch wall, which uses images and film to commemorate the Battle of Messines fought nearby in June of 1917.

In collaboration with a network of partners, Architectura Virtualis GmbH in Darmstadt puts together complete exhibition packages on the subject of the First World

Fig. 7. War in the Ploegsteert Region, illuminated model and projection on the wall (© Architectura Virtualis GmbH)

Fig. 8. War in the Ploegsteert Region, illuminated model and projection on the wall (© Architectura Virtualis GmbH)

War. The package includes the design of the exhibition, the conceptualization of the use of media, the development of scenarios and content and the installation of the hardware.

5.2   City Models

5.2.1   Model of the City of Munich

Project: Model of the city of Munich
Special feature: Large scale
Location: Munich
Type: Mono
Span: City
Scale: 1:5,000
Use of media: -
Completion: 2008, temporary exhibition

Munich celebrated the 850th anniversary of the city's foundation with an exhibition tracing its urban development. The municipal planning office developed an idea for an exhibit of a three-dimensional representation of the city. A black and white drawing of a map of modern-day Munich (scale of 1:5,000) was transferred onto an 8 × 3 m wall. The more interesting areas of the city were picked out in the form of a relief model superimposed onto the map (Fig. 9). The remit was to machine the model on the basis of the 3D dataset provided by the land survey office.

The model consists of ten individual panels (50 × 50 cm) with plaster-printed sections of the city (Fig. 10). It is planned to expand the model gradually by adding further panels.

Fig. 9. Model of the city of Munich, model for the exhibition (© Architectura Virtualis GmbH)

Fig. 10. Model of the city of Munich, model for the exhibition (© Architectura Virtualis GmbH)

5.2.2   Model of the Frankfurt Judengasse

Project:	Model of the Frankfurt Judengasse (Jewish ghetto)
Special feature:	Model on map
Location:	Jüdisches Museum Frankfurt Dependance Börneplatz
Type:	Parallel
Span:	City section
Scale:	1:1,000
Use of media:	-
Completion:	2009–2014, permanent exhibition

Frankfurt's main synagogue in the Judengasse (built in 1711) was reconstructed as a 3D computer model and presented in a film made for the exhibition *Servants of the Royal Chamber: The Emperor and the Jews of Frankfurt.* Among other things, the visualization shows the illumination of the synagogue on the occasion of the coronation of Leopold II as Holy Roman Emperor in Frankfurt in 1790.

Another exhibit dealt with the architectural history of the synagogue and its integration into its urban setting. Located east of the medieval city wall, the Judengasse ran from today's Konstablerwache to Börneplatz, near the river Main. A historical map of the city measuring 1 × 1 m and featuring the path taken by the coronation train was set onto a block (Fig. 11) with a height of 70 cm. The virtual dataset provided the basis for a plaster-printed haptic model of the crescent-shaped street and the synagogue which was set onto the mounted map (Fig. 12).

The combination of map and 3D printed city section has proved very effective. It emphasizes the salient part in a visually interesting way and anchors it in the overall

Fig. 11. Model of the Frankfurt Judengasse, model on map (© Architectura Virtualis GmbH)

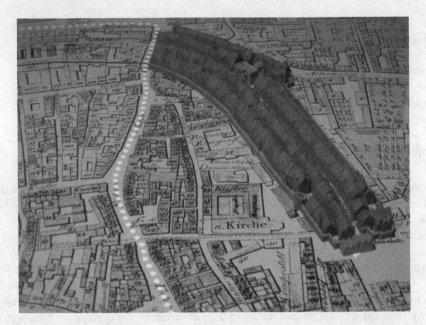

Fig. 12. Model of the Frankfurt Judengasse, model on map (© Architectura Virtualis GmbH)

urban context, obviating the need for a more comprehensive 3D model. The close focus on the Judengasse alone meant that the exhibit could be produced at a relatively modest cost.

5.2.3   Fortifications of Florence

Project:	Fortifications of Florence, Michelangelo
Special features:	Small, aesthetically appealing exhibit, inexpensive
Location:	Rheinisches LandesMuseum, Bonn
Type:	Parallel
Span:	City section
Scale:	1:1,000
Use of media:	Screen with 3D film simulation
Completion:	2007, temporary exhibition

The exhibition devoted to Michelangelo's painting *Leda and the Swan* at the Rheinisches LandesMuseum in Bonn also presented six expressive drawings of fortifications by the artist whom the Florentine Republic had tasked with the responsibility of strengthening the city's defenses against the papal army. Reminiscent of modern deconstructivist architecture, the designs take the viewer by surprise.

The drawings were made in 1529, when Michelangelo served as Governor of Fortifications. Drawing on architectural history and comparable fortifications, the two-dimensional drawings were translated into three-dimensional computer models and into an animation shown in the exhibition (Fig. 13). The focus is on a section of the fortified defenses with the Porta al Prato d'Ognissanti and the Prato d'Ognissanti bastion.

Fig. 13. Fortifications of Florence, virtual model (© Architectura Virtualis GmbH)

Fig. 14. Fortifications of Florence, model for the exhibition (© Architectura Virtualis GmbH)

The virtual dataset formed the basis for a small plaster-printed haptic model showing the simulated section of the fortifications (Fig. 14). The small size of the model (35 × 25 cm) heightened its aesthetic appeal and kept production costs low (c. €1,500).

5.2.4   The Dresden Palace Precinct

Project: The Dresden palace precinct (1678)
Special feature: Scientific soundness
Location: Dresden, Staatliche Kunstsammlungen
Type: Parallel
Span: City section
Scale: 1:300
Use of media: Virtual reconstruction
Completion: 2011, Installation in the permanent exhibition after completion of the refurbishment of the exhibition space

The Staatliche Kunstsammlungen Dresden commissioned a model to illustrate the architectural history of the Dresden royal palace for the permanent exhibition. The first step was the computer reconstruction of the building as it was in 1678. The reconstruction was masterminded by the Digital Design Unit at the Darmstadt Technical University, which produced a film with virtual zooms and tracking shots. Architectura Virtualis accepted the commission to complement the film with a haptic model of the entire palace precinct (Fig. 15). The groundwork and research that form the basis of the model took more than two years to complete.

Fig. 15. The Dresden palace precinct (1678), model for the exhibition (© Architectura Virtualis GmbH)

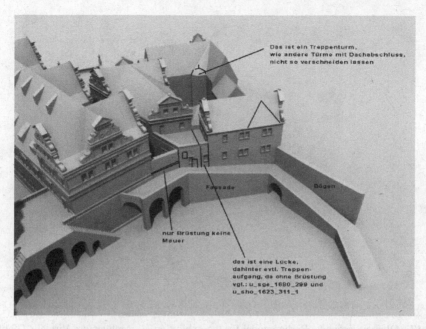

Fig. 16. The Dresden palace precinct (1678), rendering with comments from the advisor (© Architectura Virtualis GmbH)

The base plate was mill-cut from polyurethane foam (Uriol) and painted in two colors (white for the ground and powder-blue for the river). The buildings were 3D plaster-printed. Like many other projects, the Dresden model exemplifies the enormous advantage of rapid prototyping. All buildings could be checked for accuracy on the computer. Detailed renderings were emailed to the associated architectural historian, corrected and returned (Fig. 16). This was repeated until every last question was answered to everybody's satisfaction. Only then was the virtual model cleared for printing. In the event of new information on the history of the building coming to light, it is relatively easy to amend the virtual model and to reprint the section in question. The buildings are produced in blocks that are attached to the base plate by means of simple pegs to allow for updates or repairs.

5.2.5   Olympic Grounds, Berlin

Project:	Olympic grounds, Berlin
Special feature:	Color-coding provides information on the period when the existing buildings were built
Location:	Visitor Centre at the Olympic Bell Tower in Berlin
Type:	Parallel
Span:	City section
Scale:	1:1,000
Use of media:	Virtual reconstruction
Completion:	2006, permanent exhibition

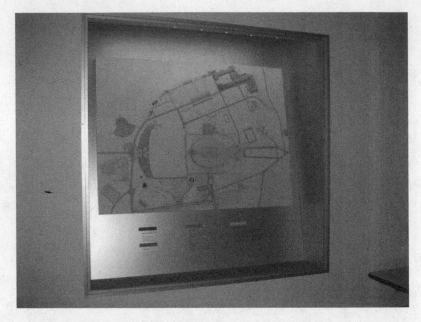

Fig. 17. Olympic grounds, Berlin, model for the exhibition (© Architectura Virtualis GmbH)

Fig. 18. Olympic grounds, Berlin, color-coding identifies different construction phases (© Architectura Virtualis GmbH)

Commissioned for a permanent exhibition in Berlin, the 3D computer reconstruction presents the history of the Berlin Olympic grounds. The film simulation of the reconstruction is complemented with a haptic model which colour-codes the key construction phases (Figs. 17 and 18).

The model was produced on the basis of the digital dataset using rapid prototyping technology. The base plate terrain was mill-cut. The buildings were 3D printed using a special synthetic material and an Objet printer and then painted. The different construction phases are color-coded: Earliest buildings and racecourse 1909, construction of the Hochschule für Leibesübungen (University for Physical Education) which became part of the German Sport Forum 1919–1930, construction of sporting facilities for the 1936 Olympic Games and, finally, post-war construction and use of the grounds from 1945 to 2004. The model is installed vertically in a display case; the film is shown in an adjacent room.

5.2.6   Frankfurt and the Staufen Period

Project:	Frankfurt and the Staufen Period
Special feature:	Model projection with an area on the model for secondary information
Location:	Historisches Museum Frankfurt, old building
Type:	Hybrid
Span:	City
Scale:	1:500
Use of media:	Projection onto the model
Completion:	2012, permanent exhibition

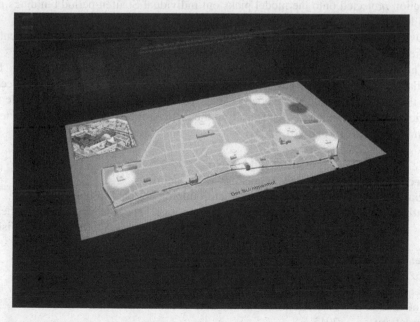

Fig. 19. Frankfurt and the Staufen Period, illuminated model (© Architectura Virtualis GmbH)

Fig. 20. Frankfurt and the Staufen Period, illuminated model (© Architectura Virtualis GmbH)

Produced for the new permanent exhibition in the old building of the Frankfurt Historical Museum, this installation presents the city during the time of the Staufen kings. The starting point is a city model showing the known buildings of the period. An animation projected onto the model picks out individual Staufen period buildings and provides further information in the form of texts and images.

Over the course of the animation, visitors can trace the history and development of the area from the time of the Romans to the present.

The terrain is mill-cut polyurethane foam (Uriol), the buildings plaster-printed. The installation is brought to life by two synchronous films, both of which are projected onto the model, one onto the model as such, the other onto the flat area outside the fortifications, which naturally lends itself to the display of additional information, texts and images (Figs. 19 and 20).

5.2.7   Urban Development of Hildesheim
Project: Urban development of Hildesheim
Special feature: Model of the terrain and buildings printed in one
Location: Temporary exhibition Roemer und Pelizaeus Museum Hildesheim. On permanent display since 2015 at the World Heritage Visitor Centre in the Tempelhaus, Hildesheim
Type: Hybrid
Span: City
Scale: 1:1,800
Use of media: Projection onto the model, screen
Completion: 2015

Commissioned by the Hildesheim Marketing GmbH, the model of Hildesheim shows the modern city as it presents itself to visitors today. It was first installed in a temporary exhibition at the Roemer und Pelizaeus Museum Hildesheim and is now on permanent display at the Hildesheim Welcome Centre.

A projection onto the model visualizes the changing urban landscape from the early Middle Ages to the present. A synchronous presentation on a screen shows images and provides further information in the form of texts (Figs. 21 and 22).

Fig. 21. Urban development of Hildesheim, model projection and film (© Architectura Virtualis GmbH)

Fig. 22. Urban development of Hildesheim, model projection of the bastion phase (© Architectura Virtualis GmbH)

The model measures 1.9 × 1.2 m and is executed on a scale of 1:800. The large number of buildings that needed to be reproduced and the available budget made it necessary to depart from our usual practice of mill-cutting the terrain and plaster-printing blocks of buildings to be attached to the base plate by means of pegs. Instead, terrain and city were 3D printed in PMMA as a unit. Buildings of special interest such as churches are rendered in greater detail, while the rest of the urban fabric is depicted in a highly pared down fashion. This process meant that the model was divided into four sections of equal size.

5.2.8   Torgau During the Reformation

Project: Torgau during the Reformation
Special feature: Virtual simulation of the exhibit in the exhibition
Location: Schloss Hartenfels, Torgau Temporary exhibition 2015. On permanent display in 2015
Type: Hybrid
Span: City
Scale: 1:400
Use of media: Projection onto the model, screen .
Completion: 2015

This model of the city of Torgau around 1600 was made for the exhibition *Luther and the Princes* shown at Schloss Hartenfels in 2015. Once again, the terrain was mill-cut and the buildings plaster-printed and attached to the base plate by means of pegs. A projection onto the model and a synchronous display on a screen thematize, locate and illuminate the momentous events of the Reformation in Torgau (Fig. 23).

The result of extensive historical and architectural research, the virtual dataset, on which the final haptic model is based, allowed not only for the correction and double-checking of details and the trialing of hypotheses, but also for the virtual

Fig. 23. Torgau during the Reformation, exhibit (© Architectura Virtualis GmbH)

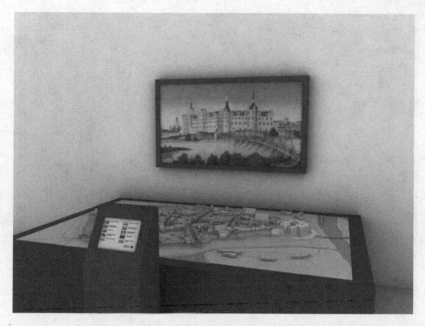

Fig. 24. Torgau during the Reformation, simulation of the exhibit (© Architectura Virtualis GmbH)

simulation of its final installation in the exhibition. Different sites, protective measures such as display cases or barriers, heights of installation and casings could be simulated and assessed, permitting the organizers of the exhibition to determine the best possible installation ahead of the exhibition (Fig. 24).

5.2.9 Cities Founded in the Middle Ages

Project: Cities founded in the Middle Ages
Special features: Special design in display case, cost, interactivity
Location: Deutsches Historisches Museum, Berlin
Type: Hybrid
Span: City
Scale: 1:500
Use of media: Projection onto the model and a rear projection screen
Completion: 2006

Commissioned by the German Historical Museum in Berlin, the installation was designed to familiarize visitors with medieval city foundations. The core of the exhibit is a reconstruction of a sixteenth-century model of the medieval city Straubing. The original wooden model, made by Jakob Sandtner, is exhibited in the Bavarian National Museum in Munich. A reconstruction in limewood would have been prohibitively expensive; rapid prototyping brought the cost down by 75 %.

Fig. 25. The Foundation of Medieval Cities, exhibit (© Architectura Virtualis GmbH)

Fig. 26. The Foundation of Medieval Cities, touch panel (© Architectura Virtualis GmbH)

The original model in Munich was photographed from all conceivable angles and reconstructed on the computer. Rapid prototyping technology was used to produce a 3D plaster-printed model on the basis of the volumetric dataset. Base plate and buildings were printed separately. 3D plaster-printing also allows for the production of full-color models. At the time of writing, almost ten years after the model was first installed, the color is as fresh as it was in 2006.

In addition to the haptic model, the exhibit also features a vertical rear projection screen behind the model. Two synchronized projectors beam information onto the model and onto the screen (Fig. 25). Thus when specific aspects of the medieval city are described on the rear projection screen, the relevant area is illuminated on the model. What is more, the buildings and urban spaces located on the model can be explored from a virtual pedestrian's perspective on the screen. A touch panel (Fig. 26) on the exhibit offers a range of options and submenus.

5.2.10   Flossenbürg Concentration Camp

Project:	Flossenbürg concentration camp
Special feature:	Duplicate on a smaller scale
Location:	Flossenbürg memorial site (KZ-Gedenkstätte) Deutsches Historisches Museum, Berlin
Type:	Hybrid
Span:	City section
Scale:	1:500
Use of media:	Projection onto the model and the wall
Completion:	Flossenbürg memorial site, permanent display since 2007 Deutsches Historisches Museum, Berlin, permanent display 2009–2014

This model of the former concentration camp was made for the entrance area of the permanent exhibition at the Flossenbürg memorial site. Two projections explain the function and history of the camp. One projection is aimed directly onto the haptic model. It picks out specific areas and buildings and also traces the gradual repurposing and development of the area by the municipality of Flossenbürg after 1945. A second synchronous projection onto the wall behind the model shows a series of complementary black and white photographs.

The haptic model of the terrain and the concentration camp buildings were machined on the basis of a digital dataset produced earlier. The grounds are made of mill-cut polyurethane foam (Uriol); the individual buildings are 3D plaster-printed (Fig. 27).

The German Historical Museum in Berlin displays a second, somewhat smaller copy of the model in its permanent exhibition (Fig. 28). Mill-cut and 3D printed like the one in Flossenbürg, it was made by simply scaling down the virtual model. The content was adapted to the requirements of the Berlin museum, where the example of the Flossenbürg camp is used to explain the layout and significance of the individual structures. The compelling interplay between model, images and texts conveys an idea of what a concentration camp was.

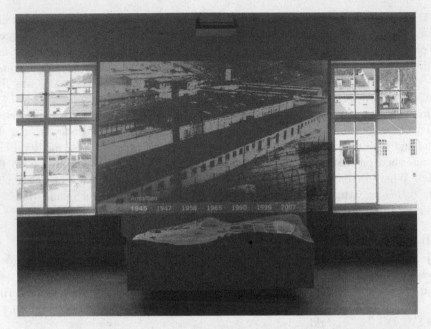

Fig. 27. KZ-Gedenkstätte Flossenbürg, exhibit (© Architectura Virtualis GmbH)

Fig. 28. Deutsches Historisches Museum Berlin, duplicated exhibit (© Architectura Virtualis GmbH)

5.3   Buildings

5.3.1   Basilica of Saint Peter, Rome

Project: Basilica of Saint Peter, Rome
Special feature: Metal print
Location: TU Darmstadt, Digital Design Unit
Type: Parallel
Span: Building
Use of media: Virtual reconstruction
Completion: Research models 2005–2013

The Digital Design Unit at the Technische Universität Darmstadt had reprocessed four design variants of the Basilica of Saint Peter in Rome – which the department had reconstructed and simulated earlier – for rapid prototyping. The resulting digital datasets of the church designs by Bramante, Sangallo, Michelangelo (Fig. 29) and Maderno allow for the production of haptic models, for example in plaster, within a relatively short time.

In 2013, the design by Michelangelo was used to investigate whether the data set could also be used for metal-printing (Fig. 30). The fact that the resolution of the selected metal-printing process was lower than that of plaster-printing meant that the detailing had to be pared back. Moreover, the sheer weight of the model made it necessary to fit it with a support structure. All things considered, the experience was hugely positive. At $3,000, the costs incurred for the 8-kg model were within

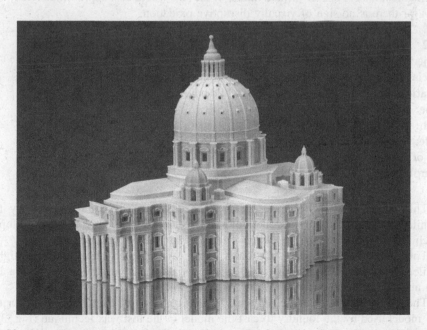

Fig. 29. Saint Peter's Basilica in Rome, plaster-printed model (© Technische Universität Darmstadt, Digital Design Unit)

Fig. 30. Saint Peter's Basilica in Rome, metal-printed model (© Technische Universität Darmstadt, Digital Design Unit)

reasonable limits. A plaster-printed model of the size would cost approximately €1,300. Thus far there is no sign of visually disruptive oxidation.

5.3.2 Hochzeitsturm, Darmstadt

Project:	Hochzeitsturm, Darmstadt
Special feature:	Cast bronze based on a plaster-printed model
Location:	Outdoors on the Mathildenhöhe
Type:	Mono
Span:	Building
Scale:	1:65
Use of media:	-
Completion:	2011

This model of the Olbrich-designed Hochzeitsturm was commissioned by the Mathildenhöhe Institute for the benefit of blind visitors. A virtual model was developed which allowed for thorough checking of the detailing before production.

The digital dataset formed the basis of a plaster-printed haptic model. Highly detailed areas were 3D printed in a synthetic material to achieve a higher resolution and then attached to the plaster model (Fig. 31).

The enhanced plaster model, in turn, formed the basis of the silicon mold for the wax model used by the foundry to cast the model in the lost wax technique (Fig. 32). This process chain was more cost-effective than the traditional casting process.

Fig. 31. Hochzeitsturm in Darmstadt, virtual model (© Architectura Virtualis GmbH)

Fig. 32. Hochzeitsturm in Darmstadt, outdoor model (© Architectura Virtualis GmbH)

5.3.3   Bell Tower in the Moscow Kremlin

Project: Bell tower in the Moscow Kremlin
Special feature: Plaster-printed in color
Location: State Historical and Cultural Museum Moscow Kremlin
Type: Parallel
Span: Building
Scale: 1:135
Use of media: Virtual reconstruction, projection
Completion: 2006

Made for the Moscow Kremlin Museum, this haptic model of the sixteenth-century Ivan the Great bell tower in the Moscow Kremlin complex was 3D plaster-printed on the basis of a digital dataset (Fig. 33). The original dataset was compiled as part of a large-scale research project of the Digital Design Unit at the Technische Universität Darmstadt and was reprocessed for rapid prototyping. The objective was to convey an impression of the bell tower's original color scheme, which was dominated by the color red before the belfry was whitewashed.

Plaster-printing allows for the admixture of color and direct color printing. The process is so precise that even the inscriptions (Fig. 34) beneath the cupola, which had been generated as textures in the virtual model, could be printed directly. The geometric transfer of the textures is very precise; obtaining the desired color, on the other hand, took some experimentation. The gilding of the cupola was done by hand.

Fig. 33. Bell tower in the Moscow Kremlin, color-printed model (© Architectura Virtualis GmbH)

Fig. 34. Bell tower in the Moscow Kremlin, detail color-printed model (© Architectura Virtualis GmbH)

5.3.4 Imperial Palace Frankfurt

Project: Imperial palace Frankfurt
Special feature: Relatively abstract model – natural appearance of plaster-printed models
Location: Archäologisches Museum Frankfurt
Type: Parallel
Span: Building
Scale: 1:100
Use of media: Virtual reconstruction, screen
Completion: 2008

The 3D virtual reconstruction of the first imperial palace of Frankfurt was produced for the Archaeological Museum in Frankfurt. It covers four distinct construction phases: the Merovingian court (AD 600–800), the Carolingian imperial court with the Aula Regia, completed in AD 822 for Emperor Louis the Pious, the extension of the palace and the construction of the Saint Saviour's Basilica, the predecessor building of today's cathedral under Louis the German in AD 855 and, finally, the further extension of the architectural complex under the Ottonians around AD 1000. The imperial palace is presented in a film which is screened in three languages. The film deals with the basis of the reconstruction and illustrates the process by which the archaeological record, the analysis of comparable buildings and contemporary depictions inform our current

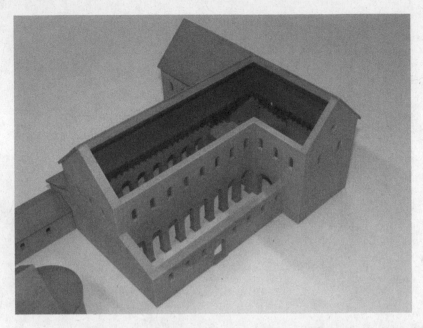

Fig. 35. Imperial palace, Frankfurt, relatively abstract model (© Architectura Virtualis GmbH)

Fig. 36. Imperial palace, Frankfurt, plaster-printed model on sandstone base (© Architectura Virtualis GmbH)

image of the imperial palace. Securely documented findings and hypotheses are separated and presented one after the other.

The museum display also includes a haptic model that was 3D plaster-printed on
the basis of the digital dataset (Fig. 35). It shows the palace as it may have presented
itself around AD 855. The absence of intricate architectural detailing is intentional and
meant to convey the hypothetical nature of the reconstruction, which is made clear in
the film simulation voiceover. The model in the Archaeological Museum is paradig-
matic for the look and feel of plaster-printed models. Compared to other materials,
which can seem rather artificial when they are not painted, plaster comes across as
fairly natural and goes well with the sandstone base (Fig. 36).

5.3.5   Staufen Tower, Frankfurt

Project:	Staufen Tower, Frankfurt
Special features:	3D viewers, different production techniques
Location:	Historisches Museum Frankfurt
Type:	Hybrid
Span:	Building
Scale:	1:50
Use of media:	3D stereo viewers, virtual reconstruction, projection onto model
Completion:	2012

This model of the medieval Staufen Tower in its original form was produced for the
new permanent exhibition in the old building of the Frankfurt Historical Museum. The
building still exists; it is part of the museum, but has undergone substantial changes
over the course of the centuries.

As with other models, it was enormously helpful to be able to simulate the original
state in a virtual model which allowed for a discussion of the reconstruction and its
correction. The model is particularly notable for three things: its large scale (1:50), the
fact that parts of it can be opened up or folded away to give the visitor a better view of
the inside and, finally, the use of 3D viewers to show stereoscopic images of the
interior (Figs. 37 and 38).

Because of the large scale and the movable parts it made sense to use traditional
model-building techniques in combination with rapid prototyping. The façade and the
roofs were made in the traditional manner, the architectural details, for example the
tracery of the windows or columns with capitals and bases, were 3D printed in a
synthetic material and fitted into the façades, which were then painted. Thus each part
was produced in the most efficient manner possible.

The other notable feature is the use of 3D viewers. Mounted on steel supports and
aimed at different interior spaces, four such viewers were affixed to the model. The
stereoscopic images – complete with furnishings and people – show how the rooms
were once used. Drawings of the individual layers of the room were modeled in the
computer and then staggered in space to achieve the stereoscopic effect.

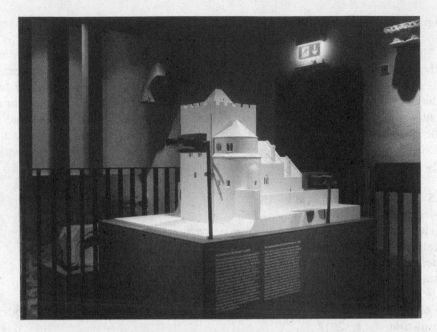

Fig. 37. Staufen Tower, Frankfurt, model + 3D viewers (© Architectura Virtualis GmbH)

Fig. 38. Staufen Tower, Frankfurt, model + 3D viewer (© Architectura Virtualis GmbH)

6 Conclusion

All of the examples presented here deal with architectural models as well as models of cities and landscapes. In addition, I would like to say that rapid prototyping plays an important and growing role in the presentation of replicas in the museum sector and in the area of digital heritage. The cost efficient reproduction of original object by means of rapid prototyping allows museum visitors to actually handle and experience objects and thus makes their visit more attractive. At the same time, it allows for the dissemination of copies to other museums and the completion of collections scattered among several institutions.

The technologies used to gather the necessary three-dimensional data, for example laser scanning, are also coming down in price. These are complemented by SfM technology, which is finding ever wider applications, and which uses specialist software to create 3D models based on a large number of systematically taken photographs. In this context one should mention projects such as CultLab3D, which seeks to develop fully automatic, low-cost 3D data gathering systems for museum objects [6]. While the digitization and reproduction of the geometric form no longer presents much of a problem, the digitization and reproduction of surfaces and textures remains a challenge. Developments at the Fraunhofer Institute in Darmstadt and elsewhere are promising. Here printers are capable of printing objects in color of a standard that is high enough for the production of excellent replicas. In the not-too-distant future, it should even be possible to color-print transparent areas.[5]

But haptic models are based not only on real objects that were fully 3D digitized, but also on virtual datasets that were modeled wholly or in part on the computer. As in architecture, where designs that were never built can be constructed virtually and then printed out, this method was used for drawings of objects and furnishings by Piranesi, among them a coffee pot, which was reconstructed on the computer and printed out [7]. 3D modeling is also the method of choice for objects that have come down to us in a fragmentary state. It allows for their virtual completion and subsequent materialization in a rapid prototyping process [8].

Compared with traditional model-making techniques, in academic contexts rapid prototyping has a number of distinct advantages, not least among them the fact the virtual model allows for all details to be checked and revised before printing.

In the context of exhibitions, the attractiveness of illuminated models and hybrid exhibits cannot be overestimated. They combine the qualities of traditional haptic models with the dynamism, flexibility, updatability and interactivity of digital media and infuse them with a new aesthetic appeal. They are part of a development in the museum sector that sets great store by "new attractive but serious exhibits" [9] in the context of digital applications.[6]

---

[5] See [5].

[6] In context of a report of the project V-MUST.NET Sofia Pescarin gives a very interesting overview of the use of various digital technologies in exhibitions and the expectations of visitors and curators. See [9, pp. 31–140].

The fast-paced development of rapid prototyping technologies in new materials such as metal and glass as well as new, cutting edge processes that improve the simulation of surfaces and cut down production time hold great promise for the future and have intriguing potential applications in the museum sector.

References

1. Grellert, M.: Immaterielle Zeugnisse – Synagogen in Deutschland, Potentiale digitaler Technologien für das Erinnern zerstörter Architektur. Bielefeld (2007)
2. Elser, O., Schmal, P.C. (eds.): Das Architekturmodell: Werkzeug, Fetisch, kleine Utopie. Zürich (2012)
3. Orcutt, M.: Printing breaks the glass barrier. MIT Technology Review, 3 September 2015. http://www.technologyreview.com/news/540926/3-d-/. Accessed 26 July 2016
4. Pandell, L: With this 3-D Printer, Objects Emerge from a Plastic Soup. Wired, 10. 01 2015. http://www.wired.com/2015/10/carbon3d/. Accessed 26 July 2016
5. Brunton, A., Arikan, C.A., Urban, P.: Pushing the Limits of 3D Color Printing: Error Diffusion with Translucent Materials. Cornell University Library (2015). http://arxiv.org/abs/1506.02400. Accessed 26 July 2016
6. CultLab3D. http://www.cultlab3d.de/. Accessed 25 July 2016
7. Starr, M.: 18th century drawings brought to life with 3D printing, 22 May 2014. http://www.cnet.com/news/18th-century-drawings-brought-to-life-with-3d-printing/. Accessed 26 July 2016
8. Flaherty, J.: Harvard's 3D-Printing Archaeologists Fix Ancient Artifacts. Wired, 12 October 2012. http://www.wired.com/2012/12/harvard-3d-printing-archaelogy/. Accessed 27 July 2016
9. Pescarin, S.: Museums and Virtual Museums in Europe: Reaching expectations. SCIRES-IT, 4(1) (2014). http://caspur-ciberpublishing.it/index.php/scires-it/article/view/10918/. Accessed 27 July 2016

Interpretation of Sensor-Based 3D Documentation

Davide Mezzino[1]([✉]), Chloe Weiyi Pei[2], and Mario E. Santana-Quintero[1]

[1] Carleton Immersive Media Studio (CIMS), 1125 Colonel by Drive, Ottawa,
ON K1S 5B6, Canada
davide.mezzino@gmail.com, mario.santana@carleton.ca
[2] Raymond Lemaire International Centre for Conservation, Kasteelpark Arenberg 1,
3001 Heverlee, Belgium
chloe.weiyipei@gmail.com

Abstract. In contemporary architectural design and conservation, digital media
has increasingly been used to generate, visualize and manage new and existing
architecture. Digital 3D architectural models play different roles in the design
process, project management and the relationship with the client. The flourishing
3D industry has given rise to various 3D documentation and modeling software
and techniques, resulting in numerous types and formats. Starting from the analysis of the state of the art and the international recommendations such as the
London Charter (2006), Seville Charter (2010) and Venice Charter (1964), this
contribution presents emerging issues and challenges in sensor-based 3D documentation, such as the relationship with end users, visualization platforms and
interpretation of digital 3D models. Two different practical applications, a designated heritage private building in Guadalajara, Mexico and a religious educational
institution in Ottawa, Canada, are presented to illustrate various digital techniques
for 3D documentation, such as Electronic Distance Meter (EDM), photogrammetry, 3D laser scanning and building information modeling (BIM). In the first
case, the clients were architects and professionals in the architecture, engineering
and construction (AEC) and conservation sector. Therefore, an information-
oriented approach was taken. In the second case, the client was not AEC related.
Hence, a visually oriented approach was chosen for straightforward information
interpretation and dissemination tailored to the client's needs. We conclude with
some recommendations, tackling several issues including the need for standards
and common methodologies in 3D documentation, to improve strategies of
knowledge management, education and engagement through 3D modeling.

Keywords: Interpretation · Sensor-based 3D documentation · 3D modeling ·
Cultural heritage · Visualization · Knowledge management

While the three authors contributed equally to the paper, Davide Mezzino wrote the introduction
and sections 1, 2.1 and 2.2; Clohe Weiyi Pei wrote sections 1.1, 2, and 2.2; and Mario E. Santana-
Quintero wrote sections 3 and 4.

S. Münster et al. (Eds.): 3D Research Challenges II, LNCS 10025, pp. 119–135, 2016.
DOI: 10.1007/978-3-319-47647-6_6

1   Introduction

3D models have been valuable tools within the practice of architecture for centuries. From ancient Greek society to the Renaissance, tangible models (made of clay, wood, etc.) were an integral part of the design workflow. The importance of the model both in forming a comprehensive understanding of the spatial relationship of a building and in analyzing the impact of new intervention on the existing structure was already stated in the 15th century by Leon Battista Alberti: "I will always comment the time-honored custom, practiced by the best builders, of preparing not only drawings and sketches but also models of wood or any other material." [1].

Alberti not only considered models to be the best means to study and develop an idea, but also the finest tools to improve drawing documentation. In Book IX of *De re Aedificatoria*, he also claimed that models are useful to correct the imperfection of ideas and how they should be used for practical purposes such as management and organization of the building site.[1]

Current practice is once again embracing the use of modeling. Moreover, the environment of model creation has extended beyond tangible physicality into the digital realm. Recently, high-resolution recording of heritage sites and cultural artifacts (as-built reality) stimulated much research in computer graphic visualization. Photo-realistic images and image-based rendering techniques, are some of the available solutions [3]. To preserve and share a record of the geometry and appearance of an existing structure photogrammetric, Reflectorless Electronic Distance Measurement (REDM) and 3D laser scanner techniques can be used. These capture chromatic, geometrical and spatial information about a site in a three-dimensional environment. A 3D model is a rich depository of information that can be analyzed and used to improve understanding and dissemination of a structure and its characteristics. For example, a virtual reproduction is capable of improving legibility of a structure by providing perspectives that are either difficult or impossible to access in real life. A virtual tour offers alternative solutions for public engagement when the actual site is temporarily closed due to maintenance [4]. In line with this, the core of the approach here is to generate photorealistic 3D models from images and scans through techniques such as photogrammetry, EDM and 3D laser scanning. Modeling in a BIM environment using survey data collected from field work has also been considered.

The use of 3D modeling and its interpretation along all its workflows from the creation to the dissemination phase is analyzed, with issues related to operators, techniques, documentation strategies and final users.

This contribution focuses on 3D documentation based on information about existing heritage objects collected through emerging recording techniques. The two cases here provide an overview of different ways of presenting and interpreting information

---

[1] "I have often conceived of projects in the mind that seemed quite commendable at the time; but when I translated them into drawings, I found several errors in the very parts that delighted them into drawings, I found several errors in the very parts that delighted me most [...] finally, when I pass from the drawings to the model, I sometimes notice further mistakes in the individual parts, even over the numbers" [2].

structured in a 3D model. In both cases, the model had been used to satisfy the different demands of the clients and the specialists, especially concerning the future management of the site. In order to ensure the "scientific transparency" [5] of the research results, both case studies used the Industry Foundation Class (IFC)[2] compatible software to generate digital products.

Both applications were essentially developed as technical workshops. The Casa Cristo Project was an international training initiative developed collaboratively between Carleton University in Canada and the Emerita Universidad de Guadalajara in Mexico. The Dominican University College project was designed specifically for the senior Architecture Conservation and Sustainability students to test various recording techniques. Both projects were intended to train emerging professionals through hands-on practice within a systematic workflow.

Digitization strategies had been developed according to the concept of efficiency under the description of the Seville Charter, for both information acquisition and long-term management. One of the most effective ways of avoiding work redundancy here involved using previously collected information. Extensive archival research was carried out before the project at both Casa Cristo and Dominican University College. Historic blueprints, written documents, photographs and periodic survey records have all aided the current field work.

2   Questions and Emerging Issues on the Interpretation of Heritage Digitization

Three-dimensional documentation of heritage structures can be a thorny problem. A metaphor for the complexity of this is the architect as a composer and architecture as a musical melody. The audience listening to a musical performance has often already listened to the piece beforehand and has a greater or lesser understanding of the music. How is this relevant to architecture and 3D modeling? A similar approach can be applied to the level of knowledge, mindset and attitude of clients and end users in general to 3D visualization. Some questions arise out of these reflections. What is the role of architects and engineers in disseminating and communicating the relevance of 3D documentation? What can be done to train the public on the potential of 3D documentation for built heritage? How can 3D visualization influence decision-making processes? What is the difference between seeing and grasping a 3D model? 3D modeling in the AEC and cultural heritage (CH) sectors, develops in dialogue between architects and clients. It is a collaborative activity through which people work, discover and learn.

How do we share information at all stages of a 3D reconstruction? How do we provide an efficient visualization for both operators and non-professionals? An analysis of recent technological developments can help answer these questions. According to Köhler, Munster and Schlenker, 3D reconstruction procedures have remained widely unchanged while visualization technologies and tools have changed user communities and usage scenarios significantly [6].

---

[2] On virtual reconstructions, see [1].

Current technological advances make it impossible to think about heritage documentation without different components working together, including 3D modeling, digital, geographic, spatial and virtual representations. Recently, Dunn, Gold and Hughes [7] outlined how built heritage documentation extensively employs digital recording and visualization techniques (e.g., EDM, photogrammetry, or 3D laser scanning) as well as digital spatial information systems (e.g., geographic information systems, or GIS, and BIM). The advantages of these techniques in term of accuracy, time and cost effectiveness, long term management and flexibility of the outputs (i.e., for operative as well as dissemination and communication purposes) are evident and widely recognized by the scientific community.

2.1   Challenges in Sensor-Based 3D Documentation

The challenge of sensor-based 3D documentation of existing structures lies in balancing a workflow that integrates available technologies while disseminating processed information. Architects and engineers use 3D digital representations of existing structures linked to other relevant information. The resulting 3D models can be complex in nature, demand substantial storage resources, have a high transfer ratio and carry significant, highly interrelated, semantic, and provenance metadata [8]. Hence, metadata on the processing workflow, information management and dissemination are relevant issues.

In 1964, the Venice Charter stated the importance of a rational, standardized terminology and methodology, as well as accepted professional principles and techniques for interpreting and presenting digital documentation and managing cultural heritage sites: [9].

> "It is essential that the principles guiding the preservation and restoration of ancient buildings should be agreed and be laid down on an international basis, with each country being responsible for applying the plan within the framework of its own culture and traditions" [10].

After almost fifty years, these issues are still relevant. Information provenance, complex metadata about model processing, formats and sources, all require further development. These metadata should not be only a repository but a working integrated platform for present and future users, experts and non-experts.

3   Practical Applications

The contribution outlines two strategies to assure scientific quality and stimulate interaction with the outputs:

- Cross-disciplinary cooperation with different techniques and tools.
- Issues and challenges related to human interpretation.

These aspects are considered in line with international recommendations, specifically in terms of the scientific rigor of the documentation process, tool compatibility, data longevity, user-friendliness, accuracy and information interpretation issues in built heritage 3D documentation. Then, human interpretation of and interaction with the 3D outputs are analyzed, presenting two different methodologies according to the needs of diverse end users. Each methodology considers the following key issues: The socio-technical system employed, sources of knowledge, and cross-disciplinary teamwork involved.

3.1 Digital Workflow for Sensor-Based 3D Documentation

Examples of sensor-based techniques for 3D documentation of built heritage are illustrated in this section. These techniques survey and document the current condition of the real subject. Hardware and software components are involved in digitally reconstructing buildings and structures from on-site measurements. In both applications, human resources included architects, engineers, and ACE students.

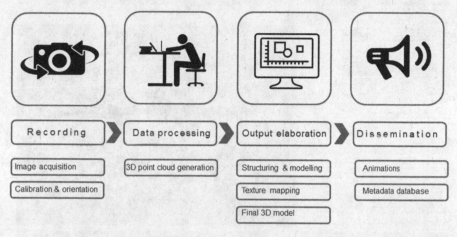

_PHOTOGRAMMETRY WORKFLOW

Fig. 1. Diagram illustrating the photogrammetry workflow employed.

The sensor-based techniques used to generate 3D models were based on passive sensor, image data [11] and classic survey.[3] They included photogrammetry, laser scanning, REDM, CAD and BIM applications to transform the 3D point cloud into 3D geometry. All these techniques were integrated to generate accurate and realistic 3D models. Technique selection followed five main parameters: accuracy, portability, cost-effectiveness, fast acquisition and flexibility. The first technique, photogrammetry, can be defined as the science of extracting metric information about objects, such as building elements and architectural spaces, from photographs. This approach is the product of recent developments in computer vision that allows us to obtain 3D scenes from 2D images using highly automated workflows. This technique can deliver accurate and detailed 3D information at any scale of application [12].

In both case studies, photogrammetry was employed for 3D documentation, effective visualizations and animations. Photogrammetry of architectural structures has

---

[3] Such as total station survey, GPS, etc.

been performed with interactive procedures.[4] The adopted workflow includes four main phases (c.f. Fig. 1):

1. Recording phase: Capturing a sequence of overlapping and oblique images taken from a scene (or subject) at the same distance. Recent algorithms allow for matching features between pairs of photographs in sequences, which, along with the information contained in the images (adequate camera motion, overlap and structure scene) uses the camera parameters to calibrate the images;
2. Data processing phase: Creating a depth map with each pixel contained in the image producing a 3D dense point cloud and/or surface model (c.f. Fig. 2);

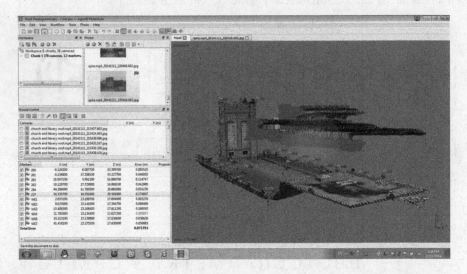

Fig. 2. Generation process of the roof point cloud of the Dominican University College. Images were captured by a Phantom 2 Vision drone.

3. Output elaboration: Creating multiple drawing types, including orthographical photos to draft the building elevation;[5]
4. Dissemination phase: Animation presentation, including explanatory video and 3D pdf.

Concerning the toolbox, in the first phase a Digital Single-Lens Reflex (DLSR) digital camera was used to capture pictures according to the 3 × 3 photogrammetric rule (ICOMOS CIPA, 2013) [13] An unmanned aerial vehicle (UAV) or drone was also used to get data from areas with low accessibility.

---

[4] Ibidem.
[5] Using the software Agisoft Photoscan it was possible to process all the photos generating a point cloud model (c.f. Fig. 2). In the same software orthophotos were generated. These were then imported into AutoCAD 2014 as raster images and then traced producing 2D drawings that later became the reference of geometrical 3D models.

Phases 2 and 3 consisted of processing the data acquired to generate the point cloud and mesh, then exporting them into a CAD environment to produce line drawings from the point cloud.

The photogrammetric image-based approach allowed surveys to operate at different levels with a high level of detail, relatively easy usage and cost-effective management of the final outcomes. User interaction was required in the different steps of generating an image-based 3D model.

Finally, in Phase 4, the data were disseminated through cloud computing, online databases, video and common formats (such as 3D pdf) easily understandable by both experts and non-professionals.

Recent developments in computer vision and sensor technology have notable benefits and possible applications for recording structures. One of these is 3D laser scanning. It was employed to record the interior and exterior of Dominican University College (DUC) buildings. The scan workflow included (c.f. Fig. 3):

- Scanning on site: A number of separate scans from different locations were required to ensure full coverage of the DUC complex;
- Scan registration: A standard coordinate system (calculated by REDM measurements and based on a local site grid) was used to position and orient individual scans[6];
- Deliverable generation: Including historical and site analysis, 2D drawings, point clouds, animations[7] and rendered images.

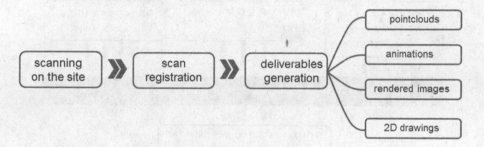

Fig. 3. Adopted laser scanning workflow

The following diagram illustrates the different phases of the adopted workflow. A management metadata has also been defined, including the following aspects:

- file name of the raw data;
- date of capture;

---

[6] The scan registration has been developed into two steps. The first one included a manual automatic raw alignment using the targets surveyed with the Total Station. The last step consisted of a global alignment based on iterative closest points.

[7] Three-dimensional geometric models can also be used to generate high-quality still or animated scenes. Movies are often successfully used to present what would otherwise be large quantities of data requiring specialist viewing software and hardware. This does serve a useful purpose in presenting an object or structure to a non-specialist group. Source: [14].

126   D. Mezzino et al.

- scanning system used (with manufacturer's serial number);
- company name;
- monument name;
- project reference number (if known);
- scan number;
- total number of points;
- point density on the object (with reference range);
- weather conditions during scanning (for outdoor scanning only) [15].

In both techniques, photogrammetry and laser scanning, the following aspects were considered in the data acquisition and processing phase:

- quality of the acquired or available data;
- relationship between time consumption and data processing;
- hardware demand for the high-resolution model;
- accuracy control through cross-referencing data from different sensors, with different geometric resolution;
- gaps and holes in 3D models due to scan blind spots;
- use of multiple techniques to solve accessibility limitations, to capture all possible spaces (i.e., using a drone to capture details of the roof inaccessible to the laser scanner and photogrammetry).

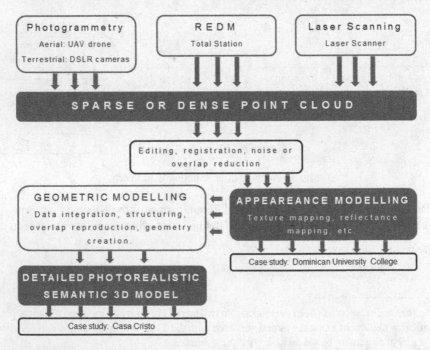

Fig. 4. Diagram of the multi-resolution sensor-based 3D documentation workflow. The two case studies are based on the integration of different techniques to generate point clouds, textured and geometrical 3D models.

To generate 2D drawings and 3D models from the obtained information, the following process was followed:

1. Orthographic photos of elevations, floorplans and cross sections obtained from the 3D point cloud were generated[8].
2. Orthographic photos exported in tiff format were imported into a CAD environment[9] as raster images, where they were traced to produce measured 2D line drawings.
3. The CAD metric drawings were then imported into a BIM environment[10] and aligned with their particular view.
4. The 3D models were constructed manually according to the CAD references.

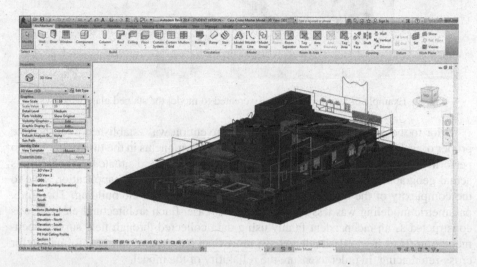

Fig. 5. Image presenting the work in progress: BIM model of Casa Cristo.

Concerning the 3D modeling phase, the construction of a geometrical model from the point cloud in a BIM environment also included the development of a semantic description of each modeled element (c.f. Figs. 4, 5). The 3D modeling workflow included the following steps:

- Naming convention: proper suffix for easy future management;
- True orientation for energy and building performance simulation;
- Set up perimeter: Constrain the model using latest plan and elevation produced from data collected during field work;
- Custom families: Created from cross-section details, plan and elevation produced from data collected during field work (c.f. Fig. 6);
- Final assembly.

---

[8] In this step the software used was Agisoft Photoscan.
[9] In this step the software used was AutoCAD 2014.
[10] In this step the software used was Autodesk Revit 2014.

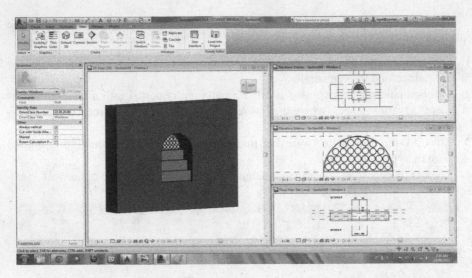

Fig. 6. Example of a customized family created to model the stained glass windows.

Prior to the modeling process, a naming convention was established to ensure the proper organization and management of modeling components in the future. In order to perform accurate energy and solar analysis, it was essential to situate the model in its actual geographical location with proper orientation within a GIS application. Due to the complexity of the design, no two elements were alike in the building. Therefore, parametric modeling was less applicable in this case. Each architectural element was constructed as an independent family using data collected through field survey documentation. Thus it was desirable to have more than one type of source information for cross-referencing, in order to ensure the reliability of the model.

In a 3D model, accuracy, scale and detail level are strongly connected to interpretation issues. Therefore, all the elements were made on a scale of 1:1 to maximize interpretability of the model in the future.

Indeed, the potential of a BIM model lies in its long-term usability for monitoring and managing building performance. Information can also be conveyed more efficiently if the model is visualized in the desirable scale within a BIM platform. Due to its flexible interpretability, BIM is a good "storyteller" for heritage structures, presenting different historical phases of the building and different elements in the desirable detail level in one single model.

3.2   3D Documentation for Knowledge Management

The first application involving 3D documentation was of a house in Guadalajara, Mexico. Casa Cristo was built by the famous architect Luis Barragán between 1927 and 1929 for Gustavo R. Cristo, mayor of the city. The house is an outstanding example of regional modern architecture, with its unique style reflecting the European influences derived from the architect's travel experience, as well as the close connection to local craftsmanship [16].

This was a case study of the role of human interpretation within the 3D documentation process in a BIM environment according to objective data surveyed in the field work phase and historical interpretative analysis.

The workflow adopted included the following phases:

- Recording: Information structure was acquired from the field survey and direct analysis/assessment;
- Attribution: Metadata related to components such as type, color, dimension, date, etc.;
- Cross-referencing: Comparison between surveyed data and historical archival sources;
- Interpretation: Analysis of the different sources to orient and support 3D modeling;
- Final output elaboration and communication: second interpretation by the end users.

In the BIM modeling phase for the digitization of Casa Cristo, user interaction played a fundamental role. The aim was to provide a flexible management tool to support and orient conservation processes, visualizing parts that could not be normally seen from a human perspective. This established a framework for modern heritage protection in the City of Guadalajara, which can be accessed by various stakeholders such as municipalities, conservation specialists, planners, architects, contractors and private owners.

Different actors collaborated in geometrical and semantic description of the model. Regarding the latter, the contribution of different people operating in different fields was essential. Last but not least a sound knowledge of geometrical rules and graphic conventions was necessary for the modeling phase. In line with this experience, Charles Hardy's

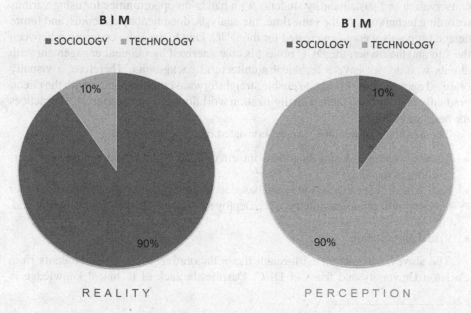

Fig. 7. Comparison between the real and perceived percentage of the sociological and technological component in BIM applications. Adapted from R. Deutsch, *BIM and Integrated Design. Strategies for Architectural Practice.* Wiley, 2011, p. x.

statement that "BIM is about 10 percent technology and 90 per cent sociology" [17] became clear (c.f. Fig. 7). In his book *BIM and Integrated Design*, Randy Deutsch explains how the accuracy and the success of a proper BIM model depends on the operators' skills, attitudes and mindsets.

The divergence between perception and reality in the above figure is relevant to understand the role of operators. In other words, how using BIM technology for digitization of built heritage structures is interpreted is very important. BIM is not only significant in the workplace due to the technological aspects or the business value proposition but because of people intended to operate and user it. This confirms the importance of the relationship between creators, users, and clients in 3D modeling.

3.3   3D Documentation for Education and Engagement

The DUC project aimed to promote the usage of 3D documentation, develop awareness of 3D modeling applications, potentials for long-term management, time and cost effective data acquisition. The first step in the project was to prepare non-specialists with the essential vocabularies and concepts to interpret 3D models of built heritage. The next step was to develop knowledge integration and competencies to manage the final outputs, including updating, monitoring and dissemination. The DUC is a religious educational institution run by Dominican friars since 1884, located on Primrose Hill in Ottawa, Canada. The structure had undergone expansion, alteration, reconstruction and renovation over the course of more than a century. A long-term partnership between Carleton University and DUC was established in 2014, which aimed to provide senior conservation and sustainability students with hands-on opportunities for using various recording techniques. At the same time, site analysis, documentation records, and future design proposals were to be created for the DUC. Due to the close connection between the site and the owner, the DUC project is characterized by frequent engagement with clients who do not have a technical architectural background. Therefore, a visually oriented approach was chosen to enable straightforward communication with the client, gradually familiarizing them with digitization workflow and best conservation practices for heritage building.

The first stage of the DUC project consisted of:

- Archival research: Using historical information to build a comprehensive understanding of the site;
- Data acquisition: Graphic and visual based techniques, such as photography, 3D laser scanning and photogrammetry were deployed to produce the desired output (c.f. Fig. 8);[11]
- Visual presentation.

The survey was completed through the collaborative effort of the students from Carleton University and friars of DUC. Despite the lack of technical knowledge in

---

[11] The outputs included 2D metric line drawings. These were obtained generating orthophotos from the point cloud using the software Agisoft Photoscan. The orthophotos were then imported into AutoCAD 2014 where they were traced.

Fig. 8. Combination of the different point clouds acquired through photogrammetry and 3D laser scanning. Software employed: Autodesk Recap.

documentation and conservation, DUC provided invaluable insights into the history and occupant experience of the building. This information laid the groundwork for establishing criteria in the upcoming survey and design.

The envelope and interior of the area of interest were documented using a 3D laser scanner at medium resolution to generate a semantic record of the structure in a time-efficient manner at the desirable level of detail, corresponding to the scale of the final drawing. Photogrammetry was used as a supplementary tool for areas that could not be scanned due to hardware limitations. Close range photogrammetry was used for elements accessible on foot, while aerial photogrammetry was used for the roof. Point

Fig. 9. Screenshot of the video animation.

cloud models generated from both photogrammetry and 3D laser scanning were assembled under the constraint of the control points. Furthermore, a virtual walk-through was produced from the complete model. The video was used in explanatory materials to help the clients understand the scope of the project (c.f. Fig. 9).

4   Future Recommendations

Both practical applications required operator decisions in the workflow. These interpretative decisions, oriented by the clients' needs and the outputs required, arose in the process of establishing perimeters for acquisition (e.g., accuracy level, scale of the outputs), tool selection and interpretation tasks (e.g., data integration and interoperability) (c.f. Table 1). The relationship between the final output and the initial decision-making process emphasized the importance of common standards for 3D documentation. As underlined by Remondino and Rizzi, current challenges in 3D documentation include selecting an appropriate methodology to ensure that final results are technically correct, allowing users to interact and verify model processes [18].

Table 1. The table presents an assessment of the interpretation tasks and related aspects in the two case studies.

Interpretation tasks and related aspects	Case study 1 casa cristo	Case study 2 Dominican University College
Client typology	Architects and professionals in the AEC and conservation sector	Non-AEC related clients
Client needs	2D drawings and 3D semantic model for managing the conservation process, monitoring and studying the development phases.	2D drawings and 3D point cloud model of record keeping, site management and interior redevelopment.
Decision making	Information-oriented approach to provide technical data needed for future management and conservation.	Visual-oriented approach for better client engagement and straightforward information dissemination.
Scientific accuracy	±2 cm	±2 mm Leica Laser ScanStation C10.
Deployed techniques	REDM Photogrammetry Photography	REDM Laser scanning Photogrammetry Photography
Interoperability	Use of IFC compatible software	Use of IFC compatible software
Interpreted outputs	2D drawings 3D point cloud model 3D semantic BIM model Recommendations for site monitoring and management	2D drawings 3D point cloud model Explanatory video 3D pdf

In line with these issues, the two case studies compared interpretation tasks with the relevant aspects of client typology, client needs, decision making, scientific accuracy, deployed techniques, interoperability and interpreted outputs.

Further recommendations to regulate modeling processes and interpretation strategies should be developed. The illustrated case studies aimed at contributing to this. Table 2 illustrates how some standards have already been developed and others are still in progress.

Table 2. The table illustrates the existing standards for 3D documentation. Source: Remondino, F., Rizzi A. "Reality-based 3D documentation of natural and cultural heritage sites techniques, problems, and examples". In Appl Geomat 2, 85-100, 2010.

Standard	Content	Country
German VDI/VDE 2634	Testing and monitoring procedures for evaluating the accuracy of close-range optical 3D vision systems	Germany
American Society for Testing and Materials E57 standards	Ongoing development of standards for 3D imaging systems for applications in surveying, preservation, construction, etc	USA
International Association for Pattern Recognition (IAPR) Technical Committee 19 (TC19): Computer Vision for Cultural Heritage Applications	Promoting Computer Vision Applications in Cultural Heritage and their integration in all aspects of IAPR activities, stimulating the development of components (both hardware and software) that can be used by researchers in cultural heritage	–
London Charter	Definition of basic objectives and principles for the use of 3D visualization methods in relation to intellectual integrity, reliability, transparency, documentation standards, sustainability and access to cultural heritage	–

The London Charter is one of the internationally recognized standards. According to the Principle 4 on documentation, the 3D models presented in this contribution, have been documented throughout their development,[12] so users can comprehend the relationships between the context and purposes for which they could be deployed. Therefore, the aim was to enable analysis and evaluation of modeling processes derived from site measurements and to ensure that end users understand 3D documentation and its

---

[12] According to Principle 4.6 of the London Charter "Documentation of the evaluative, analytical, deductive, interpretative and creative decisions made in the course of computer-based visualization should be disseminated in such a way that the relationship between research sources, implicit knowledge, explicit reasoning, and visualization-based outcomes can be understood" [19].

potentials. Then, according to the Principle 4.1, documentation strategies were adopted to support and develop the visualization of the acquired data. Finally, the Seville Charter states how 3D digitization of an existing building should involve interdisciplinary skills, specialists and techniques (Principle 4.1.2). This principle was followed in both case studies.

5   Conclusions

This contribution illustrated issues related to 3D documentation. We presented two different practical applications integrating multiple sensors and technologies to:

- Exploit the potentialities of each technique, compensating possible weaknesses with an integrated approach;
- Achieve accurate and complete geometric surveying for the correct sensor - based 3D modeling in order to have basic information about modeling sources and procedures for its correct interpretation.

The resulting 3D modeling was based on multi-scale and multi-sensor integration, yielding good results in terms of appearance and geometric detail. In the Mexican case, the model provides a standard procedure to document, visualize and disseminate data related to modern heritage. The Canadian case, however, presents a method for training non-professional clients, showing them the potentials of 3D digital documentation through attractive, easily comprehensible visualizations. These approaches arose from different geographical, social, architectural and historical contexts, using different data exchange and human interpretation, but each illustrate the challenges and opportunities involved. The challenge of the adopted approach lies in training people with different backgrounds to work together on developing a consistent 3D model. Indeed, the role of each team member in every step of a sensor-based documentation process is fundamental for the final precision of the 3D model. The main strength of this approach lies in generating 3D models for heritage buildings which can be interpreted differently according to the scopes and needs of diverse end users.

References

1. Beraldin, J.A., Picard, M., El-Hakim, S.F., Godin, G., Valzano, V., Bandiera, A.: Combining 3D technologies for cultural heritage interpretation and entertainment. In: Beraldin, J.A., El-Hakimm, S.F., Gruen, A., Walton, J. (eds.) Proceedings of Videometrics VIII, SPIE-IS&T Electronic Imaging, San Jose, USA, 18–20 January, vol. 5665, pp. 108–118 (2005)
2. Beacham, R., Denard, H., Niccolucci, F.: An introduction to the London Charter. In: Ioannides, M., et al. (eds.) Papers from the Joint Event CIPA/VAST/EG/EuroMed Event, pp. 263–269 (2006)
3. Bruno, F., et al.: From 3D reconstruction to virtual reality. A complete methodology for digital archaeological exhibition. J. Cult. Heritage **11**(1), 42–49 (2010)
4. Denard, H.: A new introduction to the London Charter. In: Bentkowska-Kafel, A., Denard, H., Baker, D. (eds.) Paradata and Transparency in Virtual Heritage, pp. 57–72. Ashgate, Burlington (2012)

5. Deutsch, R.: BIM an Integrated Design. Strategies for Architectural Practice. Wiley, Hoboken (2011)
6. Doerr, M., Tzompanaki, K., Theodoridou, M., Georgis, C., Axaridou, A., Havemann, S.: A repository for 3D model production and interpretation in culture and beyond. In: Proceedings of VAST 2010: The 11th International Symposium on Virtual Reality, Archaeology and Cultural Heritage, Palais du Louvre, Paris, France, 21–24 September 2010, pp. 97–104. Eurographics, Aire-La-Ville (2010)
7. Dunn, S., Gold, N., Hughes, L.: CHIMERA. A service oriented computing approach for archaeological research. In: 35th Computer Applications and Quantitative Methods in Archaeology Conference, Berlin, 2–6 April 2007
8. English Heritage: 3D laser scanning for heritage. Advice and guidance. English Heritage, Swindon, p. 14 (2011)
9. Fisher, C.R., Terras, M., Warwick, C.: Integrating new technologies into established systems. A case study from Roman Silchester. In: 37th Computer Applications and Quantitative Methods in Archaeology Conference, 22–26 March 2009. Williamsburg (2009)
10. ICOMOS: The Venice Charter. Adopted by ICOMOS in 1965, May 25th–31st, Venice, Italy (1964)
11. Kröber, C., Münster, S.: An App for the Cathedral in Freiberg - an interdisciplinary project seminar. In: Sampson, D.G., et al. (eds.) Proceedings of the 11th International Conference on Cognition and Exploratory Learning in Digital Age (CELDA 2014), Porto, Portugal, 25–27th October 2014, pp. 270–274 (2014)
12. Köhler, T., Münster, S., Schlenker. L.: Smart communities in virtual reality. A comparison of design approaches for academic education. Interact. Des. Archit. J. IxD&A, N.22, 48–59 (2014)
13. Lopez-Menchero, V.M., Grande, A.: The principles of the Seville Charter. In: Proceedings of XXIII CIPA Symposium, Prague, Czech Republic, 12–16 September 2011
14. Mezzino, D., Pei, W., Santana Quintero, M., Reyes Rodriguez, R.: Documenting modern mexican architectural heritage for posterity: Barragan's Casa Cristo, in Guadalajara, Mexico. In: Proceedings of ISPRS Annals of Photogrammetry, Remote Sensing and Spatial Information Sciences 08/2015, II-5/W3:199-206. doi:10.5194/isprsannals-II-5-W3-199-2015
15. Niccolucci, F., et al.: Five years after. The London Charter revisited. In: Artusi, A., et al. (eds.) 11th International Symposium on Virtual Reality, Archaeology and Cultural Heritage (VAST 2010), Eurographics Association, Paris. pp. 101–104 (2010)
16. Remondino, F., Fraser, C.: Digital camera calibration methods: considerations and comparisons. Int. Arch. Photogramm. Remote Sens. Spat. Inf. Sci. 36(5), 266–272 (2006)
17. Remondino, F., Rizzi, A.: Reality-based 3D documentation of natural and cultural heritage sites techniques, problems, and examples. Appl. Geomat. 2, 85–100 (2010)
18. Rykwert, J., Leach, N., Tavernor, R.: Leon Battista Alberti on the Art of Building in Ten Books. The MIT Press, Cambridge (1998). Trans
19. Waldhäusl, P., Ogleby, C.: 3-by-3 rules for simple photogrammetric documentation of architecture. In: Proceedings of the Symposium of Commission V of ISPRS - Close Range Techniques and Machine Vision, IAPRS XXX/5 Melbourne, Australia, 1–4 March 1994

3D Model, Linked Database, and Born-Digital E-Book: An Ideal Approach to Archaeological Research and Publication

John R. Clarke(✉)

Department of Art and Art History, University of Texas at Austin,
2301 San Jacinto Blvd., Stop D1300, Austin, TX 78712-1421, USA
j.clarke@austin.utexas.edu

Abstract. The objective of the Oplontis Project is to study and publish two UNESCO World Heritage Sites, Villa A and Villa B at Torre Annunziata, Italy, buried by the eruption of Vesuvius in 79 CE. Faced with the high costs of traditional print publication, the Project has opted for a born-digital publication. An additional publication consists of a navigable 3D model linked to a database in order to provide the fullest possible documentation both of the actual states of these Villas and proposals for their reconstructions. This article presents several of these reconstructions, highlighting the importance of digital technologies, including laser scanning and 3D modeling, for research and long-term preservation of these cultural artifacts.

Keywords: 3D model · Oplontis · E-book · Linked database · Laser scanning

Since its inception in 2005, the principal objective of the Oplontis Project has been to fully study and to publish two archaeological sites near Pompeii, Villas A and B at Oplontis. Located about five kilometers from Pompeii at the modern town of Torre Annnunziata, Italy, they lie buried beneath 8 m of hardened volcanic ash and pumice from the eruption of Vesuvius in A.D. 79. The Soprintendenza Archeologica di Pompeii partially excavated the villas between 1964 and 1984. Villa A, often called "The Villa of Poppaea," is a lavishly decorated residence consisting of 99 distinct spaces, including a 61-m swimming pool and extensive gardens. Villa B, sometimes called "The Villa of Publius Crassius Tertius, at Torre Annunziata, Italy" was a commercial center; over 1,200 wine jars as well as 54 human skeletons were discovered there. Both are UNESCO World Heritage Sites.

One of the primary responsibilities of the Oplontis Project has been to record the actual states of Villa A and Villa B. Until recently, recording methods involved standard architectural drawing techniques, including tracing walls one-to-one on enormous sheets of transparent plastic [1, 2]. A reader consulting the resulting publication must be able to understand the conventions of black-and-white line drawing, since a draftsperson must decide which details to include and which to exclude. When printed – even on large folio sheets – much detail is lost. Analogue photography also has many limitations, particularly when attempting to capture deep narrow spaces or especially long walls

© Springer International Publishing AG 2016
S. Münster et al. (Eds.): 3D Research Challenges II, LNCS 10025, pp. 136–145, 2016.
DOI: 10.1007/978-3-319-47647-6_7

(colonnades and porticoes). In order to record them, the photographer might have to rely on distorting wide-angle lenses or resort to making a photomosaic. The other major limitation for accurate documentation arises from the linear structure of print books. Largely for economic reasons, editors must group the various illustrative apparatuses in separate sections; drawings (often in folio format or reproduced as gatefolds) in one section; color plates in another; figures in another, and so on. To study these surrogate images a reader must navigate a complex system of indexing and cross-referencing. Finally, the cost of publishing actual-state drawings and photographs is very high, constraining editors to limit the number of illustrations and often favoring black-and-white rather than color photographs.

In response to the less-than-ideal results obtained by print publication, the Oplontis Project began to consider the advantages of digital publication. We determined that the Humanities E-Book series of the American Council of Learned Societies was the most successful; since its inception in 1999, with a generous grant from the Mellon Foundation, the HEB became a self-sustaining on-line collection of 4,686 books of major importance in the humanities. Twenty-seven learned societies and over one hundred publishers have contributed to this list of fully-searchable books. In addition to books acquired from other publishers, the HEB has also commissioned born-digital books that use all the potential of new media, including hyperlinks to interactive databases, archives, music, videos, and other research tools. With the publication of volume 1 of *Oplontis: Villa A ("of Poppaea") at Torre Annunziata, Italy*, the Oplontis Project joined ranks with these newly-commissioned E-books [3].

The effectiveness of the scholarly print book rests on the accuracy and efficiency of the finding tools: the table of contents, the index, figure call-out numbers, notes, and – above all – cross references. All of these tools allow a reader to find information. They allow the author to take the reader from text to image and back, to compare one set of information (such as bibliographical references or visual comparisons) with another set of information. Recasting these traditional finding tools in the born-digital environment means faster access to a much greater quantity of information than is available in print books. In the first volume of the series dedicated to Oplontis, we have resolved some of these research issues. Entitled *Ancient Landscape and Modern Discovery*, it presents the history of the site of Villa A. However, the remaining three volumes present challenges of documentation and comparative analysis that go beyond the present format of the Humanities E-Book series; [4–6] we plan to address them by integrating the 3D model and the Project database into these E-books.

1 Recording and Navigating in Real Time

Early on, the Oplontis Project decided to record the actual states of the Villas through accurate, electronic 3D models. In so doing, we realized that the potential of the 3D model went far beyond just recording the features of the sites as excavated and rebuilt. We partnered with Richard Beacham and his team at The King's Visualisation Lab, King's College, London, who specialize in visual representation for archaeology, historic buildings, and cultural heritage organizations. Beacham and his group have been prominent among those scholars and researchers who have worked both through a long series of individual projects, and extensive theoretical discussion to bring virtual reality investigations of historic artefacts into the "mainstream" of academic discourse. Their projects, many of them international in scope, meticulously researched and technologically ground-breaking, have helped to imbue such 3D visualizations with the same degree of integrity and standards of evidence and argument enjoyed by more traditional forms of scholarly publication. As an important contribution to this process, KVL conceived and have led the formulation and evolution of a major document now widely accepted as the "gold standard" for the pursuit and presentation of such work: The London Charter For the Computer-Based Visualisation of Cultural Heritage [7].

Work on the 3D model of Villa A began with blanket photography of all 99 spaces, recording in great detail their actual states. Paul Bardagjy, an experienced architectural photographer, carried out this work in 2009–2010. A crucial part of his work was post-processing the digital images. This involved stitching together the many photographs needed to create undistorted images of long walls, floors, and porticoes. The KVL team then mapped Bardagjy's images onto a 3dsMax model created by Project architects. The next step was to import the texture-mapped model into the Unity gaming engine, making a fully the model navigable. Unity is a "first-person shooter" platform that has found relatively wide use among cultural heritage modelers because it allows a user to move freely within the site [8, 9].[1]

The gaming platform allowed us to develop many features that enhance a viewer's experience of the virtual Villa. A user can turn on a popup plan of the Villa with a red arrow that tracks his or her movement through its spaces. From another popup menu, he or she can "jump" from one space to another by clicking on the desired room number. There is a time-of-day slider that allows a user to see the illumination of each space over twenty-four hours. The model also provides intuitive access to our reconstructions: the user simply presses the "R" key to toggle between actual and restored state.

As we developed the Villa A model over a period of three years, we were able to add many features that made it an advanced tool for scholarly research, far outstripping conventional print publications. In place of the conventional finding tools of printed books, such as endnotes, indexes, and cross references, we decided to locate the information gathered over the years by the Oplontis Project spatially, within the model itself. We did this by linking each feature of the Villa represented in the model directly to the Project database.

2   Exploring the Database

Within the model, whether a user is looking at an actual-state image or a reconstruction, he or she need only click on that feature (e.g., wall, floor, ceiling, sculpture, or trench) and press the "Q" (query) key to retrieve all the pertinent data. The ability to query the database directly from the model is a new scholarly experience: a user does not need to call up

---

[1] See also the following project websites with Unity 3D applications [10].

the spatial context for an object using abstract tools like plans and tables. The model locates the object of inquiry, concretely and contextually, in the spaces of Villa A.

Andrew Coulson designed the Oplontis Project database and has refined it as we continue to build data for both Villa A and Villa B. It consists of a rich user interface provided by a Java web application and leverages a MySQL relational database as the metadata information store.[2] Both the web application and the database are currently hosted on an Amazon Web Services server instance.[3] The web application stores photographs and documents uploaded by Project members in a permanent iRODS collection hosted on the Corral storage system at the Texas Advanced Computer Center.[4] The entire set of metadata is periodically exported from the database to XML and is also stored in the iRODS collection.

This agile database has allowed Project members to record and modify their research, either directly from the field (via wireless internet connections) or at their home institutions, and share it with others. There are ten categories of information within the database. "Architecture," "water and drainage," "wall and ceiling décor," "stucco," and "floors" are the categories that address the buildings and their surface decoration; included here are descriptive catalogues of paintings, stucco decorations, and pavements. "Archival materials" and "photos and files" give access to thousands of archival photographs, scanned texts, and drawings that document the history of the excavations and of the reconstruction of the Villas. "Excavations" takes the user to trench profiles and excavation notebooks, whereas "plants and animals" directs one to organic materials found in the excavations. The largest category, "objects," documents all the archaeological finds from both the original excavations and those of the Oplontis Project. These include everything from life-size sculptures to tiny objects like coins.

Because the database includes such a wealth of information, a user, located in a particular place in the model, can explore all the research of the Oplontis Project in full detail. In this way the 3D model serves not only to record actual state of Villa A (in 2010, when the blanket photography was completed); it also constitutes a tool for new research. A similar model is being planned for Villa B.

3 Digital Reconstruction of Lost Decorations

The Oplontis Project dedicated much time and energy to the "orphans," the thousands of fragments of decorated plaster left behind when excavations halted. When, in the course of studying each fragment, we found one that seemed to fit into the decorative schemes of one of the rooms of Villa A, we would directly go to that room with the fragment in hand to see if we could find a fit. Away from Oplontis, this work continued because the 3D model allowed us go to any room of the Villa (albeit virtually) and

---

[2] A relational database stores data in separate tables rather than putting all the data in one big storeroom. The MySQL relational database is one of the most reliable and popular open-source databases.

[3] The server instance is a single Java EE compatible Java Virtual Machine hosting an Application Server on a single node.

[4] For further information on iRODS, see [11, 12].

compare digital photos of fragments with those within the Villa as reconstructed. In this way we were able to determine where many of the orphans belonged.

The large fragments that we eventually connected with the imposing Second-Style schemes of rooms 5 and 15 of Villa A posed problems that could only be solved through digital means. For one thing, because of their great weight, we could not carry them to the rooms that we thought they came from for direct comparison with the standing decoration. For another, as we eventually realized, there were no clear joins – that is, there were no gaps where we could simply fit the orphans in, like puzzle pieces. A more sophisticated method was needed.

The Italian excavators had already recognized that some of the fragments belonged to the decorative scheme of room 5 (the atrium or central hall of the Villa), but only one reconstruction had been proposed; it was seriously flawed. There was a clue, however. Because there was an Ionic capital among the fragments, Project architect Timothy Liddell examined the standing Doric order on the existing west wall; he located, at the top of the Doric architrave, traces of a column base that was meant to support a second, Ionic story (Fig. 1). Using Adobe Illustrator, he composed the fragments within a perspective scheme that united the pieces of this Ionic order.

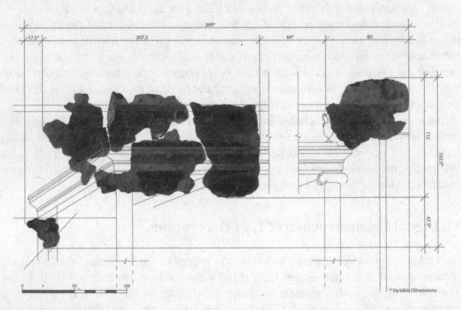

Fig. 1. Oplontis Villa A, atrium 5, west wall. Reconstruction of ionic upper order. Timothy Liddell

On the basis of Liddell's conservative rendering, Martin Blazeby of the KVL proposed a reconstruction of the entire scheme (Fig. 2). Although it is hypothetical, it is quite plausible, especially since Blazeby has recreated many similar ancient Roman painting schemes for projects of the KVL.[5]

Fig. 2. Oplontis Villa A, atrium 5, west wall, reconstruction. Martin Blazeby

The resulting reconstruction has important repercussions for our understanding of the decoration itself as well the architecture of atrium 5. Once inserted into the 3D model, this upper order revealed that the atrium was originally several meters taller than it is in modern reconstruction (Fig. 3). In short, the atrium was an even grander space than the original excavators imagined.

Room15 (an oecus, or reception space) is justly famous for its sweeping trompe l'oeil architecture, with peacocks and theatrical masks perched on fictive ledges. The surprise discovery, in 2013, of fragments that repeated motifs of the existing east wall posed even bigger challenges than those of atrium 5, since none of them fit into any of the gaps in that wall. In fact, many of the fragments repeated motifs of the east wall. It soon became clear that they had to belong to the unexcavated west wall, where excavations had halted because of the modern structures above. In fact, archival photographs showed that many pieces of the east wall were found blown out of place by volcanic forces; the same must have been true for the new fragments from the west wall.

Working on the solid hypothesis that the decorative scheme of the west wall of oecus 15 would have been the mirror reverse of the east wall, Liddell was able to reposition most of the newly-found fragments (Fig. 4). Because many of the new fragments show

---

[5] See especially the Roman Villa at Boscoreale, painted by the same workshop that created the Second-Style paintings at Oplontis: [13]; and the Skenographia Project: [14].

Fig. 3. Oplontis Villa A, atrium 5, west wall, screenshot from 3D model with ionic upper order

Fig. 4. Villa A, oecus 15. Reconstruction of upper part of west wall. Timothy Liddell

details that are missing in the standing wall, they add new information about the original appearance of both walls.

4   Laser Scanning: Sculptures and Architecture

One of the greatest disappointments for the visitor to Villa A is that none of the nineteen major pieces of sculpture is on view (Fig. 5). Although many pieces were found in their original settings, all have languished in storage for more than forty years. To address this problem, the Oplontis Project commissioned Marcus Abbott to scan the sculptures for insertion into our 3D model so that viewers could see how the sculptures fit into the décor of the Villa. Abbott combined two techniques: laser scanning and photogrammetry. With the sculptures back in place, the extensive exterior spaces of the Villa have come back to life, populated once again – albeit virtually – with statues interspersed among the garden features.

Fig. 5. Sculptures put back in place for Italian television program, July 1978. Photo S. Jashemski 2_31_78

5   Villa B

In 2008, because of the prohibitive costs of laser-scanning the 99 spaces of Villa A, Project architects used conventional Total Station data to correct the existing (but unfortunately error-filled) electronic plan provided by the Superintendency. Whereas the total station measures a few dozen individual points in the course of an afternoon, the new scanners measure many million. They bombard a space with laser beams to create a point-cloud array, recording the color and intensity of each point within a 360° radius of the sensor. Equally important is the efficiency of post-processing software that takes advantage of the high-speed capabilities of the newest computers.

The remarkable results provided by Abbott allowed Project architect Jess Galloway rapidly to create highly accurate plans, sections, and elevations, accurate to within 3 mm. Equally important is the fact that the scans of individual spaces stitch together without error, so that the resulting navigable model will be more accurate than that of Villa A.

For Villa B, the 3D scans also serve to record the positions of objects as left by the Italian excavations in 1991. For example, they show us, in three dimensions, the current disposition of the skeletons left in the north area of room 10 (Fig. 6).

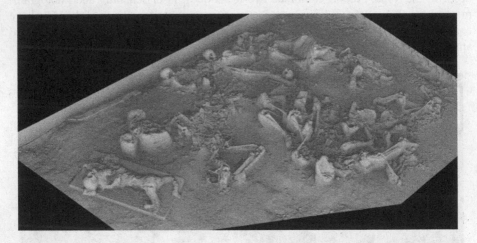

Fig. 6. Villa B, room 10, laser scan of skeletons left in situ. Image Marcus Abbott

Like many projects aiming to preserve cultural heritage sites, permanent preservation of digital data remains a great challenge [15]. Whereas the Project database itself will endure, archived in the Texas Advanced Computer Center, the software that runs the Unity interface will continue to evolve, making updates necessary. The born-digital publication of the Oplontis Villa A and Villa B will constitute another kind of secure backup: all of the digital publications in the Humanities E-Book Series of the American Council of Learned Societies are guaranteed by the University of Michigan Press to stay in print for 99 years. Despite these challenges, the digital instruments for recording and preserving archaeological heritage sites constitute the wave of the future. Whereas many 3D models provide highly accurate, interactive surrogates for the real thing, when linked, like the Oplontis Villa A model, to rich databases, they encourage users of every level to explore them and to test hypotheses. Through digital publication we have built a solid foundation for ongoing and future research on the villas of Oplontis, and we hope that our efforts will also provide a model for analogous project.

References

1. Strocka, V.M.: Häuser in Pompeji, vols. 1–11. Wasmuth, Tübingen (1984–2004)
2. Ling, R.: The Insula of the Menander at Pompeii, vol. 4. Oxford University Press, Oxford (1997–2006)
3. Clarke, J.R., Muntasser, N.K.: Oplontis: Villa A ("of Poppaea") at Torre Annunziata, Italy (50 B.C.–A.D. 79). Volume 1: Ancient Landscape and Modern Discovery. The Humanities E-Book Series of the American Council of Learned Societies, New York (2014). http://quod.lib.umich.edu/cgi/t/text/text-idx?c=acls;idno=heb90048.0001.001. Accessed 26 July 2016
4. Clarke, J.R., Muntasser, N.K.: Oplontis: Villa A ("of Poppaea") at Torre Annunziata, Italy (50 B.C.–A.D. 79). Volume 2. Decorative Ensembles: Painting, Stucco, Pavements, Sculptures. The Humanities E-Book Series of the American Council of Learned Societies, New York (forthcoming)
5. Clarke, J.R., Muntasser, N.K.: Oplontis: Villa A ("of Poppaea") at Torre Annunziata, Italy (50 B.C.–A.D. 79). Volume 3. Archaeology, Documentation, and Material Culture, 2006–2010. The Humanities E-Book Series of the American Council of Learned Societies, New York (forthcoming)
6. Clarke, J.R., Muntasser, N.K.: Oplontis: Villa A ("of Poppaea") at Torre Annunziata, Italy (50 B.C.–A.D. 79). Volume 4. Architecture. The Humanities E-Book Series of the American Council of Learned Societies, New York (forthcoming)
7. http://www.londoncharter.org/. Accessed 26 July 2016
8. Frischer, B., Fillwalk, J.: The digital Hadrian's Villa project: using virtual worlds to control suspected solar alignments. IEEE Explore 3(12), 49–55 (2012)
9. von Schwerin, J., et al.: The MayaArch3D Project: Digital Technologies for Research in Maya Archaeology. University of New Mexico, Albuquerque (2011). See also the following project websites with Unity 3D applications: http://pompeii.uark.edu/. Accessed 26 July 2016
10. http://pompeii.uark.edu/. Accessed 26 July 2016
11. http://irods.org/. Accessed 28 July 2016
12. https://www.tacc.utexas.edu/systems/corral. Accessed 26 July 2016
13. http://www.kvl.cch.kcl.ac.uk/boscoreale.html. Accessed 26 July 2016
14. http://www.skenographia.cch.kcl.ac.uk/. Accessed 26 July 2016
15. Delve, J., Anderson, D.: Preserving Complex Digital Objects. Facet Publishing, London (2014)

Innovative Concepts and Solutions for the Exchange, Management, Publishing and Visualization of Data And Knowledge Related to an Interpretative Reconstruction of Cultural Heritage

3D Models on Triple Paths - New Pathways for Documenting and Visualizing Virtual Reconstructions

Piotr Kuroczyński[1]([⊠]), Oliver Hauck[2,3], and Daniel Dworak[4,5]

[1] Herder Institute for Historical Research on East Central Europe -
Institute of the Leibniz Association, Marburg, Germany
piotr.kuroczynski@herder-institut.de
[2] Technical University of Darmstadt, Darmstadt, Germany
oha@raumdarstellung.org
[3] Institute for Space Representation, Frankfurt am Main, Germany
[4] Center for Media and Interactivity, Justus Liebig University Giessen,
Giessen, Germany
[5] Institute of Information Technology, Lodz University of Technology, Łódź, Poland
daniel.dworak@dokt.p.lodz.pl

Abstract. This paper presents the project "Virtual Reconstructions in Transnational Research Environments - the Portal: Palaces and Parks in Former East Prussia" in the light of the Semantic Web and Open Source technologies. The project examines the methodology of the computer-based 3D computer reconstruction of Cultural Heritage (CH) and the still unresolved questions of certification, classification, annotation, storage and visualization of 3D data sets. This multinational and interdisciplinary project is concerned with designing a Virtual Research Environment, based on interactive 3D objects being part of a semantic data model. Our approach effects the entire process of digital 3D reconstruction and requires the development of a data model, Cultural Heritage Markup Language (CHML) as groundwork for an application ontology for this kind of project. The preliminary results shed new light on areas such as effective data acquisition, documentation, semantic 3D modeling, data management, and 3D visualization. They may be useful for the creation of virtual museums and other forms of interactive presentation of CH that employ open source visualization platforms (e.g., WebGL technology).

Keywords: Digital 3D reconstruction · Semantic modeling · Application ontology · Documentation and visualization standards · Virtual research environments

1 Digital Heritage - 3D Preservation vs. 3D Reconstruction

One side effect of the Digital Revolution is the emerging field of digital heritage, which was recognized by the UNESCO in 2003 [1]. In the Cultural Heritage

© Springer International Publishing AG 2016
S. Münster et al. (Eds.): 3D Research Challenges II, LNCS 10025, pp. 149–172, 2016.
DOI: 10.1007/978-3-319-47647-6_8

(CH) context digital resources like digital pictures, 3D point clouds and other 3D representations, in particular the digital 3D reconstruction of CH, become part of "born-digital" heritage. Concerning tangible CH (e.g., art and architecture) a distinction between "digital 3D preservation" and "digital (hypothetical) 3D reconstruction" is relevant in terms of acquisition, process, access, and preservation, in particular for documentation and visualization.

The production processes for creating 3D data involve several stages, possible methods and techniques including, for example, automated data capture from real objects (e.g., digital images, photogrammetry, or laser scanning) and/or the interpretive (hypothetical) creation of 3D models, for example using Computer Aided Design (CAD) software.

The term "3D reconstruction" is confusingly used in the CH community for two completely different approaches: both the machine-driven algorithmic reconstruction of faces and solids from 3D point clouds and human-driven 3D modeling of disappeared or transformed objects and buildings as a critical process of source evaluation and interpretation. We prefer to call the machine-driven algorithmic approach "digital 3D preservation" because it is a digitization process for still existing objects.

In contrast "digital (hypothetical) 3D reconstruction" in our context is generally a human-driven process. This reconstruction is concerned with objects which no longer exist or never existed, such as unrealized art and architectural concepts. This modeling and 3D visualization process is based on a broad data acquisition (primary and secondary resources), the evaluation and interpretation of various sources, and finally digital molding, leading to the digital 3D object. The interpretative approach represents the creative aspect of this process. The impact of the hardware and software on the results is much lower than in the case of "digital 3D preservation". The human role in the creative process is essential.

Since the 1980s the development of information technology has led to the diffusion of digital 3D reconstruction of CH and thus to the rapid growth of 3D visualizations and extended application of 3D data. The WINSOM computer model of Old Minster [2] and the ASB BAUDAT computer model of Cluny III [3] are examples of the early use of computer-based 3D reconstructions. Visual communication, aided by digital 3D reconstruction, represents a higher form of conveying the spatial documentation and knowledge fusion of CH. Ideally, digital reconstruction is based on extensive research into and new interpretation of different kinds of sources. The holistic view of the 3D model has great potential for research as it combines views, cuts, and layouts which are traditionally drawn independently from each other [4].

Digital 3D reconstruction of extinct structures results in a digitally created (born-digital) 3D resource, ideally of lasting value in the sense of the above-mentioned UNESCO Charter. Yet this kind of research-based digital heritage often fails to meet scholarly standards, because the models are presented without any relation to the sources used to create them, and also lack documentation of the creation process and visualization methods. This raises reasonable doubts about the scholarly value of this field [5]. Moreover, the limited use of standards and rarity of applicable tools leads to an inexcusable loss of knowledge and resources.

Since the initial enthusiasm for textured geometries and rendered visualizations decreased, the critical view according the transparency, validity and long-term availability of digital 3D models and their representations prevails. The debate among architects, art historians and humanists is well documented, inter alia in the proceedings of the symposium on "The Virtue of Models: CAD and New Spaces for Art History" at Darmstadt University of Technology, one of the early centers of excellence for computer-aided digital 3D reconstruction [6].

Internationally the efforts to set standards and create scholarly approved digital 3D content were furthered within several EU projects starting with "EPOCH - European Network of Excellence in Open Cultural Heritage" (2004–2008). EPOCH produced the London Charter, which defined basic principles for computer-based visualization of CH [7]. This set of guidelines for documentation and dissemination underlines the creative process in data processing, that is, the human-driven aspects. The London Charter introduces the term "paradata" to capture the creative processes in the production chain, expanding the traditional term metadata. The London Charter gave rise to the announcement of the Principles of Seville, honing the guidelines for the emerging research field of virtual archaeology.

Beside the theoretical requirements for the digital 3D reconstruction of destroyed CH, established by the London Charter and refined by the Principles of Seville for virtual archaeology, some further basic research in the field of 3D documentation has already been done [8,9].

2   Semantic Staircase and Reference Ontology

In the light of the emerging Semantic Web the leading CH institutions are reorganizing and revising their databases towards Linked (Open) Data models. Opening up data silos and placing their data sets in a broad context enables new dimensions of knowledge representation and research possibilities. Linked Data is becoming increasingly popular in research and documentation.

The Semantic Web was introduced in 2001 by an article in Scientific American. The authors state: "Semantic Web is an extension of the current web in which information is given well-defined meaning, better enabling computers and people to work in cooperation." [10] They demonstrate the revolutionary idea of the Web of (Linked) Data, a machine and human readable network of information, presupposing the appropriate preparation of data sets, based on standards.

In the Semantic Web an ontology describes a part of the real world. At the heart of this are concepts (entities) and relationships (properties) which provide successful communication and common understanding about a domain. Ontologies realize the full potential of the Web by uniting two important aspects: On the one hand ontologies describe real-world semantics, and on the other they allow machines to process these translated formal semantics for information [11]. Blumauer and Pellegrini define a semantic staircase in which the ontology represents the highest semantic richness of all Knowledge Organization Systems (KOS) [12].

One essential aspect of the new data management is structured and harmonized data, using controlled vocabulary terms and data set definitions expressed in the Resource Description Framework (RDF) serialization format. The technical background of Semantic Web and Linked Data relies on Uniform Resource Identifiers (URI), which are crucial to handle disambiguation, RDF schemas, Web Ontology Language (OWL), and SPARQL Query Language for inference.

The CIDOC Conceptual Reference Model (CRM), an international standard since 2006 (ISO 21127:2006), is a conceptual model and reference ontology with a fundamental role in many data integration efforts in digital libraries and in the CH domain. On December 2014, a new version of the CIDOC CRM became available: ISO 21127:2014. It is currently (2014) based on 93 entities and 164 properties, which allow the human and machine readable annotation of CH. The theoretical and formal extension of the ontology to include documentation of 3D cultural objects and the digital (hypothetical) 3D reconstruction has already been initiated [13,14].

The importance of the ISO 21127:2006 as reference ontology in the CH domain is underlined by the effort to align the Europeana Data Model (EDM) to CIDOC CRM [15]. The models differ in the object-centric view of EDM in contrast to the efficient event-centric view of CIDOC CRM. Event documentation, such as creation activity, is a requirement of the cultural heritage community, as it is the most expressive way of describing all aspects of this broad domain.

3   Metadata Schema and Data Models for 3D Content

The EU funded project 3D-ICONS (2012–2015) contributed to an improved metadata schema for documentation of 3D content and delivery to the Europeana digital library. The authors of CARARE 2.0 were involved in the creation of the London Charter and were keen to implement the paradata within the metadata schema, in particular for capturing the machine-driven process (e.g., software used, technical parameters like calibration, and resolution). The schema focuses on documenting digitized 3D objects (digital 3D preservation). The schema makes marginal attempt to express and document the digital 3D reconstruction. The case study "The Hellenistic-Roman Theatre of Paphos" [16] demonstrates how this kind of project can be described.

The 3D-ICONS Guidelines [17] aim to document the complete pipeline which covers all technical and logistic aspects to create 3D models of cultural heritage objects with no established digitization. CARARE 2.0 is focused on heritage assets and their relationship to digital resources, activities and collection information [18]. The fundamental elements within its structure are as follows:

"Heritage asset identification" includes the descriptive information and metadata about the monument, historic building or artefact. The ability to create relations between heritage asset records allows the relationships between individual monuments that form parts of a larger complex to be expressed;

"Digital resources" are digital objects (3D models, images, videos) which are representations of the heritage asset and are provided to the services such as Europeana for reuse;

"Activity" is an event which took place at a heritage asset. In this case this is used to record the data capture and 3D modeling activities (paradata) which are utilized to create the 3D content;

"Collection information" is a collection level description of the data being provided to the service environment (Europeana).

The CARARE 2.0 schema follows the Europeana Data Model (EDM) from the perspective of description. As a result CARARE 2.0 is an object-centric model focused on the object described. The information comes in the form of statements that provide a direct link between the described object and its features. Most metadata practices making use of the "Dublin Core Metadata Element Set" [19] can be seen as an application of this approach. Both CARARE 2.0 and EDM, include the option to embed the activities and events that a heritage asset or digital resource took part in. For instance the element "WasDigitizedBy" marks the relation between a heritage asset and an activity in which it was digitized. It is a specialization of the element "WasPresentAt" constructing the relation between a heritage asset and an activity that it was present at, for example "a castle" > "was present at" > "a siege".

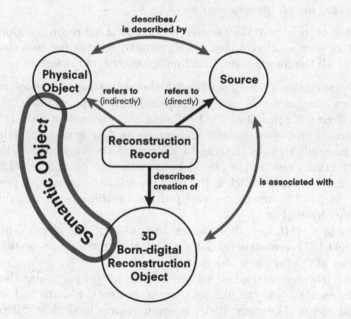

Fig. 1. Organization graph of a digital 3D reconstruction of no more existing objects.

Heritage assets and digital resources are the main themes in the CARARE core schema and it is mandatory for each CARARE record to include one heritage asset and at least one digital resource. In this way the schema provides for the description of cultural objects including historical images whose exact location is no longer certain and digitized cultural objects. The inclusion of collections and activities in CARARE 2.0 records to provide the context for the collection and information about activities is recommended, but not mandatory [20].

The CARARE 2.0 schema recommends the use of controlled vocabularies. The metadata schema mainly involves the Dublin Core Metadata Element Set from the Dublin Core Metadata Initiative (DCMI) and MIDAS heritage terms. The "HeritageAsset" set uses MIDAS to make a broad classification of the "General-Type" of the heritage asset and is intended to enable the distinction of monuments, buildings and landscape areas from artefacts, text documents (printed materials, books, articles, etc.), images (photographs, drawings etc.), audio recordings, movie references and 3D models. The "DigitalResource" recommends the use of DCMI controlled vocabulary to point out the nature or genre of the resource. The "Activity" determines the "EventType" by the use of MIDAS terms too (e.g., survey, archaeological excavation, digitization, or rebuilding). The "Activity" set makes it possible to refer to CIDOC CRM and its extensions in the following way: $HadGeneralPurpose$ (source = CIDOC CRM); $ConsistsOf$ (source = CRMdig); $HadSpecificPurpose$ (source = CIDOC CRM); HasCreated (source = CRMdig).

Cultural Heritage Markup Language [21] (CHML) differs from existing CH related schemas in two fundamental ways:

- it describes objects from the perspective of digital 3D reconstruction
- it is neither seen as a metadata nor a predated schema but as a data model containing all the information, including geometry and materials.

The reconstruction process starts with the evaluation of sources with commonly direct relation to the original physical object. In addition, there is in general no digital 3D model at the beginning. At best a digitized 3D model of physical remains (ruins) is available and can be used as source for further reconstruction. In result there is nothing to refer to at the beginning of the digital 3D reconstruction - neither the physical object that is lost in most of the cases, nor the digital 3D model which is the final result of the procedure - except the object the actors of the reconstruction process are thinking and talking about: the semantic object (Fig. 1).

This is why CHML describes the semantic object. The physical object and the born-digital 3D reconstruction object with their intrinsic properties are thus subcategories of the semantic object [22].

The data model is focused on the event/activity (in particular the "Reconstruction Record") being the glue of sources, semantic objects and actors, set in time and space. The data model is event-centric, and thus CIDOC CRM compliant.

The fundamental themes within CHML's structure are (Fig. 2):

"Activity" denotes research activities (e.g., computer-aided reconstruction) involving the semantic object. Generally in this case it is used to record the data capture and 3D modeling activities (paradata) creating 3D content;

"Source" denotes digitized sources (text, images, videos) which are representations of the "physical object", including the digital 3D preservation (e.g., 3D point clouds of physical remains);

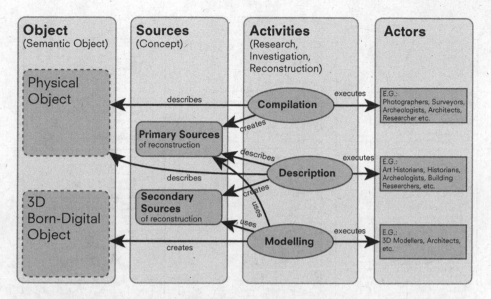

Fig. 2. Data model for mapping the digital 3D reconstruction workflow within four main themes of CHML.

"Semantic object" denotes the descriptive information and metadata about the artefact, consisting of the "physical object" (identified by a source) and the "3D born-digital reconstruction object" (represented by a digital model);

"Actor" denotes the information about the domain experts involved in the digital 3D reconstruction, legal bodies and natural persons of importance for the data provenance.

The main element set of object, source and activity themes expresses the semantic linkage between the above-mentioned themes and reflects the ideal workflow (Fig. 3). Within the activity theme the "computer aided reconstruction" record links the architect (actor) using different sources (sources used), previously analyzed and registered by domain experts (e.g., art historians), for the interpretation of an artefact. This research activity of the actor results in a digital (hypothetical) 3D reconstruction of the object (object modeled). The digital model and the activity refers to the semantic object (object). Ideally, the semantic object was identified by a domain expert (art historian) during a previous source analysis (research activity), setting the object in a relation to a structural hierarchy (IsPartOf/HasPart) and interlinking all sources representing the object (IsShownBy). The data model enables semantic enrichment of the 3D data sets uploaded.

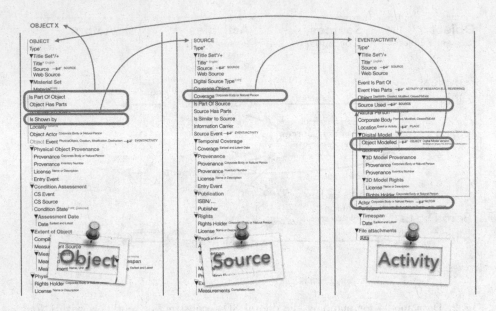

Fig. 3. Semantic linkage between the themes object, source and event/activity.

The CHML acts as groundwork for the subsequent design of an application ontology and Virtual Research Environment (VRE) for digital hypothetical 3D reconstruction in the on-going project "Virtual Reconstructions in Transnational Research Environments - the Web Portal Palaces and Parks in Former East Prussia" (2013–2016) [23]. This interdisciplinary project, coordinated by the Herder Institute for Historical Research on East Central Europe, seeks to integrate diverse information related to destroyed physical objects, the process of data acquisition, source interpretation, modeling and visualization, introducing the semantic 3D modeling method. The integration of interactive modules enables interactive collaborative research on 3D content. The result is a prototype of an interactive immersive Virtual Museum (VM) linked to scholarly approved data.

The innovation and the strength of patrimonium.net, the VRE under discussion, becomes clear in the implementation of a CHML schema with a high relational structure into an application ontology, based on CIDOC CRM as the reference ontology. The mapping of the themes, sub-themes and elements into adequate entities and properties is managed in cooperation with the University of Erlangen-Nuremberg (FAU) and Germanisches Nationalmuseum Nuremberg (GNM) and based on long-term experience from the DFG-funded research project "WissKI" [24]. To ensure sustainable data formalization and data structure, a customized application ontology has been created on the basis of the Erlangen CRM (E-CRM) [25]. The current E-CRM is an application-related interpretation of CIDOC CRM (ISO 21127:2006) and represents certified implementation of the reference ontology written in OWL DL. The designed semantic data model

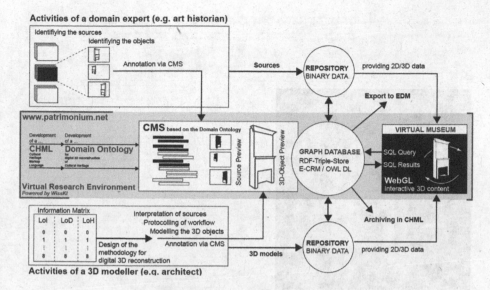

Fig. 4. Graphical abstract of the project.

embedded in an adapted Content Management System (CMS) establishes a promising VRE for spatial (space related) research according to Linked Data requirements. The VRE is set up on the Drupal 8 open source CMS.

The collaborative VRE enables the multidisciplinary research team involved to acquire data sets and to semantically enrich the records, including 3D data. While recording and editing the data, the system semi-automatically expands the graph database, interlinking the data with internal records in the database and with external Linked Data addressed by the SPARQL Endpoint.

The graphical abstract shows the central backbone of the project, represented by the coloured background (Fig. 4). The activities of the domain experts (e.g., art historians) evaluate the sources and identify the objects. Activities, sources and objects are embedded and annotated within the VRE/CMS. The 3D modeler (e.g., an architect) interprets the registered information and creates the digital 3D reconstruction. Ideally, as a result every identified object includes an interpretative (hypothetical) representation. The provenance of the digital 3D model (paradata) is annotated by the architect during the modeling process. All field-based entries and semantically enriched free-text annotations within the VRE result in graph data (E-CRM/OWL DL). The 3D scenes are integrated by queries in the VM, an immersive and interactive web-based 3D environment (WebGL). The prototype VM combines the semantic data model with 3D visualization, providing transparency and validity of the information.

The design of the application ontology is mainly concerned with defining the scientific domain, in this case digital (hypothetical) 3D reconstruction, mapping entities to E-CRM or proposing new application entities and defining their specific properties. As a result all CHML elements are expressed by triple paths

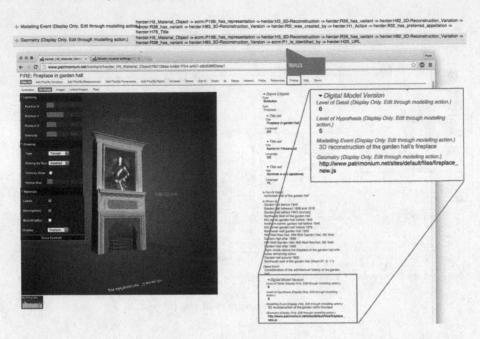

Fig. 5. The element "Modeling Event" within the object view (bottom) and the RDF triples of "Modeling Event" (top).

in Linked Data standard, hidden behind the field-based entry in the familiar environment of an indexing form. The VRE facilitates the storage of the comprehensive information in the CIDOC CRM compliant triple architecture of the RDF.

In the back-end, the application ontology entities are marked with chml:H"value", their properties with chml:R"value", in contrast to used reference ontology entities marked with ecrm:E"value", their properties with ecrm:P"value".

The "Modeling Event" element of the digital 3D model within the CHML theme "Objects" is semantically expressed in the following way (Fig. 5):

Listing 1. Object > Digital 3D Model > Modeling Event

```
chml: H5_Material_Object -> ecrm: P138i_has_representation ->
chml: H3_3D-Reconstruction -> chml: R36_has_variant ->
chml: H82_3D-Reconstruction_Variation -> chml:
R36_has_variant -> chml: H83_3D-Reconstruction_Version ->
chml: R5i_was_created_by -> chml: H1_Action -> chml:
R32_has_preferred_appellation -> chml: H76_Title
```

The vice-versa path from the Activity to the "Digital 3D Model" is represented in the following way:

Listing 2. Activity > 3D Reconstruction Model > Object Modeled

```
chml:H1_Action -> chml:R5_created -> chml:H83_3D-
Reconstruction_Version -> chml:R36i_is_variant_of ->
chml:H82_3D-Reconstruction_Variation -> chml:
R36i_is_variant_of -> chml:H3_3D-Reconstruction -> ecrm:
P138_represents -> chml:H5_Material_Object -> chml:
R32_has_preferred_appellation -> chml:H76_Title
```

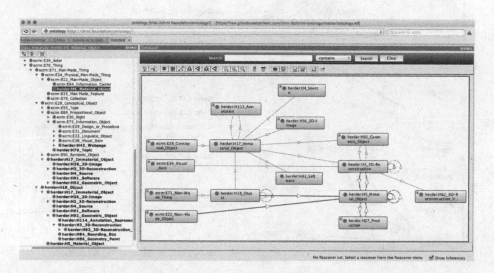

Fig. 6. Class hierarchy of the "H5_Material_Object" within the ontology editor [protégé].

The class hierarchy within the data model presents the relations in the OntoGraf (Fig. 6). The *chml : H5_Material_Object* is a subclass of *ecrm : E22_Man − Made − Object* with the *chml : H3_3D − Reconstruction*. The *chml : H3* has *chml : H82* variations and is a subclass of *chml : H17_Immaterial_Object* with annotations (i.e. paradata).

4   The TYPE Labeling System

The semantic core of CHML is a labeling system called TYPE. TYPE gives every record a meaning. It is a required attribute for every object, source, activity and actor, as well as places and historic events. The TYPE is a non-ambiguous classification. Its attribute's values are four letter abbreviations (for instance: FIRE for the object class "Fireplace") which can be linked to multilingual definitions, thesauri, authority files, Wikipedia articles, websites, e-publications, and so on. It ensures high flexibility for a variety of projects with different requirements and is the reliable basis for multilingual environments or changing terms due to linguistic development [26]. This kind of multiple linking of a label (term) to various sources is advantageous for creating Linked Data, according to Bruhn [27].

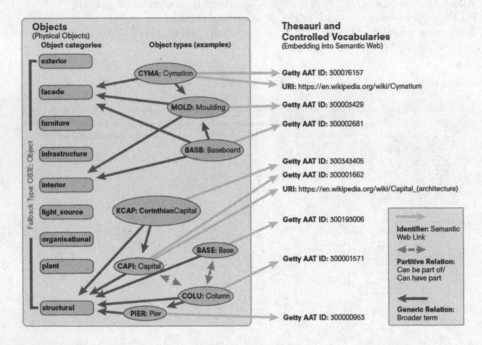

Fig. 7. Categories and relations of object terms within the TYPE system.

The TYPE labeling system is explained in more detail from a Linked Data perspective in Fig. 7. This figure shows three possible relations of terms for objects: two of them are internal and one is the link to the Semantic Web.

The identifier links to URIs of controlled vocabularies and thesauri or to other URIs such as Wikipedia articles or any website with information about the term.

The generic relation is the most important relation. It relates broader and narrower terms, the narrower term being more specific than the broader one according to ISO 2788. An example: All Corinthian capitals can be seen as capitals, but not all capitals are Corinthian capitals. Therefore "capital" is a broader term for "Corinthian capital" and "Corinthian capital" is a narrower term for "capital".

The partitive relation is specific for object TYPEs: A capital "can be part of" a column. A wall "can have a part" which is an opening or fireplace. It is defined as "can" not as "is" because walls without openings or fireplaces exist and capitals have often been re-used as spoils serving as bases (a famous example is the Basilica Cistern in Istanbul).

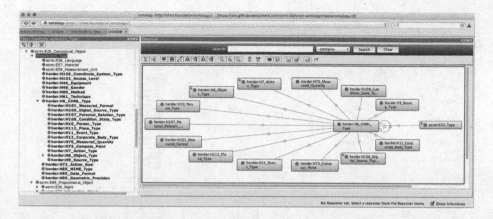

Fig. 8. Class hierarchy of the "H6_CHML_Type" within the ontology editor [protégé].

Every CHML theme record is classified by TYPE. Semantically the CHML TYPE is an application entity H6_CHML_Type referring to the sub-class ecrm:E55 (CIDOC CRM Type) of the class ecrm:E28 (CIDOC CRM Conceptual Object). Several classes are derived from the entity H6_CHML_Type including the sub-classes H8_Object_Type, and H41_Interior (Fig. 8).

Within the CMS the TYPE:FIRE (for the object fireplace) is a narrower term of the class interior (H41_Interior). The labeling system is a powerful feature integrated in the CMS-based editor of TYPEs. In defining the TYPEs (such as fireplace) the domain expert is encouraged to semantically enrich the record by linking the title sets for the TYPE with several SKOS controlled vocabularies and thesauri. It is recommended to use the controlled vocabularies of the Getty Institute (AAT for architectural objects, TGN for places, CONA for cultural objects and ULAN for artists) [28]. The TYPE editor allows access to all kinds of sources, and authority files, such as the German National Library's "Gemeinsame Normdatei" [29] (GND, Integrated Authority File). The additional usage of national thesauri, like the Polish "Tezaurus Dziedzictwa Kulturowego" [30] (Cultural Heritage Thesaurus) enhances the accuracy of the classification, and is highly recommended. Semantic Web technologies, in particular essential controlled vocabularies, thesauri and other authority files, are currently being developed. Therefore the proposed labeling system seems to be a flexible and adequate approach. Specialists can design their domain specific thesauri embedded within the Linked Data controlled vocabularies (Fig. 9). This allows the user to deal with local phenomena and terms: for example, many construction techniques are restricted to small areas and historical uses and thus hard to find in most thesauri. The proposed labeling system is the gate to the Semantic Web, linking the entries in the project specific environment with the Linked Open Data.

For geographical places, the use of GeoNames [31] and OpenStreetMap [32] (OSM) open source service is recommended. Both are highly participatory: The implementation of OSM IDs and the ability to draw and mark up areas, buildings

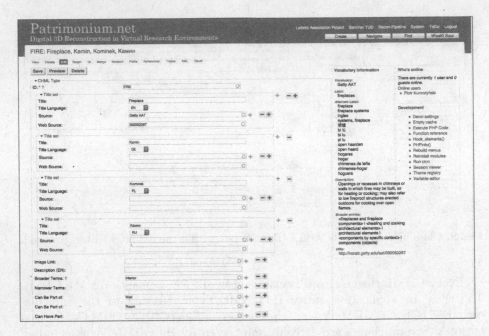

Fig. 9. Edition of the TYPE "FIRE" within the CMS of WissKI at patrimonium.net.

and ruins within the OSM database achieve a new dimension of accuracy and visibility. In addition, the OSM map can be embedded in a CMS window within the place entry. Places are used only for locations outside the area modeled in 3D. Localization of objects inside the 3D model works with the XYZ coordinates related to the common pole (origin of the scene) of the model.

The 3D extension of the open source CMS modules enables comprehensive research into 3D data sets. The VRE in development combines different physical object representations. For instance, the presentation of the object within patrimonium.net compiles the 3D point cloud created from Structure from Motion (SfM) technology with the CAD 3D model shaped via an interpretative reconstruction process (Fig. 10). The 3D data sets are visualized by the adaptation and integration of WebGL technology within the CMS. The supported formats are OBJ (with MTL for materials and linking to texture images), DAE, JSON, and PLY (for point clouds).

The object "Fireplace of the Green room" is embedded within activities (digitization and computer-aided reconstruction) with extended provenance entries and comprehensive annotation possibilities. A structured format in the back-end according to the CIDOC CRM documentation standards is used to capture the data process leading to the digital representations (3D models).

Extensive documentation of the technical and creative processes, associating the digitization process with the interpretative (hypothetical) 3D reconstruction, generally occurs in the WissKI "free text input" (Fig. 11). The WissKI CMS enables to create Full HTML and WissKI Annotated HTML text input, as

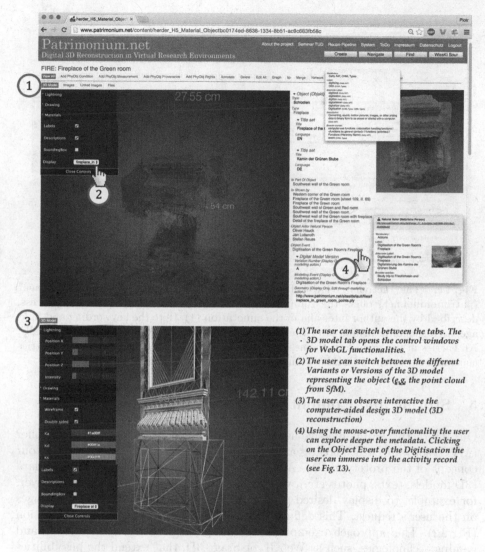

(1) The user can switch between the tabs. The 3D model tab opens the control windows for WebGL functionalities.

(2) The user can switch between the different Variants or Versions of the 3D model representing the object (e.g. the point cloud from SfM).

(3) The user can observe interactive the computer-aided design 3D model (3D reconstruction)

(4) Using the mouse-over functionality the user can explore deeper the metadata. Clicking on the Object Event of the Digitisation the user can immerse into the activity record (see Fig. 13).

Fig. 10. Object view within the virtual research environment [patrimonium.net].

descriptive paradata in the database. WissKI Annotated HTML has the advantage of enabling linkage (keywording) of the written words (terms) with existing semantic instances from all CHML themes and sub-themes. As a result the free text, including the paradata, is semantically enriched. It follows that the digital 3D objects are semantically enriched and users are not limited in their description of the processes and the artefacts under investigation.

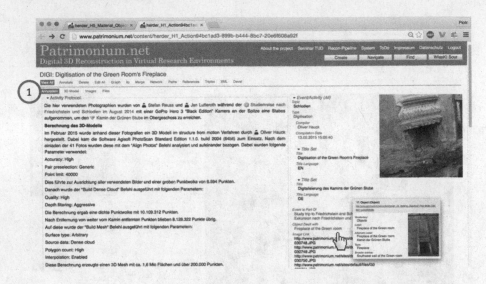

Fig. 11. The activity view "Digitisation of the Green Room's Fireplace" (patrimonium.net) offers the comprehensive inside view of the digitisation process, described by the author inter alia in the annotation (1). Here the keywording and linkage with semantic instances in the graph data base can be done semi-automatically. All entries in the main four themes of CHML are supported by the field-based entries accompanied by the Full HTML and Wisski annotated HTML tool.

5   Storing and Computing 3D Data

Our interactive and immersive user interface is based on Model-View-Controller (MVC) software, which creates a background layer for storing and designing our concept of the prototype VM. A model layer is a storage for any kind of data (3D models, texts, photos etc.), which can be manipulated by a controller layer, for example, to display desired content in the database. A view layer changes on the user's request. This defines the final result of information visualization (Fig. 12). This approach exemplifies the adoption of new web standards and gaming technologies, such as WebGL or Stage 3D, that extend the possibilities for visualizing 3D data.

The VM connects many techniques and standards that are commonly used in virtual reconstructions. There are existing and ready-made solutions like X3D, which enable the creation of a virtual world. These are insufficient for our research and limited by external libraries. Despite this, we have attempted to create a container for 3D geometry that would compress the required files, reduce the time for decoding such data or complexity of existing models. In fact, our solution also uses a lot of authors' ideas for digital reconstructions to overcome the above problems.

The interactive form of the VM allows the user to visit places that do not exist, such as the Garden Room (Fig. 13). The whole scene is composed of actual 3D geometry (saved in a PNG file by author's algorithm) with textures. After

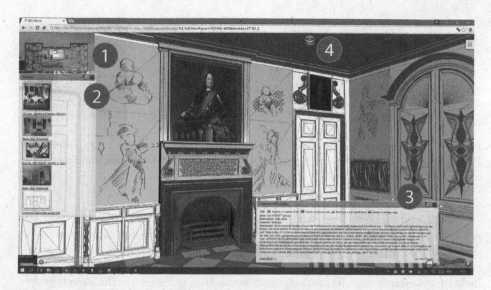

Fig. 12. Prototype of the Virtual Museum: Integration of interactive semantic 3D objects in WebGL. (1) The real-time rendered map of the surroundings with user's focus area and position; (2) Visual information; (3) Metadata and textual content; (4) Paronamic view option.

the user selects an element of interest, such as the fireplace, semantic content is loaded from the database and displayed. As point (2) shows, there is visual information (images, movies) connected with this specific element. Moreover, there is paradata, metadata and textual content (3) with complex data about the historical background, names in different languages and a link to the database page of this model within patrimonium.net. Some of the places are associated with a panoramic view (4) of the state of the existing site, making it possible to compare past and digital form with its present appearance. There is also a list of initially prepared points of interest which can be changed or generated by the user (with the add or remove functions) for future use. If the user wants to share some view with others or return to it later, the website link contains a position and vector, which is called deep linking.

The accumulation of many models of buildings, trees and so on results in a considerable increase in the number of vertices and faces and produces huge data sets. They need to be stored, sent and decoded on the client side. Most current technologies for 3D graphics are limited to drawing only 65,536 vertices per segment of the model. This is caused by 16-bit vertex buffer due to the backward compatibility of graphics cards. The technique of splitting models with a huge number of vertices is frequently used to reduce the file size; then a portaling method [33] can be applied. There is also a LoD (Level of Detail) method [34] which requires few representations of the same object with a different number of vertices. If the user is far away from the model, an algorithm loads the object with the smallest number of vertices. When this distance decreases, a model with more vertices should be loaded.

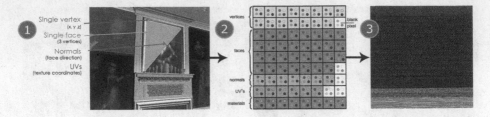

Fig. 13. (1) Elements of geometry - vertices, faces, normal and UVs. (2) Stucture of PNG file (3) PNG output file with geometry for testing model of fireplace and prototype of the Virtual Museum.

There are also problems with diverse users' computers, platforms, browsers and computing power. Although there are special formats for the transmission of audio (MP3), video (H.264) and images (JPEG), optimized for web applications, a standard format for 3D graphics transmission is still lacking. The lack of standards for 3D data transmission has resulted in the development of the new Graphics Library Transmission Format (glTF) by Khronos Group. Trevett notes [35] that COLLADA is not a web transport format, therefore glTF is JSON based.

Another aspect that needs to be improved concerns coding and uploading large 3D data sets using alternative formats, with an emphasis on architectural models. We have developed a technique for storing 3D geometrical data in 2D PNG files, which are characterized by small sizes and lossless compression (Fig. 13). PNG can also be used for the long-term preservation of information, due to its portable and standardized form.

Our idea for optimizing the transfer of large 3D data sets consists of storing geometry in 2D, lossless formats. This concept is based on saving data to RGB channels of 2D graphic file. First of all, the geometry is scaled down if needed. Every vertex coordination is then split into integer and fractional parts and then encoded to the red, green and blue (R, G and B) channels. Information about faces is somewhat unusually encoded. The face flag and their indices are encoded one by one for vertices, material, texture UVs, normals and colors. Every face value is an integer number and also requires three color channels. Normals are stored similarly to faces, but it is needed to store a sign of the value in the blue channel. Finally, UVs values are stored similarly to normal values, but UVs are not signed. Material storage is another stage. They are separated from geometry by two transparent pixels and by one pixel if there is more than one material. The alpha channel of the PNG file is also used for separation of geometry's elements data. Vertices are saved first, then transparent pixels, faces, transparent pixels, normals, transparent pixels and UVs (Fig. 13). The alpha channel cannot be used to store any important data, because WebGL (like other JavaScript technologies) uses pre-multiplied values for R, G and B channels when the alpha channel is used. This produces inaccurate output data. Data are stored with accuracy to four decimal places. This process is reversible data from PNG files can therefore be decoded easily.

Table 1. File size comparison for architectural models, according to OBJ and PNG format.

Model	No. vertices	OBJ [KB]	PNG [KB]	Ratio OBJ:PNG
Portrait	11 439	2 124	518	**4,1**
Chairs	12 618	2 098	462	**4,54**
Column	17 901	3 083	709	**4,35**
Sala001	24 958	3 727	807	**4,62**
Sala002	28 480	12 971	2 334	**5,56**
Sala112	39 202	6 882	1 370	**5,02**
Stairways	44 525	9 246	1 372	**6,74**

Table 2. Uploading time comparison for different file formats of sphere (550,000 vertices).

	1 Mb/s	2 Mb/s	4 Mb/s	8 Mb/s	12 Mb/s
OBJ	15min 26s	7min 43s	3min 52s	1min 56s	1min 18s
PNG	2min 15s	1min 8s	0min 34s	0min 17s	0min 15s

We decided to use a PNG file because it supports lossless data compression and was designed to be transferred over the Internet. The compression algorithm implemented for PNG files is called DEFLATE and it builds a data dictionary of information occurring in an original stream. This method eliminates redundant data because, when any part of the data occurs once, it may be used many times. This is an important point in our research, because many architectural models are symmetrical and tend to have a lot of common vertices, faces and other characteristics.

This approach is likely to help decrease the size of files (Table 1). For example, in the case of raw 3D data with 550,000 vertices stored in OBJ we have a 79 MB file. After saving it as PNG we only have approximately 11.5 MB. There was also an improvement for small objects (35,000 vertices) - the OBJ file was about 3.5 MB, and a PNG file was only 0.76 MB (780 KB).

Moreover, modern web technologies are optimized for streaming pictures and movies. This reduces the uploading time of a PNG file, compared to OBJ file. The time of decoding data from OBJ and PNG files is similar (about 100 ms for the test model), therefore, there is no change. Decreased file sizes also affect the time of transferring the data over the Web (Table 2.).

There are other steps in the decoding process that can be performed on Graphics Processing Unit (GPU). Research has also been done to reduce the time taken to decode PNG files with 3D geometry. It has been proved that the time to load 3D geometry from a PNG file on GPU dropped significantly (540 ms instead of 6900 ms). This improves most of the aspects described in this paper; storing, sending and displaying 3D geometry.

Fig. 14. Prototype of the Virtual Museum. Foreground: interactive, procedural real-time generated trees; background: billboarding trees.

Since WebGL restrictions and hardware incompatibility are well-known, we also decided to generate trees in real time. It has been decided to use an open source library called proctree.js which generates complicated trees using GLGE, a library for direct access to OpenGL. Every tree is described by 25 parameters (including height, size of leaves, root, drop amount, twig scale, and textures) and its position. The average number of vertices per object is about 4,000, depending on its parameters. The whole prototype of VM consists of about 350 trees, resulting in a great number of vertices in this case. It is not possible to display such complicated geometry in real time, so we combined two well-known techniques: billboarding (two crossed textures) and LoD. The basic version of LoD technique needs to load the whole geometry at the beginning and hide or display what is needed on demand. This caused display problems on an average laptop and stopped working when displaying about 60 trees. Therefore we introduced a modified LoD technique that we called Progressive LoD (PLoD), based on billboarding which is exchanged for more complicated, real-time generated objects for closer viewing (Fig. 14). This appeared to be a very efficient method, highly interactive and seems to be golden mean between performance and appearance.

6   Conclusions on Combined Schema and Prospects for Common Application Ontology

The increased digitization efforts within the CH sector (e.g., in museums, archives, libraries, or research institutions) require strategies to improve documentation standards serving the transparency (validity), interoperability, long-term access and preservation of information, in particular for 3D data sets.

Beside domain-driven documentation standards in museums, archives and libraries, applicable documentation standards for digital 3D preservation, specialized to capture and express a broad range of requirements for 3D digitization, already exist.

The London Charter provides the overall guidelines for scholarly approved computer-based visualization and the documentation of 3D data sets. Europeana and supporting EU projects serving the delivery of 3D content to digital libraries still promote the development of improved 3D documentation standards, expressed in metadata schemas such as CARARE 2.0.

We recognize the current lack of documentation standards for digital 3D reconstruction, based on a different procedure in data acquisition and data processing, and leading to various 3D visualization applications.

As the massive demand on 3D digitization of cultural objects and cultural sites still takes priority, unsolved issues of the complementary domain of interpretative digital 3D reconstruction of lost and/or never existing CH objects has been marginalized.

The Semantic Web is changing scientific methodologies and documentation standards. Digital-driven scholars in particular have recognized its potential and see the challenges involved in establishing an infrastructure and new methodology for future research work. CIDOC CRM is the leading, and only approved "semantic glue" (reference ontology) for scientific domains concerned with the broad field of CH.

CHML is a tailor-made data model for the digital 3D reconstruction of lost and/or never existing CH 3D objects. This event-centric data model is mapped to CIDOC CRM, implemented in OWL DL (E-CRM) and ready to use as a proven way of indexing the CH objects within a Virtual Research Environment (VRE).

Our approach sets benchmarks in two ways:

(1) It is the first application ontology for digital (hypothetical) 3D reconstructions according to the international documentation standard CIDOC CRM.
(2) It is the first collaborative and interactive VRE for spatial research on digital 3D content (patrimonium.net) delivering Linked (Open) Data.

The interactive visualization of integrated 3D point clouds and hand-modeled 3D data sets accompanied by the semantic 3D annotation tool (in development) will have a significant impact on immediate research on 3D data sets, the documentation and dissemination of our common digital heritage, which is what this representation of CH means in the broader sense.

The mid-term challenge is to improve the documentation of the provenance and paradata, recently expressed in the WissKI field-based entry and free text input. Interesting prospects for more structured annotations include the CIDOC CRM extensions CRMinf and CRMsci. The challenge will be to examine the formal expression of these extensions and their proper implementation in structured (predefined) editor systems. Successful integration would mean facing the fear of "killing the humanities" by restricting metadata schemas and formal expressions within ontologies.

Modern Web trends are actually aimed to visualization of large tridimensional data sets in the most attractive and interactive form. There are many technologies (for example WebGL, Stage 3D) and techniques which are usually used in the Internet, neverless they are still in development. In fact, to provide real time and realistic 3D scene simultaneously, it causes really quick increase of data to be displayed. Most of current technologies for tridimensional graphics are limited to draw only 65,536 vertices per frame for single objects segment, due to harware's backward compatibility. It is a real problem to solve because of geometry's complexity and, what is more, time needed to transfer a whole scene. The technologies in question are no standard and there is considerable scope for improvement. The combination of solutions applied during our project is promising, in order to increase the performance of the whole Web 3D environment. Our proposed solutions for the interactive integration of semantic 3D objects in WebGL environment are in development, but the authors' ideas of coding, storing and decoding 3D content is a promising solution for current problems with transferring 3D data sets in real time, prooved by the reached results.

Acknowledgments. The international, collaborative research project and the resulting Virtual Research Environment (patrimonium.net) under discussion, as well the findings concerned with the prototype of the Virtual Museum, are funded by the German Leibniz Association from 2013 to 2016. The project is coordinated by the Herder Institute for Historical Research on East Central Europe in Marburg, Germany. Part of this work was supported by German "Federal Government Commissioner for Culture and the Media" and the European Cooperation in Science and Research (COST) Action TD1201 "Colour and Space in Cultural Heritage" (cosch.info). The basic development of CHML has been undertaken by O. Hauck and A. Noback between 2000 and 2004 (chml. Foundation).

References

1. UNESCO: Charter on the Preservation of Digital Heritage. Records of the General Conference, Paris, 29 September to 17 October 2003, pp. 74–77 (2003)
2. Burridge, J.M., Collins, B.M., Galton, B.N., Halbert, A.R., et al.: The WINSOM solid modeller and its application to data visualisation. IBM Syst. J. **28**(4), 548–568 (1989)
3. Cramer, H., Koob, M.: Cluny Architektur als Vision. Edition Braus, Heidelberg (1993)
4. Kuroczyński, P.: 3D reconstruction of the architectural history of the city of Vratislavia. A progress report (3D-Computer-Rekonstruktion der Baugeschichte Breslaus. Ein Erfahrungsbericht). In: The Annual of the Polish Academy of Sciences, Scientific Centre Vienna, pp. 201–213 (2012)
5. Bentkowska-Kafel, A.: Digital visualization of cultural heritage and its scholarly value in art history, visual resources. Int. J. Documentation **29**(1), 38–46 (2013). Special Issue on Digital Art History edited by Murtha Baca et al
6. The Virtue of Models. CAD and New Spaces for Art History (Der Modelle Tugend CAD und die neuen Räume der Kunstgeschichte), Frings M. (ed.), Weimar (2001)

7. Denard, H.: A New introduction to the london charter. In: Bentkowska-Kafel, A., Baker, D., Denard, H. (eds.) Paradata and Transparency in Virtual Heritage, Ashgate, pp. 57–71 (2012)
8. Pfarr, M.: Dokumentationssystem für Digitale Rekonstruktionen am Beispiel der Grabanlage Zhaoling, Provinz Shaanxi (China). Diss. Technische Universität Darmstadt (2010)
9. Blümel, I.: Metadatenbasierte Kontextualisierung architektonischer 3D Modelle, Diss. Humboldt-Universität zu Berlin (2013)
10. Berners-Lee, T., Hendler, J., Lassila, O.: The semantic web. In: Scientific American, May 2001
11. Olensky M.: http://www.ieee-tcdl.org/Bulletin/v6n2/Olensky/olensky.html#2. Accessed 15 Oct 2015
12. Blumauer, A., Pellegrini, T.: Semantic web und semantische technologien. In: Pellegrini, T., Blumauer, A. (eds.) Semantic Web: Wege zur vernetzten Wissensgesellschaft. X.media.press, pp. 9–15. Springer, Heidelberg (2006)
13. Niccolucci, F.: Setting standards for 3D visualization of cultural heritage in Europe and beyond. In: Bentkowska-Kafel, A., Baker, D., Denard, H. (eds.) Paradata and Transparency in Virtual Heritage, Ashgate, pp. 23–36 (2012)
14. Ronzino, P.: CIDOC CRM$_{BA}$ - a CRM extension for buildings archaeology information modelling. Dissertation, The Cyprus Institute (2015)
15. Doerr, M., et al.: The Europeana data model (EDM). In: Proceedings of the 76th IFLA General Cconference and Assembly, Gothenburg/Sweden, p. 9 (2010). http://conference.ifla.org/past-wlic/2010/149-doerr-en.pdf. Accessed 15 Oct 2015
16. http://www.carare.eu/eng/Media/Files/Paphos-Case-Study. Accessed 15 Oct 2015
17. 3D-Icons Guidelines. http://3dicons-project.eu/eng/Guidelines-Case-Studies/Guidelines2. Accessed 15 Oct 2015
18. CARARE metadata schema V 2.0.pdf, p. 3. http://www.carare.eu/slv/Support/CARARE-metadata-schema Accessed 15 Oct 2015
19. http://dublincore.org/documents/dces/. Accessed 15 Oct 2015
20. Hansen, H.J., Fernie, K.: CARARE - connecting archeology and architecture in Europeana. In: Ioannides, M., et al. (eds.) Proceedings of Third International Euro-Mediterranean Conference, Lemesos, p. 456 (2010)
21. Hauck, O., Noback, A.: CHML - Cultural Heritage Markup Language. EineAuszeichnungssprache für das gebaute Weltkulturerbe, Presentation at CeBit 2003. https://www.academia.edu/12617393/CHML. Accessed 15 Oct 2015
22. Kuroczyński, P., et al.: Virtual museum of destroyed culturalheritage - 3D documentation, reconstruction and visualisation in the semantic web. In: Proceedings of the 2nd International Conference on Virtual Archaeology, Hermitage Museum, St. Petersburg/Russia, pp.54-61. http://www.virtualarchaeology.ru/pdf/281_va-book2015.pdf. Accessed 15 Oct 2015
23. www.herder-institut.de/en/research-projects/current-projects/virtual-reconstructions-in-transnational-research-environments-the-web-portal-palaces-and-parks-in-former-east-prussia.html. Accessed 15 Oct 2015
24. Scientific Communication Infrastructure (WissenschaftlicheKommunikationsInfrastruktur). http://wiss-ki.eu/. Accessed 15 Oct 2015
25. Görz, G., Schiemann, B., Oischinger, M.: An implementation of the CIDOC conceptual reference model (4.2.4) in OWL-DL. http://erlangen-crm.org/docs/crm_owl_cidoc2008.pdf. Accessed 15 Oct 2015

26. Hauck, O., Kuroczyński, P.: Cultural heritage markup language -designing a domain ontology for digital reconstructions. In: Proceedings of the 2nd International Conference on Virtual Archaeology, Hermitage Museum, St. Petersburg/Russia, pp. 250-255. http://www.virtualarchaeology.ru/pdf/281_va_book2015.pdf. Accessed 15 Oct 2015

27. Bruhn, K.-Ch.: The labeling system: a new approach to overcome the vocabulary bottleneck. In: DH-CASE II: Collaborative Annotations on Shared Environments: Metadata, Tools and Techniques in the Digital Humanities (2014). https://www.academia.edu/12055632/. Accessed 15 Oct 2015

28. http://www.getty.edu/research/tools/vocabularies/. Accessed 15 Oct 2015

29. http://www.dnb.de/gnd. Accessed 15 Oct 2015

30. http://historiasztuki.uni.wroc.pl/tezaurus.html. Accessed 15 Oct 2015

31. http://www.geonames.org/. Accessed 15 Oct 2015

32. http://www.openstreetmap.org/. Accessed 15 Oct 2015

33. Lowe, N., Datta, A.: A technique for rendering complex portals. IEEE Trans. IEEE Vis. Comput. Graph. **11**, 81–90 (2005)

34. Tan, K.H., Daut, D.: A review on level of detail. In: Computer Graphics, Imaging and Visualization. CGIV 2004, pp. 70–75 (2004)

35. Trevett, N.: 3D Transmission Format. In: NVIDIA, June 2013

36. Stead, S., et. al.: CRMinf: the argumentation model - an extension of CIDOC-CRM to support argumentation, produced by Paveprime Ltd and collaborators. http://www.cidoc-crm.org/docs/cidoc_crm_sig/CRMinf-0.7.pdf

37. Doerr, M., et al.: CRMsci: the scientific observation model - an extension of CIDOC-CRM to support scientific observation, producedby FORTH and collaborators, version 1.2. http://www.cidoc-crm.org/docs/cidoc_crm_sig/CRMsci1.2.pdf

Classification Schemes for Visualization of Uncertainty in Digital Hypothetical Reconstruction

Fabrizio I. Apollonio[✉]

Department of Architecture, Alma Mater Studiorum - University of Bologna,
viale Risorgimento, 2, Bologna, Italy
fabrizio.apollonio@unibo.it

Abstract. The chapter presents the methodology that has been adopted to develop a process for acquiring knowledge that is able to note and make the analysis of preliminary data and interpretation criteria used through a 3D modeling reconstructive process understandable. The classification schemes and criteria adopted aimed to validate the entire process, giving us the ability to visually assess the proper level of knowledge related to the reconstructive process, with its flaws and lacunae, and to carry out comparative operations on the set of data and information held.

Keywords: Classification scheme · Knowledge system · Architectural heritage · Semantic structure · 3D modeling · Uncertainty visualization

1 Introduction

During the last two decades, a wide series of reconstruction works have been dedicated to the visualization of no longer extant historic artifacts. This field of work dates back as early as 1990, as Paul Reilly first used the term Virtual Archaeology at the 1990 CAA Conference [1, 2]. With his work, he opened the debate on the multi-disciplinary approach to a huge amount of virtual reconstruction projects applied to architecture and archaeology. The virtual reconstruction practices over past years have showed many theoretical problems related to documentation, analysis and interpretations of artifacts [3], mainly because different disciplines have their own methodologies and because, although the theme of transparency in virtual reconstruction is largely discussed, it has rarely been applied [4]. Köller et al. [5], in the resettlement of the general framework of the challenges and opportunities offered by 3D model digital archives related to cultural heritage, recognized the need to make visible the traceability of all additions, subtractions, and changes to 3D models to make understandable the calculation and display of differences between 3D models of the object/artifact.

Within this context, a huge amount of studies have been carried out to define new protocols for processing spatial data (acquisition, manipulation and management) and to offer new opportunities to the reconstruction offered of no longer extant historic objects [6, 7].

In addition to in the context of archeology, virtual reconstruction (considered to be a series of steps that includes the documenting, interpretation, and visualization of "lost"

S. Münster et al. (Eds.): 3D Research Challenges II, LNCS 10025, pp. 173–197, 2016.
DOI: 10.1007/978-3-319-47647-6_9

archaeological contexts), according to some authors, is not yet a very clearly delineated discipline. From a methodological point of view, both in terms of data transparency and the definition of common standards [8, 9], this application has been widely recognized by other scientific communities [10–16], ranging from communications to museum exhibition, from medicine to geographical analysis, from paleontology to legal sciences.

The development achieved by digital technologies, i.e., knowledge/building information systems, real-time rendering of 3D models, multimedia techniques, animations and simulations, has opened new scenarios for reading and interpreting architectural and archaeological heritage, allowing all the information to be made available in a visual and integrated manner [17].

Thanks to ICT and 3D web technologies, it is currently possible to use a 3D model as an interface for localizing and querying data associated with it (pair physical objects/documentary), turning an Information System into a de facto Cognitive one. That is a real 3D system able to provide a uniform framework for scientific display, allowing effective integration and presentation of web-based heterogeneous data and exploration and analysis of large volumes of data with geo-spatial, temporal and semantic characteristics. Within a Cognitive Information System, it becomes evident the need to prepare an exhaustive documentary base, covering the entire process of research and data collection - moreover, characterized by different degrees of uncertainty and irregularity - related to the creation of digital content within the reconstruction. This documentary base can be qualified through a full transparency of analytical methods, surveying techniques and the criteria used.

Therefore, 3D architectural models have become "spatial metaphors", enabling the distribution of pieces of information in time and space [18], to be used as an interface for the localization and retrieval of associated data. To validate the entire 3D modeling reconstruction process and to facilitate the exchange and reuse of information and collaboration between experts in various disciplines, new standards are necessary due to the reusability and accessibility of knowledge of 3D digital models. For a better interpretation of a digital heritage artifact, a comprehensive interpretive method is needed. Because many hypothetical reconstructions are the result of highly complex design decisions [5], we have to focus attention on the cognitive process.

Through the semantic structuring of digital models, it is possible to develop a process of acquiring knowledge that is able to note and make understandable and reusable the analysis of preliminary data and interpretation criteria used to validate the entire process. It gives the ability to visually assess our level of knowledge, with its flaws and lacunae, and to carry out comparative operations on the set of data and information held, allowing the compatibility of the digital model with alternative modes of representation. The digital display allows for the activation of types of surveys previously unthinkable in the fields of archiving and accessing data, spatial analysis, simulation of unbuilt projects, etc.

The process of reconstruction is essentially composed by decisions based on various sets of assumptions that may be obvious to the scientific curator of the reconstruction process but not to public, the final user or those who later could view the final project. This subjectivity, if not correctly reported, compromises the validity of an entire virtual reconstruction. In response to this problem, the "The London Charter" [19] was drafted in 2006 to set principles for visualization methods and their outcomes in heritage contexts and, lately, the Sevilla Principles [20], which have highlighted the need for the formalization of reconstructive processes, lacking, anyway, proposals for a unique and agreed-upon solution. Within this framework, the granularity of data relies on the different types, typologies and characteristics of sources used, which is tightly connected to the proper segmentation adopted for the reconstruction process (i.e., finds, ruins, ancient drawings, literary sources, etc.). It defines, according to the assumptions adopted by evidence, inference or conjecture, the different degrees of certainty and the levels of confidence [21] of the solution adopted or proposed, which can be shown through the visual representation of the certainty.

The purpose of this chapter is to present a methodology framework adopted to define a process of acquiring knowledge that is able to note and make understandable, as well as reusable, the analysis of preliminary data and interpretation criteria used to validate the entire process. It is also meant to give the ability to visually assess the proper level of knowledge related to the reconstructive process, with its flaws and lacunae, and to carry out comparative operations on the set of data and information held, allowing for compatibility of the digital model with alternative techniques of visualization [22].

2 Visualizing Uncertainty in Virtual Reconstruction

Over the last few years, several projects of virtual/digital reconstruction have attempted to solve the connate issue of showing not just the complete interpretational process but also the reliability of its different components, proposing different solutions [23–25] focused mainly on ways of sharing the lack of knowledge with scholars and the public.

At the dawn of the of Virtual Reality era, higher expectations were pinned on the achievement of an appropriate level of photorealism [26], at that time, certainly, one of the objectives more felt and more desired. Roussou and Drettakis [27] focused on the differences between Photo-Realistic and Non-Photo-Realistic rendering - within the archaeological reconstructions field - suggesting that both approaches could greatly aid heritage visualization related to the targeted audience.

The simplest solution, obvious and also most appropriate for allowing a correct and detailed contextualization of reconstructive hypotheses adopted, to assess the degree the uncertainty is that aimed to produce multiple models of the same object, giving the opportunity to allow comparisons between different theories [28] and different versions. The limit of this type of application is related to the opportunities to make them available an adequate number of alternative solutions, and consequently, it requires modeling different and new features from the same documentary sources.

Kensek [21] presents a wide review of the methods used, in many disciplines, to represent uncertainty in reconstructions, which include (a) "coloration" schemes, (b) patterns, hatches, and line types, (c) materials, (d) rendering type, and (e) transparency.

Some of these methods have successfully been applied in the field of architectural and archaeological virtual reconstruction. Kensek [21] and Pang et al. [29] proposed using variations in the thickness of the lines to mark the variations in reliability; meanwhile, Zuk et al. [30] proposed darkening or lightening certain features for the visualization of chronological uncertainty.

Kensek et al. [24] proposed one of the most interesting and articulated solutions, which consists of adding the information related to the lack or uncertainty of knowledge as a new layer using a color map (e.g., red-green scale), mixed opacity, a combination of both those indicators, or using different rendering types, such as wireframe and texture.

Pollini et al. [31] proposed a method for uncertainty charts representing ambiguity in virtual reconstructions. D'Arcangelo and Della Schiava [32] referred to the use of different colors to mark those items whose uncertainty reconstructive invites taking greater caution. Perlinska [33] proposed adopting a 'probability map' with the green-red color scale to describe the certitude regarding each part and introduced a new quality to it, the possibility to import the model into 3D GIS, adding a database which will show the reasoning adopted for modeling each single part.

Stefani et al. [34] used colors to define a temporal correspondence, while other authors [3, 35–39] used it to depict uncertainty. Some authors, however, have followed other paths in an effort to establish a "model validation" process. They proposed making more than one reconstruction hypothesis available to scholars and the public through the use of an interactive solution [40].

In some cases, the validation of the model passes through "gradients of consistency" and is based on documentary sources [36, 41]. In other cases, such sources may be grouped according to "levels" and "classes" [42] or simply according to "typologies" [3].

Hermon et al., on the case study of the Roman Theater of Paphos, based their proposal on fuzzy logic quantitative methods [43] for quantifying reliability in virtual reconstructions. The validation of the model is numerically calculated as an "Index of Reliability" (IR). In their approach, based on the "Level of Existence" (LOE) and on the "Level of Geometrical Reality" (LOGR), the granularity of the 3D model's semantic annotation is object-based and not source-based.

Other case studies show a connection between the archaeological sources and the detail of the 3D model, but only in terms of elements such as the architecture's static aspects [41]. Meanwhile, others focus on an "experimental approach" in which 3D reconstruction modeling is used to verify a hypothesis and results in a cyclical validation process [42, 44].

Demetrescu [45] proposed a typical "archaeological approach," aiming to define a formal language based on existing archaeological standards, and an annotation system with which to document reconstruction processes to link them to both the survey and interpretation procedures within the same framework and to attempt to formalize the steps involved in each reliability evaluation and visualization.

All of these methods and attempts show us, regardless of their proposals and solutions from the theoretical concepts (plausibility, uncertainty, probability, etc.) to which they refer, that the goal of all researchers is to be able to make explicit, or at least intelligible, through a graphical system a synthetic/communicative level representative or the value of the reconstructive process that is behind a particular result.

The result of a reconstructive process acts in the definition of three areas intimately related one each other that concur to define the digital consistency of the artifact object of study (Fig. 1):

- Shape (geometry, size, spatial position)
- Material (physical form, stratification of building/manufacturing systems)
- Appearance (surface features)

Fig. 1. The three areas that concur to define the digital consistency of an artifact's reconstructive process: stone molding

In the digital reconstruction process, two of those areas (appearance and material) are subordinated to that of shape, which along the modeling process (not by-object) constitutes the object of the other two fields that become the attributes.

The assessment (and consequently the explication) of the uncertainty degree of the reconstructive process, although the three areas should be considered jointly and continuously, in the first instance it is mainly based on the evaluation of the reconstructive process adapted to determine the shape of that case study.

The determination of the shape is based on procedures that provide, for the definition of the measure, the geometry and the topology of the elements that are composed or in which an object can be decomposed. This procedure a 'playback' of the design and construction process - is embodied through the definition of a given degree of accuracy, connected, in turn, with the scale to which the process of modeling could be related to.

2.1   The Scale of Representation/Degree of Accuracy

If, in the pre-digital design process, the scale at which a given object/artifact was rebuilt/ designed defined the accuracy obtainable, that duality has failed in the digital age, losing all significance.

In the pre-digital era, in fact, the size of the line (thickness) and the capacity of the human eye to see separately (resolve) two close lines defined the threshold beyond which it was not possible to define the geometry and size of an element. With the advent of digital tools for vector representation/modeling of geometric/mathematical forms, modeling and representation can coexist separated. The former (modeling) defines the shape of an object in 1:1 (related to dimensional accuracy chosen based on the unit's working environment in which it operates); the latter (representation) displays the model with attributes and the desired level of detail.

The form (dimensional and geometric consistency) of a case study becomes the first area where one needs to clarify the level of geometric accuracy of the reconstruction process, and therefore it defines its semantic structure that hinges the same valuation method.

Therefore, the resulting uncertainty validation of the reconstructed model is based on different levels of interpretation of source data, characterized by a progressively increasing level of uncertainty of the geometrical definition (accuracy) of constitutive elements making up the artifact.

This process can be developed according to the following operational pipeline (Figs. 2 and 3):

1. collection of documentary sources
2. semantic structuring of the artifact
3. analysis of documentary sources and extrapolation of information on the consistency of the artifact (geometrical shape, surface appearance, physical characteristics)

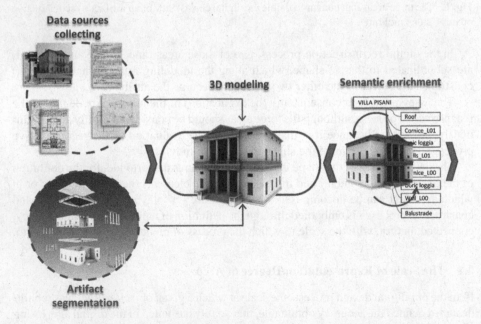

Fig. 2. The operational pipeline of reconstructive process

through a process of analysis/interpretation (induction/deduction/analogy)/decision assumed to extract the data based on the evidence, the relationship between information, deduction or conjecture

4. correlation between data used in the process of reconstruction and the level of uncertainty that characterizes each constitutive element
5. reconstructive modeling 3D
6. semantic enrichment of 3D reconstructed model
7. validation of the reconstructive hypothesis obtained through the data enrichment of each constitutive element and its displaying.

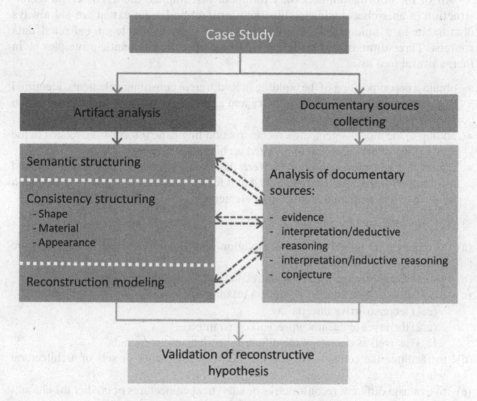

Fig. 3. Diagram of validation of reconstructive process

In the following sections, we analyze methods that allow for the semantic structuring of an artifact, the criteria for determining the different uncertainty degree that characterizes the process of reconstruction of a particular item, and the methods to make clear (visible and understandable) the degree of uncertainty that characterizes/qualifies/validates the obtained reconstructive model.

2.2 3D Modeling Semantic Structure

The use of a semantic structure in digital modeling is a useful technique for making clear the relationship between the archaeological/architectural object and the documentation sources (drawings, text and more). It can be usefully used to reconstruct the hypothetical model, for identifying the characters, limitations and inconsistencies of those sources, for displaying the reconstructive conjectures adopted and not documented in the same documentation, and the reconstructive solutions more likely, giving back self-representation to the same instrument.

All of the information necessary to model or complete the hypothetical reconstruction of an archaeological/architectural artifact no longer extant are not always obtainable in a unique and unambiguous way from available or collected data sources. Three-dimensional modeling based on structured semantic principles is, in fact, a useful tool to:

- obtain a decomposition of the building in its different constituent elements, identified through the analysis of their geometry and aggregation between them according to precise compositional/logic rules
- adding to the model's geometric reconstruction linguistic information, related to the recognition of the signs and of a shared architectural language
- identifying a further connection between the three-dimensional model rendered and information stored in a database linked to it for the purposes of a full documentation relating to that particular architectural element.

The semantic structure allows us:

(a) to manage 3D models in multi-resolution and divide them into subsets that are hierarchically consistent
(b) to efficiently manage the metadata related to the models themselves
(c) the ability to view and represent data relating to
    (c.1) reconstructive uncertainty
    (c.2) the level of accuracy/precision guaranteed,
    (c.3) as well as control of the different versions of the models
(d) to facilitate the comparative analysis between the parties or sets of architectural works
(e) to evaluate different reconstructive or analytical conjectures or predict the chronological development of a building over its life [46].

The methodology used to structure the 3D models began, along with topological information, with the concept of a structured 3D information system using semantics that follows the 'shape grammar' for architectural elements, as introduced by Stiny and Mitchell [47] and Stiny [48], and the classification method is based on the criteria of Tzonis and Oorschot [49]. According to Quintrand et al. [50], the artifact has to be seen as a system of knowledge, an association of semantics and shape, where the model is extracted from its description, while its representation is defined according to the objectives of the analysis. De Luca et al. [51] have subsequently developed an application that allows comparative studies starting from heterogeneous data and models using a simple and intuitive web-based interface. In this case, the multiple representations of buildings and their associated information have been organized around semantic models. Ullrich et al. [52] defined two types of approaches for describing the shape of 3D objects: descriptions following the composition of a primitive approach and descriptions based on procedural shape representations. This semantic 3D modeling methodology has been largely applied in different fields (archaeological [53] and architectural [54]) as well as on different types of artifacts, from a typological point of view (size, geometry, surface and textural properties, and semantics) and ranging from simple decorative apparatus to entire buildings, showing the opportunities and the advantages it makes available [55].

The construction rules do not determine the appearance; they define the assemblage of physical objects in 3D space. The adopted method refers to the hypothetical appearances of Shape (geometry, size) Appearance (surface features) and Material (physical form, stratification of building systems) of the case study. Therefore, not only the schema but also the constructive rules can be identified, highlighted and discussed, and it addresses a wider gamma of objects that range from a simple vase or bas-relief to an entire building, and not only architectural objects.

The semantic organization of a 3D digital model of an artifact can be defined, taking into account the definition/identification of the nodes that make up the single element, the identification of the origin of geometric elements and construction of the relationship between the elements identified and their groupings into macro-groups. The artifact is then decomposed by a morphological, design and constructive point of view, defining elements organized on several levels.

The number of typological/morphological/elementary units depends on the criteria followed in the distinction of the minimum units and their subsequent combination. This combination can be defined according to the change of material, the recognition of type elements, morphologically homogeneous (for a building, e.g., frames, windows, moldings, capitals, etc.), whose boundaries are defined by geometric transitions in the presence of the same element on different levels of the building.

The method requirements consist of the following steps:

- encoding the finds;
- identifying the number of elements corresponding to the definition of each individual part;
- verifying the element and class of item naming;
- defining volumes underlying 3D modeled surfaces.

From this, derive two different levels of interpretation and structural formulation for the final archaeological/architectural artifacts:

- a first level made up of individual elements derived from pure geometric primitives and built up using unambiguous logic
- a second level referring to the construction of complex parts, e.g., an architectural whole (a cornice, window, basement, internal and external volumes, etc.). The transposition of these levels of interpretation was implemented by defining a structure based on individual components using an acyclic graph (Figs. 4 and 5).

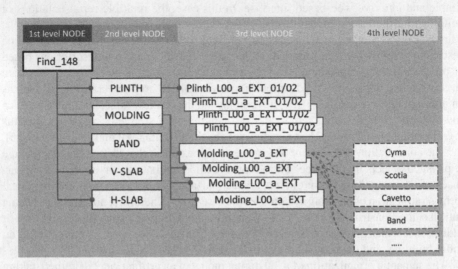

Fig. 4. Semantic structure criteria of 3D model of an archaeological artifact (Pompeii: Find_148).

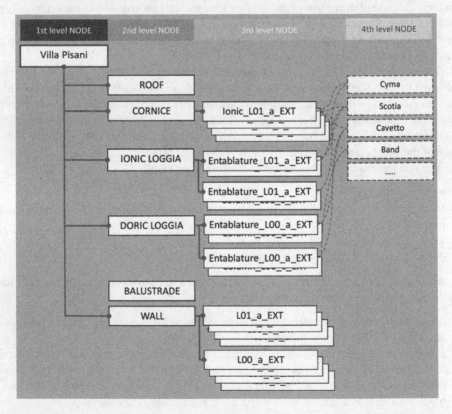

Fig. 5. Semantic structure criteria of 3D model of an architectural building (A. Palladio, Villa Pisani)

2.2.1 3D Model Encoding Method

Organized according to taxonomic criteria, the result of the semantic segmentation procedure is expressed in the combination of the different sub-elements, declined according to the building/artifact system that characterizes the case study and according to the styles referring to the different epochs that give rise to the shape of the graph characterizing each artifact (Fig. 4, bottom).

To organize the information and linkage coming from this semantic structure, it is necessary to adopt systems, processes, and encoding rules based on a structured set of names and descriptions in a consistent manner [56, 57] (Fig. 6).

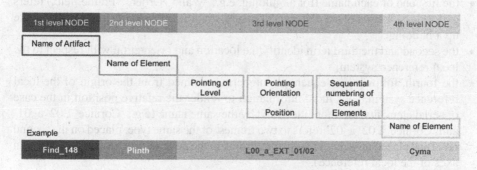

Fig. 6. Encoding criteria of element item

A key point in this procedure is the operation code/label uniquely assigned to each 'element,' which derives from the definition of the criteria and segmentation rules and that, in turn, must take into account the following factors:

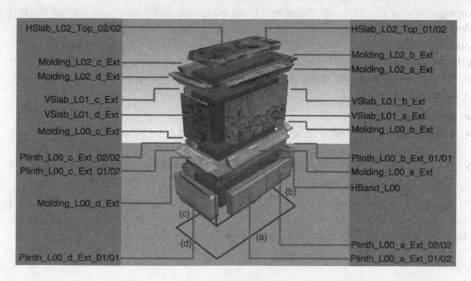

Fig. 7. Encoding and semantic structure of 3D model of an archaeological artifact (Pompeii: Find_148)

- recognition of the shape/geometry of each 'element,' corresponding to a certain level of detail and a certain manufacturing or architectural component;
- identification of the location of each 'element' with respect to a reference system relative to the single artifact (level/altitude, interior/exterior, side/orientation);
- distinction through a progressive number of 'elements' repeated and/or in series that are of the same type and will identify the reference position and orientation (Fig. 7).

The criteria used to define the name/code of a single item and the corresponding morphological/architectural unit are:

- the first end of each name (for a building, e.g., 'Wall,' 'Order,' 'Frame,' etc.) refers to the classification of the elements of nature, architectural or construction that make up a building;
- the second and the third term identify the location and orientation with respect to the local reference system;
- the fourth, following a sequential numbering, defined from the origin of the local reference system, adds more information to render the relative position in the case of serial elements, therefore identified by the same name (e.g., 'Cornice_L02_a_01' and 'Cornice_L02_a_02' refers to two frames, of the same type, placed on the second level and placed in ascending order according to the positive direction of the Cartesian axes of the local reference).

The name of each item and the corresponding typological/morphological unit are defined following the Art & Architecture Thesaurus of the Getty Foundation [58], which defines a glossary of terms related to art and architecture. The name of each item that belongs to an architectural structure corresponds to a portion of the geometry of the 3D model; the tree-shaped structure of the node report defines the various sub-elements in which the workpiece and its constituent elements are divided. Defined univocally and recalled within the entity of the article (root node) are the typological/morphological determined entities (node family), which consist, in turn, of the individual elements (leaf nodes). The number of typological/morphological and elementary units depends on the criteria used to distinguish the minimum units and their subsequent combination. In particular, the elementary units can be distinguished according to the contact surfaces, which correspond to:

- a material change;
- recognition of element type/morphologically uniform (e.g., window frames, moldings, capitals, etc.), whose boundaries are defined by geometric transitions;
- the presence of the element on different levels of the article (defines the placement and alignment of the single element with respect to the reference system).

Encoding methods have been applied in previous experiences, carried out in different fields (archaeological [59] and architectural [54]), providing opportunities to go beyond the required fragmentation and reconstructing the entire knowledge.

3   Criteria for the Definition of Uncertainty

Investigating the evolution of patrimonial architecture or designing a hypothetical reconstruction of a no longer extant artifact requires gathering and often analyzing a wide amount of documentary sources, the interpretation of which may support researchers in proposing a digital model or a morphological evolution of edifices. To qualify and authenticate products of scientific research within the field of documentation and the study of architecture, and aiming at improving the comprehension of the complex and discontinuous process of knowledge acquisition [60] and derived conjecture, it is necessary that the 3D geometric models relating to archaeological/architectural heritage be demonstrative of the solutions adopted to meet the uncertainties and the lack of information.

Many of these 3D models are, in fact, reconstructions of buildings just designed or no longer existing nor fully documented; therefore, it is inevitable that such reconstructions contain a small or large amount of hypothetical elements, characterized by their specific degree of uncertainty.

This is due to a number of clear factors: the need to make up for the missing parts in today's structure, the need to implement a hypothesis in the reconstruction of a 2D drawing in a spatial shape, the temporalization of the various layers to decide an original state or, most simply, the different conformations in time.

In the field of architectural/archaeological heritage, we very often are faced with the combination of 3D physical objects and 2D and textual documentary sources in which both elements are subject to uncertainties and inaccuracies. The three-dimensional nature of the object itself has led, however, to seeking to exploit its same representation for displaying information related to it, as well as the development of visualization techniques able to make manifest the latent uncertainties.

Zuk et al. presented an application that enables integrating and visualizing the temporal uncertainty for multiple 3D archaeological data sets with different dating. They introduced a temporal time window for dealing with the uncertainty and review various visual cues appropriate for revealing the uncertainty within the time window. The interactive animation of the time window allows a unique exploration of the temporal uncertainty [61]. De Luca et al. described a methodological approach to make existing iconographic corpus usable for the analysis and the 3D management of building transformations. The aim was to establish a relation between the iconography used for the hypothetical reconstruction and the 3D representation that depends on it [62]. In a recent paper, De Luca and Lo Buglio addressed the issue of the review of the methodological aspects concerning the collection of information that describes an architectural object [63], offering an approach to the creation of representation systems that articulate the digital instance with the geometric/semantic model.

Recent work of other researchers included within the series of experiences carried out regarding 3D modeling reconstructive process [22] provides some significant innovations with regard to:

- analysis of different types of sources and the related degree of certainty of deducted data [64];

- the use of a semantic construction of the digital model, not only as a means to look for a building or such a cognitive system (Fig. 8).

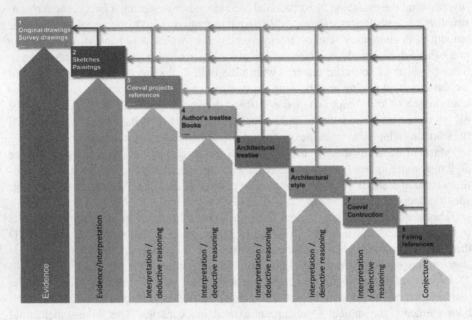

Fig. 8. The diagram of relationship between different level of uncertainty

The reconstruction process from a given set of documentary sources requires a construction pipeline the analytical type, based on a semantic system, because all of the information necessary for completing the model is not always obtainable in a unique and unambiguous way from data sources or by drawings that we have at our disposal.

Therefore, it is necessary to define a series of preparatory and operational phases, complementary between them, to investigate the sources and integrative design references that are able to provide useful information to model the project, even for those parts not explicitly or comprehensively documented, related to:

- architectural/structural elements, archaeological evidence;
- size/geometry;
- stylistic/formal;
- temporal correspondence;
- building materials.

Such types of information may be conveyed using different technologies of visualization, defining a modeling structured procedure based on different levels of interpretation, characterized by a progressively increasing ordinal scale of uncertainty. This scale ranges in the interval from 0 to 1, where 0 (zero) uncertainty means a modeled element is totally certain and 1 (one) means it is absolutely uncertain (Table 1):

Table 1. Uncertainty gradient color code

Color code (R,G,B)	Uncertainty value
255,0,255	r.c. based on archaeological/architectural evidence (reality-based data; stratigraphic record, etc.)
	r.c. based on original drawings
0,180,255	r.c. based on design data related to stylistic similarities
0,255,210	r.c. on treaties, books, ecc. written by the author
0,255,60	r.c. based on reference to treaties books, journals, ecc.
235,255,0	r.c. based on reference to a specific architectural style and/or historical period
255,195,0	r.c. based on reference to coeval building systems
	reconstructive conjectures failing references.

1. reconstruction based on archaeological/architectural evidence (reality-based data; stratigraphic record);
2. reconstruction based on original drawings (survey/projects/scratches and therefore affected by a low level of dimensional accuracy, etc.)
3. reconstruction based on design data related to stylistic/coeval similarities (e.g., coverage, type of roof, gutter frame, frames, roof, basement, or the openings and decorative system);
4. reference to treaties, books, journals, articles or architectural guidelines written by the author (architect/artist) of the artifact studied;
5. reference to treaties, books, journals, articles or the manual that the author (if known) has or could have used as his own reference (e.g., measurements of the rooms, stair design, detail design and equipment, the architectural orders, if any, as well as for the definition of the height of the internal doors or types and sets the height of the time);

6. interpretative hypotheses related to a specific architectural style and/or historical period;
7. interpretative hypotheses more thrusts, referring to coeval construction systems at that time to achieve solutions constructively plausible and compatible with the project, by which, however, is not always possible to reach conjecture or univocal solutions;
8. reconstructive conjectures failing references.

Each of these categories is defined by the degree of accuracy of data geometric, dimensional, formal, material and construction (v. infra paragraph 2) that can be derived, infer or assume from the documentary source available for that particular element of case study.

The first category refers to the hypothetical reconstruction based on evidence derived from the architectural or archaeological artifacts or real items. The level of accuracy of real based data, therefore, is determined only by the intrinsic accuracy of the instrument or by the surveying and measuring technology used to detect the object.

The last category refers to the conjectural hypothetical reconstruction, made, due to the lack of any documentary source or references, by using the "common/scientific sense" of the researchers, based on their accumulated knowledge or, when also necessary, to their imagination.

Beyond the analysis specifically conducted (ex-post), digital systems allow, in fact, the collection and systematization (ex-ante) of operations to determine the geometry of the elements that contribute to the definition of an architectural work, becoming in fact themselves explanatory values of the geometric-formal genesis of that edifice. The possibility, in fact, to examine the collection of data containing large amounts of records, such as geometric analysis and semantic characterizations of artifacts, offer new approaches to the classification and the comparison.

4   Uncertainty Visualization Through a Density Slicing Color

Among all methods adopted and proposed for representing probability, ambiguity, reliability or uncertainty in 3D reconstructions, the use of color is undoubtedly the most efficient method and unambiguous because it allows for understanding in a clear manner and according to widely shared semantic codes, the degree of uncertainty surrounding the hypothetical reconstruction of each element of an artifact.

The use of a color scale seems to be almost frequent [21] within disciplines that utilize the virtual reconstruction as an investigative tool. False-color images, in fact, even sacrificing natural color rendition (in contrast to a true-color image) have long been used to ease the detection of features that are not readily discernible otherwise (e.g., the use of near infrared for the detection of vegetation in satellite images, remote sensing satellites, space telescopes or space probes, or even weather satellites that produce grayscale images from the visible or infrared spectrum). Therefore, the use of colors in 3D visualization could be considered as a symbology able to allow the traceability of uncertainty that characterizes each element based on a subjective but controlled understanding and interpretation of data objects [65]. As seen before in many other disciplines, color visualization schemes are extremely useful for increasing the information content of certain images. Encoded colors, overlaying additional information, can make some details more visible or ease the detection of features that are not readily discernible otherwise, providing an easy way to visualize the magnitude of some values in relation to each other.

False color and its variants, such as pseudo color, density slicing, and choropleths, refer to a group of color-rendering methods used for representing varying values using a sequence of colors and/or information visualization of either data gathered by a single grayscale channel or data not depicting parts of the electromagnetic spectrum (e.g., elevation in relief maps or tissue types in magnetic resonance imaging). While pseudo color are typically used when a single channel of data is available (e.g., temperature, elevation, soil composition, tissue type, and so on), false color is commonly used to display three channels of data using solely the visual spectrum (e.g., to accentuate color differences), and typically some or all data used is from electromagnetic radiation outside the visual spectrum (e.g., infrared, ultraviolet or X-ray) (Figs. 9 and 10).

Fig. 9. Reconstructive hypothesis of Palladio 'Project for a twin' [22]: Photo-Realistic rendering

False color used for satellite and space images, space telescopes or space probes, and weather satellites analysis/reports, cartography, GIS, engineering metrology, medicine, thermography etc. provides a mature reference framework to define a proper methodology of color mapping to visually represent uncertainty levels, especially using a perceptually ordered ordinal sequence of density-slicing color. Within those disciplines, to map quantitative data, a specific color progression is used to depict the data properly. There are several different types of color progressions used by cartographers [66]. One

Fig. 10. Reconstructive hypothesis of Palladio 'Project for a twin' [22]: displaying uncertainty of reconstructive hypothetical model and related documentary sources.

of these methods is density slicing, which divides the values of associated data into a few colored bands. In the analysis of remote sensing images [67], the range of grayscale levels of an image is divided into certain intervals, with each interval assigned to one of a few discrete colors [68].

The usability of a density slicing - as well as of other color progressions - is granted by the principles of human visual perception. Acc[70]; while there are millions of color variations, the human eye is limited in how many colors it can easily distinguish. Therefore, a full spectral progression, containing a hue from blue through red, sliced in eight categories, seems to be the most suitable method to represent uncertainty of a hypothetical reconstructive process [71]. Furthermore, the spectral progression can be combined with a partial spectral hue progression to map mixtures of two distinct sets of data or to show the sub-range of values of some sub-categories, i.e., using a blend of two adjacent opponent hues and showing the magnitude of the mixed data classes. A spectral hue progression based on an ordinal color-graded sequence is able to allow the visual perception of the ordering of values, in which the darkest hue represents the greatest number (highest value of certainty) in the data set and the lightest shade represents the least number (lowest value of certainty, which means the highest value of uncertainty) (Fig. 11).

Fig. 11. Reconstructive hypothesis of Palladio 'Project for a twin' [22]: Corinthian order, uncertainty level of reconstructive hypothesis and related data sources

The ordinal scale of uncertainty presented in Sect. 4 can be displayed using a density-slicing color code, which divides the rendering objects into a few color bands, corresponding to each level of interpretation/uncertainty: each degree of uncertainty is, therefore, identified by a corresponding RGB-HSV color space (Table 1).

Each unit element of the reconstructed model is therefore identified by its corresponding degree of uncertainty, which will be used to visually assess the proper level of knowledge related to the reconstructive process.

In addition to the visualization of the uncertainty degree related to the hypothetical reconstructive process, using this ordinal density-slicing color scale, it is necessary to systematize geometric-formal information relating to a building with those relating to the data available that have allowed the formulation of a reconstructive hypothesis. As we have seen, it is necessary to take into account uncertain and heterogeneous information that is able to consider the evolution of our knowledge, producing 2D/3D dynamic graphics and adapting our practices to the specific realities of the heritage field where uncertainty should forbid graphic assertions, highlighting what is unknown rather than hiding it.

Studying and displaying the evolution of an artifact (or ensemble of artifacts) or a hypothetical reconstruction related to a certain age requires the introduction of temporal and additional documentary dimensions.

A temporal dimension allows distributing pieces of information in space and in time, in a certain position, at that time of the study, at that moment of the history.

A documentary dimension allows displaying or making understandable and evaluable the methodology used in analyzing the architectural evolutions of that artifact, based on interpretation and comparison of different and heterogeneous types of documentation.

3D model representation, as a metaphor of a cognitive system related to architectural corpus, does not show us the 'real' object but instead how we understand it: different pieces of documentation in relation to architectural elements could become a browsing tool, allowing for mediating between the information to be handled and users able to investigate sets of data or information element-by-element.

Behind this process, there is a cognitive graph as a visual metaphor of the case study, which aims to restore the hierarchical structure that governs the geometric definition of the 3D model and gives access to documents about that studied artifact.

Through this structure, exploiting the semantic graphic code, representation is able to:

- underline inconsistency in the documentation or its analysis;
- indicate the level of incompleteness concerning the investigation;
- provide an updated visualization of our knowledge on an object (Fig. 12).

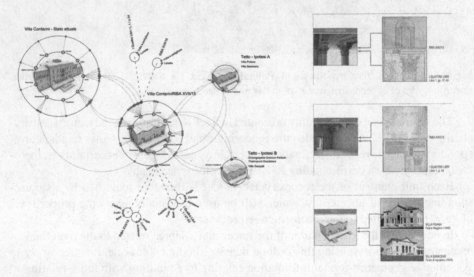

Fig. 12. Reconstructive hypothesis of Palladio 'Project for a twin' [22]: Cognitive graph and related documentary sources of reconstructive hypothesis

5   Conclusion

The proposal of a methodology framework adopted to define a process of acquiring knowledge is able to note and make understandable, as well as reusable, the analysis of preliminary data and interpretation criteria used to validate the entire process. This framework gives us the ability to visually assess the proper level of knowledge related to the hypothetical reconstructive process, with its flaws and lacunae, and to carry out comparative operations on the set of data and information held, allowing for compatibility of the 3D digital model with alternative techniques of visualization. Further more, it introduces new and meaningful innovations to the archaeological/architectural interpretation methods and techniques of representation.

The proposal framework is based on the critical analysis and interpretation of documentary source data that are able to express the intrinsic value of each modeling reconstructive process. Each different type of source (physical, textual and/or graphical) is characterized by its own specific grade of information granularity that can be transformed into a hypothetical 3D model with its own level of detail. The geometrical definition of each constitutive elementary unit is, therefore, not dependent on the level of detail of the source data (e.g., scale of representation of 2D drawing) but by the type of information that has to be induced, deduced or interpreted.

The classification scheme represents a truly interpretative work that is obtained from the simplification operation and is inherent to the schemata embedded in the concept of 'model.' This simplification allows for visualization by an interpretative code of the uncertainty level of the reconstructive hypothesis. The solution, that has just been applied in many case studies, should be addressed and tested over a wider range, covering different types of source data and different types of artifacts (age, styles and constructive technologies) to validate or eventually improve the proposed method. In this context, further significant developments can be achieved using BIM (Building Information Modeling). This platform, in fact, constitutes a powerful information parametric modeling system [39], able to allow procedural-relational methods (tree of history), variational methods (constraints/degrees of freedom), associative methods and generative techniques.

Acknowledgments. I want to express my thanks to Marco Gaiani for his long last and profitable 3D digital reconstruction carried out on the work of Palladio, to Guido Beltramini for the valuable assignment of Palladio's 'Project for a twin' to villa Contarini and to Giacomo Fabbi for the digital reconstruction of 'Project for a twin' after the drawing stored up at RIBA, London.

References

1. Reilly, P.: Towards a virtual archaeology. In: Proceedings of Computer Applications in Archaeology, pp. 133–139 (1990)
2. Miller, P., Richards, J.: The good, the bad and the downright misleading: archaeological adoption of computer visualization. In: Hugget, J., Ryan, N. (eds.) CAA 1994 Proceedings of the 22nd CAA Conference, Glasgow, vol. 60. Tempus Reparatum BAR International Series, Oxford (1994)
3. Dell'Unto, N., Leander, A.M., Ferdani, D., Dellepiane, M., Callieri, M., Lindgren, S.: Digital reconstruction and visualization in archaeology: case-study drawn from the work of the Swedish Pompeii Project. In: 2013 Digital Heritage International Congress, pp. 621–628. IEEE, Marseille (2013)
4. Hermon, S., Sugimoto, G., Mara, H.: The London charter and its applicability. In: Future Technologies to Empower Heritage Professionals: VAST 2007, pp. 11–14. Eurographics Association, Geneva (2007)

5. Kőller, D., Frischer, B., Humphreys, G.: Research challenges for digital archives of 3D cultural heritage models. ACM J. Comput. Cultural Herit. **2**(3), Article 7 (2009)
6. Münster, S.: Workflows and the role of images for virtual 3D reconstruction of no longer extant historic objects. ISPRS Ann. Photogrammetry, Remote Sens. Spat. Inf. Sci. ISPRS II-5/W1, pp. 197–202 (2013)
7. Grellert, M., Pfarr-Harfst, M.: 25 Years of virtual reconstructions project report of department information and communication technology in architecture at Technische Universität Darmstadt. In: Proceedings of the 18th International Conference on Cultural Heritage and New Technologies 2013 (CHNT 18, 2013). Wien (2014)
8. Beacham, R., Denard, H., Niccolucci, F.: An introduction to the London Charter. In: Proceeding of Joint Event CIPA/VAST/EG/EuroMed (2006)
9. Denard, H.: A new introduction to the London charter. In: Paradata and Transparency in Virtual Heritage Digital Research in the Arts and Humanities Series, pp. 57–71. Ashgate (2012)
10. Ryan, N.: Documenting and validating virtual archaeology. In: Archeologia e Calcolatori, XII, pp. 245–273 (2001)
11. Ryan, N.S., Frischer, B., Niccolucci, F., Barceló, J.A.: From CVR to CVRO: the past, present, and future of cultural virtual reality. In: Virtual Archaeology: Proceedings of the VAST Euroconference, Arezzo 24–25 November 2000, pp. 7–18 (2002)
12. Hermon, S.: Reasoning in 3D: a critical appraisal of the role of 3D modelling and virtual reconstructions in archaeology. In: Beyond Illustration: 2D and 3D Digital Technologies as Tools for Discovery in Archaeology, pp. 36–45 (2008)
13. Hermon, S., Nikodem, J.: 3D modeling as a scientific research tool in archaeology. In: International Conference on Computer Applications and Quantitative Methods in Archaeology (CAA) (2007)
14. Hermon, S., Niccolucci, F., D'Andrea, A.: Some evaluations on the potential impact of virtual reality on the archaeological scientific research. In: Proceedings of the VSMM 2005, Ghent, Belgium, pp. 105–114 (2005)
15. Cerato, I., Pescarin, S.: Reconstructing past landscapes for virtual museums. In: Corsi, C., Slapšak, B., Vermeulen, F. (eds.) Good Practice in Archaeological Diagnostics. Non-invasive Survey of Complex Archaeological Sites, pp. 285–296. Springer, Heidelberg (2013)
16. Sifniotis, M.: Representing archaeological uncertainty in cultural informatics. Ph.D. thesis, University of Sussex, July 2012
17. Kuroczyński, P., Hauck, O.B., Dworak, D.: Digital reconstruction of cultural heritage – questions of documentation and visualisation standards for 3D content. In: Klein, R., Santos, P. (eds.) EUROGRAPHICS Workshops on Graphics and Cultural Heritage (2014)
18. Blaise, J.-Y., Dudek, I.: Visual tools decipher historic artefacts documentation. In: Journal of Universal Computer Science. 7th International Conference on Knowledge Management, pp. 456–463. Know-Center (2007)
19. www.londoncharter.org. Accessed 27 July 2016
20. www.arqueologiavirtual.com/carta/. Accessed 27 July 2016
21. Kensek, A.: Survey of methods for showing missing data, multiple alternatives, and uncertainty in reconstructions. In: CSA Newsletter, vol. XIX, no. 3. Winter (2007)
22. Apollonio, F.I., Beltramini, G., Fabbi, G., Gaiani, M.: Villa Contarini a Piazzola sul Brenta: studi per un'ipotesi di attribuzione palladiana servendosi di modelli tridimensionali. Disegnare Idee Immagini, vol. 42, pp. 42–55 (2011)
23. Strothotte, T., Masuch, M., Isenberg, T.: Visualizing knowledge about virtual reconstructions of ancient architecture. In: Proceedings of Computer Graphics International, pp. 36–43 (1999)

24. Kensek, K.M., Dodd, L.S., Cipolla, N.: Fantastic reconstructions or reconstructions of the fantastic? Tracking and presenting ambiguity, alternatives, and documentation in virtual worlds. Autom. Constr. **13**(2), 175–186 (2004)
25. Pollini, J., Dodd, L.S., Kensek, K.M.: Problematics of making ambiguity explicit in virtual reconstructions: a case study of the Mausoleum of Augustus (2006). http://www.chart.ac.uk/chart2005/papers/pollini.html
26. Roberts, J.C., Ryan, N.: Alternative archaeological representations within virtual worlds. In: Bowden, R. (ed.) Proceedings of the 4th UK Virtual Reality Specialist Interest Group Conference Brunel University, Uxbridge, Middlesex, pp. 179–188 (1997)
27. Roussou, M., Drettakis, G.: Photorealism and non-photorealism in virtual heritage representation. In: Proceedings of VAST International Symposium on Virtual Reality, Archaeology and Cultural Heritage (2003)
28. Cargill, R.R.: The Qumran digital model. An argument for archaeological reconstruction in virtual reality. Near East. Archaeol. **72**(1), 28–41 (2003). http://www-sop.inria.fr/reves/publications/data/2003/RD03c. Accessed 27 July 2016
29. Pang, A.T., Wittenbrink, C.M., Lodha, S.K.: Approaches to uncertainty visualization. Vis. Comput. **13**(8), 370–390 (1997)
30. Zuk, T., Carpendale, S., Glanzman, W.D.: Visualizing temporal uncertainty in 3D virtual reconstructions. In: Proceedings of the 6th International Conference on Virtual Reality, Archaeology and Intelligent Cultural Heritage, VAST 2005, pp. 99–106. Eurographics Association, Aire-la-Ville (2005)
31. Pollini, J., Dodd, L.S., Kensek, K., Cipolla, N.: Problematics of making ambiguity explicit in virtual reconstructions: a case study of the Mausoleum of Augustus. In: Theory and Practice, Proceedings of the 21st Annual Conference of CHArt: Computers and the History of Art. British Academy, London (2005)
32. D'Arcangelo, M., Della Schiava, F.: Dall'antiquaria umanistica alla modellazione 3D: una proposta di lavoro tra testo e immagine. Camenae **10**, 23 (2012)
33. Perlinska, M.: Palette of possibilities. Lund University, Department of Archaeology and Ancient History, Ph.D. thesis (2014)
34. Stefani, C., Busayarat, C., Renaudin, N., De Luca, L., Véron, P., Florenzano, M.: Une approche de modélisation basée sur l'iconographie pour l'analyse spatio-temporelle du patrimoine architectural. In: Colloque Arch-I-Tech, November 17–19. Ausonius, France (2010)
35. Bakker, G., Meulenberg, F., Rode, J.D.: Truth and credibility as a double ambition: reconstruction of the built past, experiences and dilemmas. J. Vis. Comput. Anim. **14**(3), 159–167 (2003)
36. Borra, D.: Sulla verità del modello 3D. un metodo per comunicare la validità dell'anastilosi virtuale. In: Proceeding of eArcom 04 tecnologie per comunicare l'architettura, pp. 132–137. Ancona: CLUA edizioni (2004)
37. Borghini, S., Carlani, R.: La restituzione virtuale dell'architettura antica come strumento di ricerca e comunicazione dei beni culturali: ricerca estetica e gestione delle fonti. Disegnarecon **4**(8), 71–79 (2011)
38. Apollonio, F.I., Gaiani, M., Zheng, S.: Characterization of uncertainty and approximation in digital reconstruction of CH artifacts. In: Le vie dei Mercanti. XI Forum Internazionale di Studi, pp. 860–869. La scuola di Pitagora editrice, Napoli (2013)
39. Apollonio, F.I., Gaiani, M., Zheng, S.: 3D modeling and data enrichment in digital reconstruction of Architectural Heritage. In: XXIV International CIPA Symposium, ISPRS XL-5/W2, pp. 43–48. ISPRS, Strasbourg (2013)

40. Bonde, S., Maines, C., Mylonas, E., Flanders, J.: The virtual monastery: representing time, human movement, and uncertainty at Saint-Jean-des-Vignes, Soissons. Vis. Resour. **25**(4), 363–377 (2009)
41. Vico Lopez, M.D.: La "Restauración Virtual" según la interpretación arquitectonico constructiva: metodologia y aplicación al caso de la Villa de Livia. Ph.D. thesis, p. 117 (2012)
42. Viscogliosi, A.: L'uso delle ricostruzioni virtuali tridimensionali nella storia dell'architettura: immaginare la Domus Aurea. J. Roman Archaeol. **61**, 207–219 (2006). Supplementary series
43. Georgiou, R., Hermon, S.: A London Charter's visualization: the ancient hellenistic-roman theatre in Paphos. In: VAST: International Symposium on Virtual Reality, Archaeology and Intelligent Cultural Heritage-Short and Project Papers, pp. 53–56 (2011)
44. Lulof, P., Opgenhaffen, L., Sepers, M.: The art of reconstruction documenting the process of 3D modeling: some preliminary results. In: Proceedings of International Conference on Digital Heritage, pp. 333–336 (2013)
45. Demetrescu, E.: Archaeological Stratigraphy as a formal language for virtual reconstruction. Theory and practice. J. Archaeol. Sci. **57**, 42–55 (2015)
46. Stefani, C., De Luca, L., Véron, P., Florenzano, M.: Modeling building historical evolutions. In: Proceedings of Focus K3D Conference on Semantic 3D Media and Content. INRIA, Sophia Antipolis (2010)
47. Stiny, G., Mitchell, W.J.: The Palladian grammar. Environ. Plann. B **5**, 5–18 (1978)
48. Stiny, G.: Introduction to shape and shape grammars. Environ. Plann. B **7**, 343–351 (1980)
49. Tzonis, A., Oorschot, L.: Frames, Plans, Representation Concept dicta at Inleiding Programmatische en Functionele Analyse. Technical report, Delft, University of Technology (1987)
50. Quintrand, P., Autran, J., Florenzano, M., Fregier, M., Zoller, J.: La CAO en Architecture. Hermes, Paris (1985)
51. De Luca, L., Florenzano, M., Veron, P.: A generic formalism for the semantic modeling and representation of architectural elements. Vis. Comput. **23**, 181–205 (2007)
52. Ullrich, T., Settgast, V., Fellner, D.W.: Semantic fitting and reconstruction. ACM J. Comput. Cult. Herit. **1**(2), 1–20 (2008)
53. Apollonio, F.I., Gaiani, M., Benedetti, B.: 3D reality-based artefact models for the management of archaeological sites using 3D GIS: a framework starting from the case study of the Pompeii Archaeological area. J. Archaeol. Sci. **39**, 1271–1287 (2012)
54. Apollonio, F.I., Gaiani, M., Corsi, C.: A semantic and parametric method for 3D models used in 3D cognitive-information system. In: Schmitt, G., Hoverstadt, L., Van Gool, L., Bosché, F., Burkhard, R., Coleman, S., Halatsch, J., Hansmeyer, M., Konsorski-Lang, S., Kunze, A., Sehmi-Luck, M. (eds.) Future Cities, 28th eCAADe 2010 Conference, pp. 717–726. ECAADE – ETH Zurich, Zurich (2010)
55. Apollonio, F.I.: Architettura in 3D. Modelli digitali per i sistemi cognitivi, Bruno Mondadori, Milano (2012)
56. Lambe, P.: Organising Knowledge. Taxonomies Knowledge and Organisational Effectiveness. Chandos Publishing, Oxford (2007)
57. Malafsky, G.P., Newman, B.D.: Organizing Knowledge with Ontologies and Taxonomies. TechI LLC, Fairfax (2009)
58. http://www.getty.edu/research/tools/vocabularies/aat/. Accessed 26 July 2016
59. Apollonio, F.I., Benedetti, B., Gaiani, M., Baldissini, S.: Construction, management and visualization of 3D models of large archeological and architectural sites for e-Heritage GIS systems. In: Pavelka, K. (ed.) XXIIIrd International CIPA Symposium Proceedings, Czech Technical University in Prague, pp. B.2.97–B.2.104 (2011)

60. Pfarr, M.: Dokumentationsystem für Digitale Rekonstruktionen am Beisèiel der Grabanlage Zhaoling, Provinz Shaanxi. Technische Universitat Darmastadt, China (2010)

61. Zuk, T., et al.: Visualizing temporal uncertainty in 3D virtual reconstructions. In: Mudge, M., Ryan, N., Scopigno, R. (eds.) VAST 2005, The 6th International Symposium on Virtual Reality, Archaeology and Intelligent Cultural Heritage, pp. 99–106. ISTI-CNR, Pisa (2005)

62. De Luca, L., Busarayat, C., Stefani, C., Renaudin, N., Florenzano, M., Véron, P.: An iconography-based modeling approach for the spatio-temporal analysis of architectural heritage. In: Proceedings of the 2010 Shape Modeling International Conference (SMI 2010), pp. 78–89. IEEE Computer Society, Washington (2010)

63. Lo Buglio, D., De Luca, L.: Representation of architectural artifacts: definition of an approach combining the complexity of the 3D digital instance with the intelligibility of the theoretical model. SCIRES-IT 2(2), 63–76 (2012)

64. Beltramini, G.: Andrea Palladio. Plan and elevation of a villa for two brothers (Villa Contrarini at Piazzola?). In: Hind, C., Murray, I. (eds.) Palladio and His Legacy, A Transatlantic Journey, pp. 75–76. Marsilio, Venezia (2010)

65. Bentkowska-Kafel, A., Denard, H., Baker, D.: Paradata and Transparency in Virtual Heritage. Ashgate, Farnham (2012)

66. Robinson, A.H., Morrison, J.L., Muehrke, P.C., Kimmerling, A.J., Guptill, S.C.: Elements of Cartography, 6th edn. Wiley, New York (1995)

67. Richards, J.A., Jia, X.: Remote Sensing Digital Image Analysis: An Introduction, 4th edn, pp. 102–104. Birkhäuser, Boston (2006)

68. Campbell, J.B.: Introduction to Remote Sensing, 4th edn, p. 626. Taylor & Francis, London (2007)

69. Light, A., Bartlein, P.J.: The end of the rainbow? Color schemes for improved data graphics. EOS 85(40), 385–391 (2004). Transactions American Geophysical Union

70. Stone, M.: Choosing colors for data visualization. Business Intelligence Network (2006). http://www.perceptualedge.com/articles/b-eye/choosing_colors.pdf. Accessed 26 July 2016

71. Reichert, P., Borsuk, M.E.: Does high forecast uncertainty preclude effective decision support? Environ. Model Softw. 20(8), 991–1001 (2005)

Show Me the Data!: Structuring Archaeological Data to Deliver Interactive, Transparent 3D Reconstructions in a 3D WebGIS

Jennifer von Schwerin[1]([⊠]), Mike Lyons[1], Lukas Loos[2],
Nicolas Billen[2], Michael Auer[2], and Alexander Zipf[2]

[1] Commission for the Archaeology of Non-European Cultures (KAAK),
German Archaeological Institute, Bonn, Germany
`jennifer.vonschwerin@dainst.de`,
`mikelyons0@googlemail.com`
[2] Institute of Geography, Heidelberg University, Heidelberg, Germany
`{lukas.loos,nicolas.billen,michael.auer,`
`alexander.zipf}@geog.uni-heidelberg.de`

Abstract. Creating 3D reconstructions is a common approach today in archaeology and cultural heritage. The problem is that 3D models in online virtual research environments may tempt users to believe them as historical truth. What must be done to enable the public to view a 3D reconstruction as a hypothesis and have access to the supporting data? This paper explains – via use-case examples from the ancient Maya city of Copan, Honduras – a procedure for structuring heterogeneous data to enable interactive, web-based access to 3D reconstructions of cultural heritage. A prototype 3D WebGIS system was built that can store, manage, and visualize 3D models and integrates these with georeferenced archaeological data. An ontology was created, a segmentation pipeline was developed, and databases and services were designed to structure and integrate the data in the 3D WebGIS. Results include two interactive 3D reconstructions: a city model and a temple model – these demonstrate how proper data structuring can deliver transparent models for archaeological argumentation.

Keywords: Semantic data structuring · Ontologies · Research data management · Virtual research environments · 3D webgis · 3D digital reconstructions · Metadata · Paradata · Maya architecture · Maya archaeology · Copan

1 Introduction

Archaeological projects are increasingly acquiring and processing 3D data sets of individual finds, as well as whole sites. The archaeologists often make or commission 3D reconstructions of ancient buildings or city landscapes to demonstrate what they know or believe to have existed. Although these high quality models are valuable sources of knowledge and archaeological argumentation, the public and even researchers cannot evaluate the quality of the reconstructions, nor do they know where

© Springer International Publishing AG 2016
S. Münster et al. (Eds.): 3D Research Challenges II, LNCS 10025, pp. 198–230, 2016.
DOI: 10.1007/978-3-319-47647-6_10

to turn for information about them. Usually the argumentation for the reconstructions is contained in journal articles, the original data in field reports, the photographs in a photo archive, and these separate data sets are not linked to each other or the 3D model in any way. Moreover, although 3D remote sensing and CAD modeling technology is being used to create more realistic or accurate models, the delivery medium remains largely print or film. Images of these 3D models are published in a journal or displayed in a video in a museum exhibit and the pipeline usually ends here – with an image of the hypothesized form of the ancient structure or cityscape. Therefore, a real problem faced by 3D modelers is how to publish the actual 3D models for interactive use, and how to visually represent these hypothetical reconstructions in a way that better informs a user of the underlying hypothesis and the actual supporting data that exists.

Given today's web technologies, it is possible to remind the viewer of the uncertainty of a hypothetical reconstruction not only by making indications within the 3D model itself, but also by providing interactive 3D models online in which the user can access the archaeological data and argumentation for the 3D reconstruction. An interactive, 3D simulation that provides such supporting information can be called "transparent" [1]. A transparent model, for example, would allow a user to click on a reconstructed feature (starting with the structure as a whole down to its component parts) to see what kind of data is connected to it – for example, photos of the feature's original appearance, type classifications of that feature, literature references, argumentation, and levels of uncertainty, etc. One should be able to move back and forth between the reality-based model and the reconstruction as well. In this way, archaeologists can publish their 3D reconstructions directly with the supporting data. Such 3D models can be more informative and transparent, provide information as to how they were created, and thus facilitate discussion and provide greater value for research. This recording and communication of the process of interpretation, what becomes the "paradata", is an essential aspect of providing a transparent model [2].

To present transparent models in the most interactive way, we need a virtual research environment that can link 3D models, field reports, archaeological data, photos, drawings and maps together online so that future researchers can find, view, evaluate, and further analyze the 3D reconstructions, as well as their supporting data. In short, what is necessary is a system that can handle the management, visualization, and analysis of geo-referenced, 3D data [3]. In this case, a fundamental problem emerges: how to structure and represent the data that one does have, in order to make a transparent, visual argument for the reconstruction that is directly related to the supporting data?

The solution should have two requirements: 1. Technical reproducibility of data: The metadata on acquisition and processing should be provided. 2. Archaeological plausibility: The attribute data for each of the object elements should be available, as well as the paradata about the reconstruction process (e.g. reconstruction drawings, maps, plans, text documents). Ideally this information should all be semantically segmented within an overarching ontology so that it can be linked to sub-components of the 3D object.

This paper introduces a prototype virtual research environment created by the MayaArch3D project that can present interactive transparent models connected to complex archaeological data and in particular, explains how the data was structured for use in this system. After a brief discussion of how transparent models can address several problems in archaeological reconstructions, the paper introduces the MayaArch3D-WebGIS and then walks through the practical workflow of how this project structures and segments its data to prepare interactive 3D reconstructions that are linked to their supporting data for visualization online. Offering two examples, a city model and a temple model, the paper surveys the methods used to both conceptually and digitally segment these 3D models and their attribute data. A presentation of the results is followed by a discussion of the challenges and lessons learned, and the strengths and limits of this 3D WebGIS system for linking data to 3D models. A discussion of areas for future research precedes the paper's summary conclusion.

2   Related Work: Moving from 3D Reconstruction to 3D Argumentation, and from Metadata to Paradata

Here we mention a few projects that have been involved with 3D reconstructions, and propose that transparent models can address problems such as uncertainty by linking the 3D models directly to their supporting data.

2.1   Representing Hypothetical Reconstructions

Archaeologists researching ancient American cultures have sought since the 18th century to create visual reconstructions to express their understandings of the form of ancient structures or cities, whether in drawings, plastic models or reconstructions of actual buildings (for a review of these see [4, 5]). One of the earliest efforts to indicate uncertainty in reconstruction drawings of ancient architecture in the Americas was Tatiana Proskouriakoff's book An Album of Maya Architecture [6]. In her drawings, the known details of a building were drawn in solid lines, and the hypothetical reconstruction was articulated in dotted lines; next to these line drawings was a reconstruction of the building as it might have appeared in the past.

These images captivated the imaginations of a generation of archaeologists and the convention for using dotted lines to indicate hypothetical reconstructions is one still used in illustrations in Maya archaeology today (Fig. 1). For physical reconstructions of the ancient buildings themselves (until the Charter of Venice in 1964 recommended against onsite reconstructions) small cobbles were placed in the mortar of fully restored walls at the ancient city of Teotihuacan in Central Mexico to differentiate these reconstructed sections from the original walls found in situ. Such methods help the public to differentiate the real from the reconstructed.

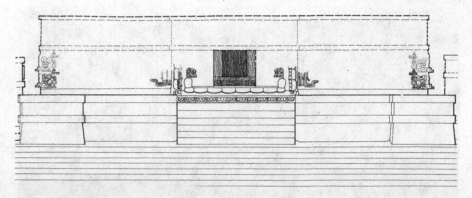

Fig. 1. Reconstruction drawing of a temple (Structure 10L-22) at the Maya city of Copan, Honduras, with the hypothesized form of the structure indicated by dotted lines extending from the existing ruins ([32]: Fig. 315).

To differentiate between the known vs. the hypothesized in computer-assisted 3D simulations of ancient structures or landscapes is also important, since virtual reconstructions, such as this simulated landscape setting for the ancient Maya city of Copan in Honduras (Fig. 2) can entice the viewer into forgetting they are viewing a hypothesis. This is often referred to as the authority that a reconstruction commands on a viewer [7]. With photorealism, a lack of supporting data or a single model unchallenged by alternative hypotheses, it has been proposed numerous times that a viewer is more likely to interpret a model as the "truth" regardless of the actual case [e.g. 8]. The concern with authoritative, non-transparent reconstructions eventually led to the development of the London Charter (2006) in addition to the Seville Principles specific to archaeology [8] in attempts to guide the production of 3D reconstructions so that authority and authenticity can be accounted for.

One way that archaeological projects have worked towards more transparent reconstructions is by visualizing uncertainty in several levels. One solution is to color-code the uncertainty [10, 11]. Concerning Maya archaeology, the Dzehkabtún 3D project did this with shades ranging from black to white [11].

Another solution is to overlay the reality-based model (state-model) and the reconstruction providing a direct comparison between the two, such as was done in the Via Appia Project [12]. In some cases, both methods are used such as the more recent reconstruction work of a Hellenistic-Roman theater in Paphos (Figs. 10 and 11) [13]. This project was designed with the specific intent of being in accordance with the principles of the London Charter and represents an exceptional case-study. They not only visually represent the uncertainty of the reconstructions with the previous two methods (color-coding and overlay), but work with a segmented structure ontology to link this color-coding to specific architectural elements to better convey reliability. The argumentation and supporting data, however, is not linked to these specific components, although the infrastructure is in place. Instead the reasoning behind the reconstructions is provided on a more general level via links to relevant articles and/or text that does not link to each individual component. While these approaches towards

Fig. 2. 3D Simulation of the Copan valley looking north with the Copan river in the foreground (Marleen de Kramer, 7 Reasons GmbH)

transparency offer solutions for representing uncertainty via the form and colors of the 3D models, an additional approach would be to guide the viewer directly to the supporting data sources as they explore the 3D model so that they themselves may evaluate the hypotheses that are presented. Journals such as Digital Applications in Archaeology and Cultural Heritage or the Journal of Archaeological Science now offer the possibility to publish the 3D model online and the related data in the form of a journal article. These are great steps forward. But an even more immediate and intuitive way for the viewer to access the data tied to the reconstruction would be to link the data to

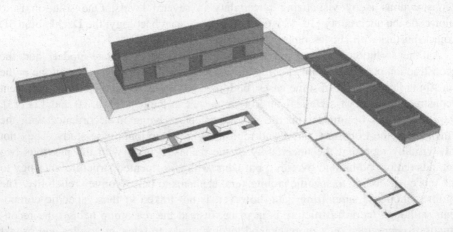

Fig. 3. Dzehkabtún structures represented in shades of grey to indicate levels of certainty ([11], Fig. 3)

the model itself. In this case, our research question becomes not how to represent uncertainty visually, but rather, how to represent the data that one does have, how to make the argumentation for the reconstruction visual but also data-based? Using the medium of 3D online is a natural solution for this problem, for by segmenting 3D models, one can structure the 3D data for interactive exploration online.

2.2 Online 3D Visualization Systems for Transparent Models

The concept of segmenting models to attach data to them initially was presented by Manferdini et al. [14] and more recently summarized by Manferdini and Remondino [15]. The start-up phase of the MayaArch3D project demonstrated this approach using Unity3D [3, 16]. Initially the 3D models were segmented because they were too large and it was a way to deliver 3D data in segments, so that when one clicked on a segment of a structure feature, a new model of that particular feature would load in a higher level of detail. But segmentation is also a way to link attribute data via the geometric segments of a model. However segmenting 3D models alone does not solve the problem; the related attribute data also must be structured appropriately in databases, and there must be a virtual research environment that can visualize and link together these models and the database information and offer query capabilities. In the last few years, several new 3D visualization platforms (e.g. SketchFab at www.sketchfab.com, Clara.io at www.clara.io) and frameworks (e.g. 3DHOP at www.3dhop.net, X3DOM at www.x3dom.org) have been released that allow the user to present their CAD models online in a way that allows the public to interact with the models. The viewers can rotate the models, shift lighting, and sometimes even annotate them. The NUBES VISUM platform moves beyond these to offer a web-based interface that links heterogeneous data within semantically enriched 3D models of heritage buildings [17]. The project, Palaces and Parks in Former East Prussia also is working on semantic mapping of data to architectural reconstructions delivered online [18]. However these systems while elegant and cutting-edge, are designed to work at an architectural scale and thus do not enable the linking of complex, spatially-referenced archaeological data within a whole georeferenced archaeological landscape or city model composed of many separate architectural models that have to be related to each other in space. Web-based, geographic information systems (WebGIS) that can also manage three-dimensional spatial data have been shown to hold great promise as an interface for virtual research environments for integrating, analyzing and publishing complex archaeological data and they can also be used for publishing transparent, three-dimensional reconstructions. One project is currently underway that can do this, but the results remain to be seen [19]. Therefore we focus here on the experiences learned by structuring data for 3D models for the MayaArch3D-WebGIS.

2.3 The MayaArch3D-WebGIS

The MayaArch3D project (MayaArch3D.org) developed a prototype 3D WebGIS system that can store, manage, and visualize 3D models of different formats and resolutions, and integrates these with other types of georeferenced archaeological data in a single, open-source, online platform [20–26]. This was developed from 2012–2015 in a research and development project led by the German Archaeological Institute's Commission for the Archaeology of Non-European Cultures and the GIScience research group at the Institute of Geography of Heidelberg University. This 3D WebGIS system is useful for the 3D documentation, visualization, and analysis of complex archaeological sites and landscapes. It goes beyond a simple visualization tool, for it makes these models available for analysis within an online, virtual research environment (VRE) and uses the models as visual storage containers by linking them to spatially-referenced archaeological data. The structure of the system is the following: on the backend are three databases: two PostgreSQL databases that hold the geometries of

Fig. 4. 2D Geobrowser of the MayaArch3D project focused on the Maya archaeological region

Fig. 5. 3D Scene Viewer of the MayaArch3D project

the digital objects - one for 3D objects, and one for 2D geometries. Then there is the archaeological database in Filemaker Pro that contains the attributes for each archaeological object (such as site, structure, sculpture), as well as the metadata for each digital object (such as photo, 3D model, archival file). Geometries and attributes are linked together by a common identifier which enables the front-end to asynchronously query the associated archaeological data to an already visualized object via an attribute service. Within the MayaArch3D-WebGIS platform the user can access the georeferenced data via a 2D Geobrowser (Fig. 4) or a 3D Scene Viewer (Fig. 5). Additionally the user can

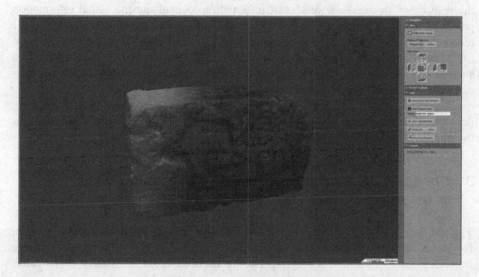

Fig. 6. 3D single object viewer of the MayaArch3D project

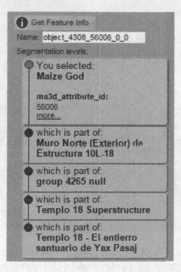

Fig. 7. Example of the semantic hierarchy

browse and edit the 3D database directly and visualize individual representations in a 3D Single Object Viewer (3DSOV) (Fig. 6) which can also be used as a standalone viewer for investigating higher resolution models. Access to the related archaeological data is provided through a Query Builder which can combine spatial, temporal and attributional criteria. Apart from the Query Builder individual sets of attributes can be obtained by a "Get Feature Info" function that allows the user to browse through the semantic hierarchy of segmented models (Fig. 7) [20]. This function is available in both the 3D Scene Viewer and the 3DSOV.

The user-interface for accessing the related data inside the semantic hierarchy gives the researcher an overview of textual information to evaluate the visual information provided by the hypothetical reconstruction model. It is part of the efforts to make 3D reconstructions in cultural heritage more traceable and transparent. Other available functions of the viewers, e.g. measuring distances and angles, and various lighting and surface shading options also support the aim to give the researcher all the tools necessary to assess the given model or even stimulate new hypotheses.

Aspects of this system have been discussed in detail elsewhere [20–26]. Having developed the system architecture, the next step was to collect and prepare the data for the particular use case.

3   Use Case: 3D Reconstructions of Architecture at the Ancient Maya City of Copan

The test data for the 3D WebGIS is mainly from the ancient Maya kingdom of Copan, Honduras. Copan is a Maya archaeological site situated in a lush river valley on the western border of Honduras (Fig. 8). During its occupation, a dynasty of 16 rulers

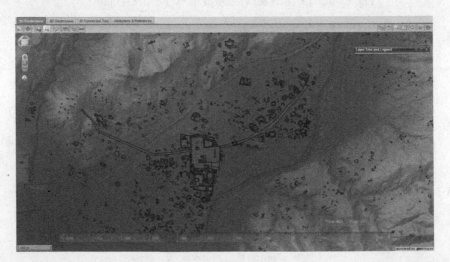

Fig. 8. View of the settlement plan of ancient Copan in the 2D geobrowswer of the 3D WebGIS system, with the principal group of ceremonial architecture in the center and two large (hypothetically reconstructed) causeways

emerged in the 5th century AD lasting roughly 400 years. At its apogee, Copan was estimated to have had a population upwards of 20,000 inhabitants. However, Copan, a UNESCO World Heritage site since 1980, is most renowned for its monumental architecture and exquisite stone carvings considered by many to be some of the most beautiful from the Classic Maya period.

Many archaeological projects have worked at Copan [27, 28] and the resulting data is stored in archives and museums throughout the world. One of the goals of our project is to use the 3D WebGIS to collaborate with colleagues to bring much of this data together in an online venue where researchers can interactively analyze this data with the aid of 3D simulations.

At the time of the dynasty's collapse around AD 822, the city settlement contained about 3500 structures with a principal group of temples and plazas in the center. Data recovered here by international projects over the last two centuries include the longest hieroglyphic inscription in the new world, a sequence of architectural change spanning five centuries, human remains, ceramics, stone sculpture, archaeo-botanical remains, etc. Archaeologists have worked for decades to map the extent of the city

Fig. 9. Structure 10L-18 (Temple 18) at Copan. View into the north room looking southwest. Photo from PAC excavations taken in 1980 shortly after consolidation/reconstruction. (Courtesy of IHAH)

settlement. A derived 3D reconstruction of the city from archaeological survey maps [29, 30] now serves as an interface for organizing and analyzing the spatial and temporal distribution of this data, and as a new data set for running GIS analyses of visibility and orientation on the landscape. One of the structures included in this city reconstruction, Temple 18, has been further hypothetically reconstructed and serves as a higher detail example of an interactive, transparent 3D model.

Fig. 10. Yax Pasaj as Warrior, Doorjamb of Temple 18 (Courtesy of IHAH)

Temple 18 is believed to be the burial shrine of the 16th and last dynastic ruler of Copan, Yax Pasaj (circa AD 800). It is a modest structure located on the eastern edge of the Copan acropolis (Fig. 9). The facade and interior walls are decorated in carved ashlars with motifs representing Classic Maya religious beliefs as well as depictions of Yax Pasaj dressed as a warrior (Fig. 10). Carved hieroglyphic texts in the structure provide dedicatory dates and also name the 16th ruler while a burial chamber is located below the southern room where Yax Pasaj was presumably interred (Fig. 11).

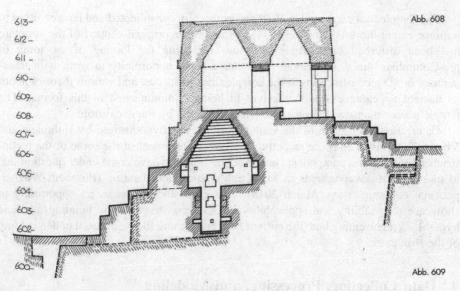

Fig. 11. Elevation of Structure 10L-18 with tomb and hypothesized vaulting ([32]: Fig. 608)

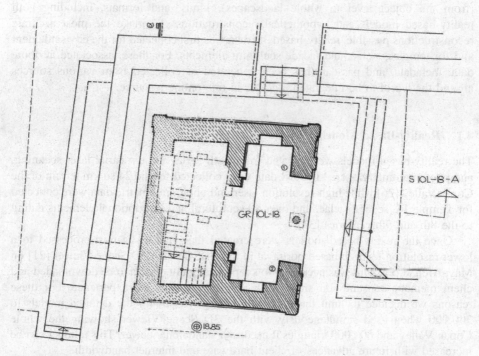

Fig. 12. Floorplan of Structure 10L-18 with hypothetical walls indicated by dotted lines ([32]: Fig. 602)

The temple was excavated in 1979 and physically consolidated and reconstructed to a minor extent the following year [31]. Although the original context of the structure had been disturbed on multiple occasions including the looting of the tomb in pre-Columbian times, the temple represents a great opportunity to work with transparency in 3D reconstructions as the complexities of its past and various theories about its ancient appearance lend themselves to being communicated in this format. The temple's floor plan was hypothetically reconstructed by the excavators.

Later, a reconstruction of the vaulted roofing was hypothesized by Hohmann and Vogrin [32] (Fig. 12). More recently, the correct placement of the some of the reconstructed architectural components on the actual building have come under question due to more recent advancements in Maya epigraphic understanding (Elisabeth Wagner, personal communication, March 2015). This case study provides an opportunity to showcase the viability and applicability of 3D reconstructions by building alternate hypotheses representing both the current state and a more likely, updated understanding of the structure.

4   Data Collection, Processing, and Modeling

The digital collection available in the 3D WebGIS includes data of varying extents (from the object level to whole landscapes), kinds, and formats, including both reality-based models and hypothetical reconstructions. To make the most accurate reconstructions possible, reality-based 3D data was first collected for the city settlement and for temples, stelae, and facade sculpture elements. For these, associated attribute data, metadata, and paradata has been generated or collected from various sources around the world to be integrated together in one online resource.

4.1   Reality-Based Models

The reality-based models were created from both aerial and terrestrial laser scanning, and photogrammetry. Aerial LiDAR data were collected for the 24 sq km terrain of the Copan valley [26] while high-resolution laser and photogrammetric data were collected for Temple 18, several stelae, and over 40 sculptural and inscriptional elements dating to the 8th and 9th centuries [33].

Once the reality-based models were created they had to be post-processed to a lower resolution for web based portrayal in our 3DSOV and 3D Scene Viewer [21] on MayaArch3d.org. This was necessary to keep the amount of data to be downloaded and client memory consumption small for a responsive real-time experience. For these reasons we decided to limit the maximum triangle count for the detailed models to 300.000 when used simultaneously with the 3D Scene Viewer showing the whole Copan Valley and 600,000 triangles if used as a standalone viewer. This number can be increased with future advances of client hardware and internet bandwidth.

4.2   3D CAD Reconstructions

One of the project objectives was to use the reality-based models to create interactive "transparent" 3D reconstructions and make them available within the 3D WebGIS system for analysis. The CAD models developed by the project were created in either SketchUp, 3D Studio Max, Mudbox and/or 3DCoat. Based on archaeological data and/or developed from reality-based models, they were converted to .obj files and segmented so that one can select different segments of the model to receive additional information [20]. Here we discuss the two 3D reconstructions in our system: (1) the city model, and (2) the temple model.

4.2.1   City Model of Copan Circa AD 822

This 3D city model contains 3500 low-resolution models of single structures and was designed for a previous project [3, 15]. It was created from archaeological survey data from Copan [28] in which the settlement plan maps were digitized and georeferenced by Heather Richards-Rissetto [30]. Then the building footprints were extruded by Giorgio Agugiaro to create 3D building models. The models are not intended to represent the appearance of the ancient structures. Rather, these schematic representations indicate the supposed height of the ancient structures, as well as their locations on the landscape. Thus these 3D reconstructions not only serve as virtual "containers" for their associated archaeological data (see Fig. 5), but also provide new data for visibility and orientation analyses.

4.2.2   A CAD Model of Temple 18 Circa AD 800

The second 3D reconstruction in this system is of Temple 18. This model, created in 3D Studio Max, contains more detail than the schematic structures in the city model, and suggests an informed hypothesis of the placement of now-collapsed façade sculpture. The workflow was to first use the reality-based, laser scan model of the existing remains of the ruined structure (Fig. 13) to establish basic dimensions for a CAD model, as well as to use photogrammetric models of various sculpture elements from the collapsed façade to develop the components of the reconstruction. In doing this, we also worked closely with Mayanist Elisabeth Wagner, who supplied drawings of the hypothesized form and reasoning behind reconstructed elements. Together, this information was used as a basis to create a hypothetical reconstruction of the temples' ancient appearance, which includes the reconstructed upper zone and roof (Fig. 14). However, an important point to note is that the model was not built with the aim of creating a photo-realistic reproduction. Instead, it was designed to illustrate the general, hypothetical form of the structure with the locations and relationships of the motifs and themes adorning its walls.

In order to communicate the authenticity or reliability of the reconstruction, we separated the structure into various levels of certainty and represented them visually as several projects have done before. Because there is no standard, each segment of the reconstruction was given one of four basic levels of certainty. Each of these levels reflects the different supporting data we have to describe the likelihood of a segment being historically accurate; they are in situ, physically reconstructed based on matching adjacent blocks, inference from structural form, and hypothesis. Each of these levels is to be color coded on the texture of the model (Fig. 15).

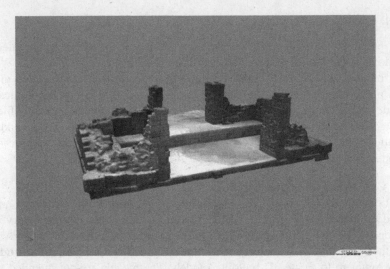

Fig. 13. Reality-Based Model of the remains of Temple 18, Copan (circa AD 800), created by Belen Jiménez Fernández-Palacios and Fabio Remondino

Fig. 14. CAD Model of partial hypothetical reconstruction of Temple 18 overlaid on laser scan model

Finally, to link data to the 3D model, we collected archaeological data about the temple (including excavation reports, maps, photographs, technical illustrations, iconographic interpretation). This as well as the argumentation, or theoretical basis, for the hypothetical reconstruction was structured and entered into an archaeological database in order to provide the reasoning behind each component of the reconstruction and to fit our ontological model (see below).

Fig. 15. The NW jamb of the Temple 18 3D reconstruction, featuring three of four levels of certainty

5 Methods of Data Structuring and Integration

Having collected and (where necessary) created the 3D data and the associated attributes, the next challenge was to structure them in such a way that they could be integrated and visualized in the 3D WebGIS as interactive, "transparent" models. First a database scheme was designed and implemented, and the attribute, metadata, and paradata structured accordingly. Then the 3D models first were segmented conceptually into an ontology, and then segmented technically into objects that matched this ontology. These data were then integrated and linked together for both visualization and analysis in the 3D WebGIS.

5.1 Database Schema and Data Structuring

5.1.1 Archaeological Database

The archaeological database used by the DAI to manage its excavation data is iDAI.field. Based on Filemaker Pro 12 (FM Pro), its schema has been used and extended over the last 9 years by 30 DAI projects [34]. It was chosen because it has a robust foundation for storing archaeological data, in addition to the FM Pro client providing a user-friendly interface for structuring and storing data.

An overview of the contents of the MayaArch3D archaeological database is given on its start page and gives a sense of its structuring scheme (Fig. 16). Each word links to a separate table in the database. These include, for example, archaeological sites, sub-sites, structures, features, objects of different materials (stone, bone, ceramic), as well as tables for individuals and organizations, projects, sub-projects, units, and lots. Additional tables exist for parties and organizations, coordinates, photographs, drawings and maps, 3D models, etc. Together these tables contain over 50,000 records.

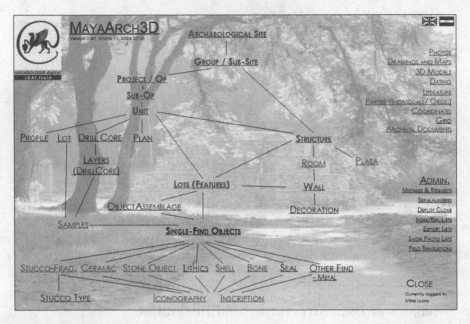

Fig. 16. Start Page of the MayaArch3D project's iteration of the archaeological database of the German Archaeological Institute, iDAI.field

While iDAI.field can hold digital images and drawings in a variety of formats (PDF documents, sound and video files, flash animations and attributes of selected artifacts and architecture), this database was not designed to handle spatial data such as 3D models. Therefore in the MayaArch3D system, we are using iDAI.field not to administer 3D geometries, but to record attribute data about archaeological objects and the metadata and paradata about their representations (whether photos or 3D models). Because the database cannot hold actual 3D data, and because iDAI.field has primarily been used for classical archaeological field campaigns, we have had to adjust the iDAI.field database schema to structure our data in three significant ways:

1. to accommodate the requirements of Maya Archaeology
2. to introduce a time model that accounts for temporal uncertainty
3. to manage the information about new 3D data that projects are now creating.

To accommodate for Maya archaeology, we first added an overarching table for Archaeological Sites, since our project database also needed to manage data on multiple sites in Central America for other project activities. This was necessary because previous iterations of iDAI.field were used for only one site. Then we added a table for sub-sites/groups because for instance at Copan there are over 800 architectural groupings that are classified as groups. We also added tables for Maya iconography and inscriptions which were previously combined in a "decorations" table. Finally, the fields in the various tables had to be adjusted accordingly to fit typologies in Maya archaeology (dates, period names, ceramic types, structure types, Maya epigraphic standards) (Fig. 17).

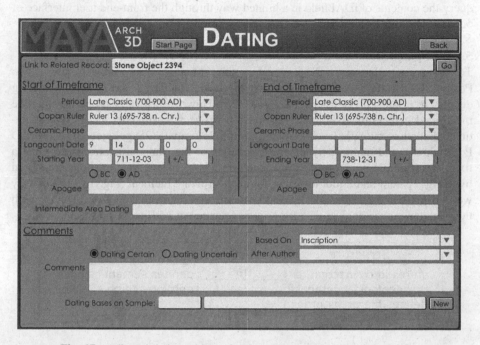

Fig. 17. Adjusted dating table to fit Maya typologies and Maya calendar

In a few cases it was necessary to change the data structure to match the structure that is required by the Query Tool to perform temporal queriestherefore, we redesigned the dating table. In this table dates can be recorded according to the Maya Long-count, Gregorian calendar, ceramic periods, or ruler's reigns. These dates are then linked to the scientific basis for the date, and the data source. We also began to record dates in iso format (8601) so that the time service developed for the Query Tool can handle the dates in a standardized and interoperable way and translate them as needed to the Maya Calendar [21]. One problem that we had to solve was to find a temporal model that on the one hand represents an often uncertain life-cycle of a structure but at the same time allows one to define temporal search criteria for complex queries. In our database, we have to provide a start and end-date for each object – but what is the end-date of a ceramic vessel or a structure? Is the "end point" of a structure defined by its initial abandonment, or when it is destroyed? Depending on the information one is interested in, this end date can vary. We decided that most queries would have to do with production dates, so we decided, for example, that an end date of a building should be the last date of the reign of the ruler in which the structure was built or dedicated.

As for recording the metadata and paradata about the 3D models, we developed a dedicated table. Here we worked with Fabio Remondino and Fabio Menna at the Bruno Kessler Foundation (FBK) to determine the most important information to record. Fields include: total polygons, file format, modeler, resolution, etc. In the 3D WebGIS system, each of these fields is visible in our Query-Builder tool. Here, the public can query the contents of iDAI.field in a limited way through the front-end user interface of our free and open-source 3D WebGIS.

5.1.2   Spatial Databases

To organize 2D and 3D geodata, the MayaArch3D project uses two PostgreSQL/PostGIS databases of which the data structuring and schema modeling details are discussed elsewhere [13, 19–21, 25]. However, two key properties shall be mentioned here 1) the 1-to-many relationship between a structure and its representations, that allow multiple levels-of-details, multiple formats (2D polygon, 3D Mesh, 3D Point cloud), and multiple hypothetical versions of the same structure. And 2) that a fixed set of ontology classes define a structure whose hierarchical relations are stored by using a parent and a root identifier for each structure element (Fig. 18). In this way we can present the hierarchically and semantically segmented models together with their related archaeological data for a more transparent and interactive result.

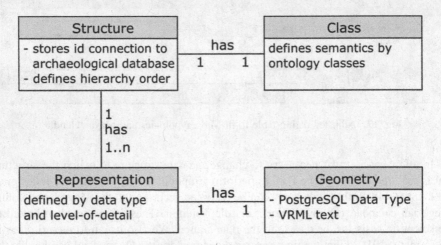

Fig. 18. Function and relations of tables in the spatial 3D model database

5.2   Post-processing: 3D Model Segmentation and Adding Semantic Information

After settling on a data structure and building the databases, the next step was to post-process the 3D models in order to digitally segment them. This allows, for example, the wall of a building to be linked to its archaeological data and metadata in the iDAI.field database, such as measurements, photographs, material, date excavated, and importantly the argumentation behind reconstructed components, or the paradata associated with it. Before this could be accomplished, a conceptual structure ontology had to be designed for segmenting these models.

5.2.1 Ontologies for 3D Model Segmentation (Conceptual Segmentation)

One set of data that were segmented is the Copan city model. Here the ontology is extremely simple and consists of three classes: structure (includes buildings, roads, and paved plazas), altar, or stela [16]. In order to accommodate the 3D model of Temple 18, we had to extend our ontology to encompass the subcomponents of a Maya structure, so that each conceivable component could allow for the retrieval of its relevant data. Although The Lexicon of Maya Architecture [35] is helpful to use as a standard for architectural descriptions, a semantic ontology that defines a hierarchy of relationships of Maya architectural parts that could be used in a database system does not yet exist.

Therefore, we designed an ontology ourselves. Beginning with the model of Temple 18 in its most comprehensive form, we conceptually segmented its component pieces and structured them to fit our archaeological database hierarchy (Fig. 19).

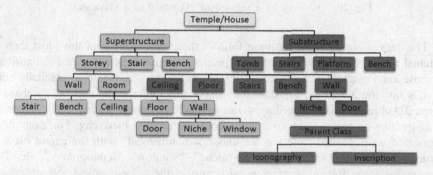

Fig. 19. Ontology for a segmented 3D model of a Maya structure (temple, house, etc.)

Generally, our segmentation process is based on three criteria:

1. Segmentation is based on structural components. For example, it is common in Maya architecture that structures are built on top of platforms, whether of river-cobbles, or multiple terraces. These are called substructures. So in our ontology, a whole structure may consist of two parts, a substructure and a super-structure. The superstructure and substructure are then segmented into their component parts, such as stairs and walls.
2. Almost all segments can be further segmented into iconographic and epigraphic/inscription components due to the great variation in where these components are found.
3. Because we must segment the total surface of the object, any leftover "uninteresting areas" are grouped together as "other".

We also developed a base ontology for Maya stelae. In this case, the stela is segmented into the pedestal and body (all parts above the pedestal). Both the body and pedestal then follow the same hierarchical segmentation scheme. They are each seg-mented into iconography and inscription. Iconography is segmented into motifs, and inscription is segmented into individual glyphs (Fig. 20).

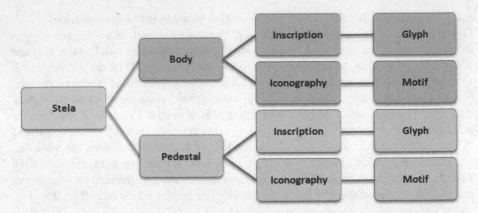

Fig. 20. Ontology for a segmented 3D model of a Maya stela.

The data in our attribute database follows these ontologies, but this must then be matched to the 3D models. In order for proper communication between the attribute database and PostgreSQL database, an ID-connection tool allows us to manually enter the IDs into the 3D Postgresql database. Using this tool we can edit the database to assign 3D objects classes according to our semantic ontology, so that each component of a structure or object is given a class from our defined hierarchy. For example, a segmented wall of a structure has the class "structure wall" with the parent class of "structure room", and child classes of "niche", "window", "iconography", etc. This remains the same for any segmented structure in the system unless the underlying hierarchy is changed, in which case it would change for all previously segmented structures.

5.2.2   3D Model Segmentation - Digital

Once the conceptual aspect has been addressed, the models have to be physically segmented. This consists of "cutting up" the model into separate models for each segment on the lowest level of the hierarchy - the leaf nodes of the hierarchy tree. This was carried out in 3DS Max and Blender. For example, although the superstructure (the temple proper, not including the platform) is a single segment, it is not cut into its own model. Instead, its component parts that make up the superstructure are cut into individual models and only later combined within our 3D object viewer to represent the superstructure segment. For Temple 18, this covered the entire structure including the motifs, such as the feathered serpent decorations on its northern façade (Fig. 21). In addition, each individual segment can be georeferenced in order to visualize it in the 3D Scene Viewer. In this way it is able to be examined in a more realistic context as opposed to isolation.

When all of the segments are stored properly in the 3D database they can be requested through a geometry service developed during this project as a hierarchically structured scenegraph [20, 21]. To create standalone models manually to be used with the 3DSOV, but without using the 3D database and services, the following procedure can be applied: the segment models are stored in a folder as .obj files titled with their

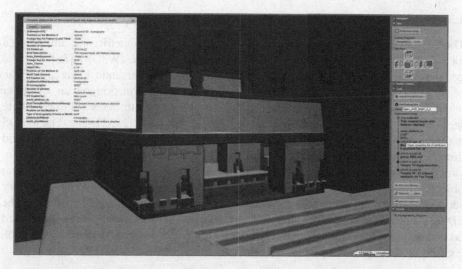

Fig. 21. Optimized and segmented CAD reconstruction of Temple 18, available in the MayaArch3D single object viewer

respective identifier number from the iDAI.field attribute database. Within this folder lies an additional folder containing the textures. A converter script provided by the Three.js JavaScript framework (www.threejs.org) reformats them to its own JSON based model format (Three.js JSON model format 3.1). An online tool, the "3D DB - Structure Hierarchy Viewer and Segmented Model Builder" (Fig. 22), retrieves the model hierarchy from the 3D database and allows the user to attach the previously generated JSON Models to finally export a combined hierarchical segmented model stored as a scenegraph in another JSON format for scenes (Three.js JSON scene format 3.2), also defined by the Three.js framework.

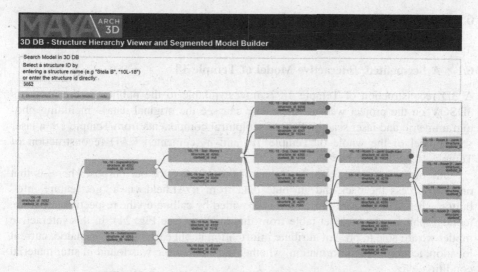

Fig. 22. Screenshot – Segmented model builder tool

5.3   Client-Service Architecture for Semantically Segmented Models

The MayaArch3D system uses three services to retrieve geometric and attributional data from two distributed databases. The Web 3D Service (W3DS) [36] and the geometry service deliver a scenegraph that represents the semantic hierarchy of the segmentation ontology described above and includes information on an identifier which the client can use later to retrieve the corresponding attributes via the attribute service (Fig. 23). This architecture has been related earlier in [20, 21, 26]. The W3DS is used to spatially request 3D Models by specifying bounding boxes or tile indices and thus is limited to deliver georeferenced data only by their location, e.g. the reconstruction of the city model together with its surrounding terrain model. To retrieve objects directly by their id regardless of being georeferenced or not, the geometry service has been implemented. A visualization of textured segmented models in the 3DSOV client is also possible directly from the file system of a web server if prepared according to the procedure described above with the "Segmented Model Builder" tool, e.g. the models from our project website.

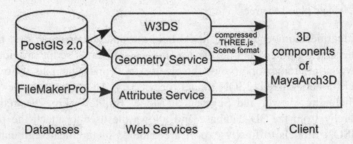

Fig. 23. MayaArch3D-WebGIS system structure (after [20], Fig. 4)

6   Results: "Transparent" Reconstructions of Maya Architecture Available Online

6.1   A Segmented, Interactive Model of Temple 18

A 3D reconstruction of Temple 18 is now available to the public via the project's 3DSOV on the project website. Here one can see the original data – including photogrammetric and laser scan models of sculptural components from Temple 18, a laser scan model of the whole of Temple 18, and a segmented CAD reconstruction of Temple 18.

One of the most important functions of the 3DSOV for our purposes here, is that one can access the back-end attribute data from iDAI.field via a "get feature info" button where descriptive information is provided by calling up the respective structure, iconographic or stone-object table from the database (see Fig. 21). In this interactive model we are able to present attribute information about each object – its name, current location, iconographic information, whether the stone piece was found in situ, material condition, etc.

Additionally, the 3DSOV allows for access to this information in hierarchical form. This means that not only can an individual component be selected and investigated, but the object hierarchy can be traversed in order to investigate the greater component that a specific element is a part of. For example, each piece of an iconographic motif (such as a human figure) can be individually selected and information about that specific piece is provided. Then by traversing up the hierarchy a single level, the entire motif is now the subject of inquiry and information regarding the motif as a whole is provided (e.g. the subject and its relation to surrounding iconography) (Fig. 24). Furthermore, this traversing of the hierarchy is enabled up to the highest level of the developed ontology, which in this case, would be Structure 10L-18 as a whole.

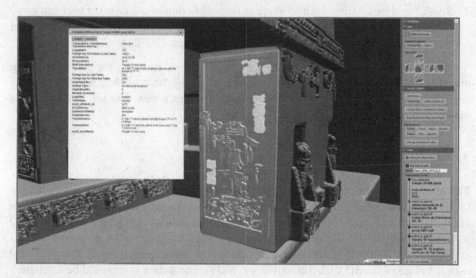

Fig. 24. Traversing the data hierarchy to change subject of inquiry on the NW door jamb of Temple 18

6.2   Segmented, Interactive Copan City Model in the 3D WebGIS

To understand the context of Temple 18 within the urban landscape of Copan, one can interact with a schematic reconstruction of the settlement of the ancient city of Copan circa AD 822. This more sensitive information is available to registered users via the 3D WebGIS[1], which allows for the query, visualization and analysis of 3D models of objects or structures within their larger context and in connection with heterogeneous archaeological data. Within this 3D environment, users can run queries about this city model in four ways:

---

[1] For log-in access, please contact the first author of this paper.

1. Querying the Query Builder. This allows queries by space, time, and attribute. For example, one can query "all structures excavated by M. Becker at Copan between 1960 and 1980", and resulting structures will be highlighted in the 3D scene.
2. Comparisons. The results of queries are also highlighted in the 2D geobrowser, so that one can compare the results in the 3D Scene Viewer (for the 3D model of the city) and the 2D geobrowser to check reconstructions against 2D maps and more detailed landscape data.
3. Individual structures and monuments. The low-resolution 3D models also serve as visual storage containers, so that by clicking on a structure, altar or stela one can access a single record about its excavation history, date of construction, current condition, associated artifacts, etc.
4. Spatial analyses. Using the hypothetical reconstruction of the city, the user can carry out 3D analyses of lighting, line of sight and orientation to analyze potential relationships between architecture and the landscape [20, 26].

This last query or analytical tool is important because it moves the user from using the 3D models as storage containers for data, to using them as data sets for 3D GIS analyses. So the 3D reconstructions become themselves a new data set, thus making a transparent reconstruction all the more crucial.

7   Discussion

The research on data structuring for this project focused on the semantic segmentation of 3D models according to a new ontology as well as the revision of the data schema of an archaeological database. Linking these two data structures together and to the 3D models allows for the detailed inspection of particular features of an object and its attribute data. Following this research, there are some points about the graphical user-interface of the 3D WebGIS, ontology, and segmentation that should be discussed.

7.1   Limitations of the Filemaker Server JDBC Interface and the Graphical User Interface

The MayaArch3D WebGIS system is a prototype that enables the storage, visualization and querying of 3D models and their related heterogeneous data. It is a useful system to publish 3D reconstructions, as it can manage knowledge about the 3D models and the objects they depict, and visualize them in direct relationship to the 3D reconstruction.

At this point however, the knowledge is all accessible in the system, but not all directly via the 3D models themselves. For instance, although users can find attribute data and limited paradata directly by interacting with the model, if users would like to view the metadata about the various 3D models, they have to exit the WebGIS and search directly in the iDAI.field database via the QueryBuilder. This is because the Filemaker server via its JDBC interface only provides access to its data fields (text, numbers, dates etc.) but not to the attached files, like images, drawings or pdfs. To circumvent this problem partly, there is a prototypical implementation of an image viewer that can retrieve image and drawings data via an image service interface. All images from the project database have been imported into the DAIs image database, Arachne. Unfortunately, due to lack of time in the project this could not be fully tested and implemented but demonstrates the applicability of the concept for future developments. Providing interactive visual media together with textual para- and meta-data is crucial to support the "transparent" documentation and should be added in the future.

7.2   Conflicting Ontologies: What Works for 3D Models Does not Always Work in Archaeological Practice - Accommodating Existing Data Structures

Both sets of data – the 3D data and the related archaeological data – need to fit the same ontology. The most difficult process of structuring our data for use with a 3D WebGIS was to match the existing iDAI.field database to the new PostGreSQL database. While the iDAI.field database contains the data we want to link to the model segments, the PostGreSQL database contains the hierarchical relationships between the different segments of a model. Each segment has a specific ID in the PostGreSQL database, and then each of these PostGreSQL IDs must be linked to a specific iDAI.field ID. This required that we rethink how we structure our archaeological data and revise the archaeological database to accommodate the way that 3D models are segmented. In practice there is one major issue: although we have a set of ontological classes in the 3D database for 3D model segments, these do not match one to one with the structure in our archaeological database. This is because the archaeological database schema reflects the classifications that are made in the field during the process of excavation. It is primarily a tool for researchers to structure, enter and search for archaeological data. In many cases, iDAI.field is not ideally structured to fit the segmentation hierarchy while still maintaining this primary purpose.

For example, archaeologists classify elements beyond individual structures as simply "features" which are then given names, numbers and types. We could not remove this structure from our archaeological database, nor can we change the methods that archaeologists use in the field, so it was necessary simply to indicate on a case-by-case basis, which instance of which class element corresponded to which table in the archaeological database (Fig. 25).

This is one of the lessons learned from our project, that new technologies can assist us in our research, and in some cases they fundamentally change the way we work, but in other cases, the technologies must be adjusted to accommodate the way we do our research - even if it means a great deal more work on the technical side of things.

It is crucial that we maintain the usability of the iDAI.field database while adapting it to be compatible with the PostGreSql database. Therefore, in the case of this 3D WebGIS it is useful to have two separate data structures that can be linked - one for the disciplinary practice, and one for the 3D model segmentation.

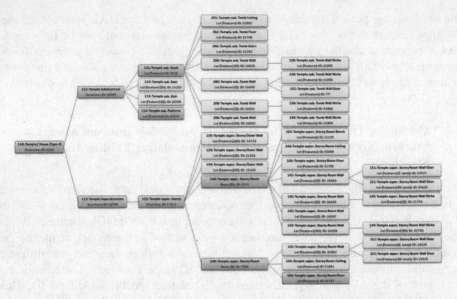

Fig. 25. Ontology for a segmented 3D model of a structure matched to the data schema for a structure in iDAI.field. Black text = GUI Class Number: GUI Title, Red text = Associated FM Pro table (if applicable, cardinal side); Serial ID.

7.3   Challenges in Post-processing and Segmentation

Providing 3D models online requires a strong consideration for the end-user who has to download them. In order to ensure that a 3D reconstruction will be useful for scientific research even after it is completed, and that it can be made available on the web and linked to other sets of data, there is still a great deal of post-processing work to complete, and decisions to be made in order to optimize it and segment it as necessary. To structure the 3D Models for online viewing, we have found that mesh models should not be larger than 600,000 polygons if they are to be visualized in the 3D WebGIS. Some improvements of the appearance can be achieved by using normal maps, textures that store surface orientation for triangle faces that otherwise would appear flat. Further implementation of technology used to vary the detail by increasing or decreasing the polygon count based on object proximity may be a viable solution.

Structuring metadata to match the segmentation of a 3D model according to its object hierarchy requires knowledge of both 3D segmentation and archaeological data. It requires a collaborative effort in which those who generate the 3D models and the disciplinary specialist who must structure attribute data to fit the model, must work together. Throughout the process we have had to maintain a consistent dialog between these two working groups in order to accomplish our goals.

Although our current segmentation methodology of cutting the models into pieces worked for the project's needs, it is not an ideal solution. The process is time consuming and limiting in several ways. For example, we cannot segment a model according to its component parts, and then again according to its levels of certainty as these will almost certainly not match up. Other options are being considered (see future work). Another seemingly simple issue is deciding the physical limits of a segment. For example, if we want to segment two adjacent walls, the stones making up the corner where these walls meet are actually part of both walls (or part of two separate segments in the model). In order to resolve this, we made the decision to cut stones that occupy a corner at the corner itself. This is a less than ideal solution because it undermines the work on segmentation, but due to limitations in our current segmentation process, we are not able to have any overlap of segments.

8 Future Work

8.1 Determining a Data Structure for Managing Differing Attribute Data, Metadata, and Paradata Sets for the Same Object

Now that the segments of the 3D models can be linked to the data, the next step in our research will be to improve the ability of the archaeological database to structure archaeological data to link to 3D models to do the following: (1) indicate and visualize uncertainty (either physical or temporal), (2) indicate and visualize an object's change over time and (3) accommodate both reality based models and their analogous reconstructions (i.e. physical, evidence-based information vs. hypothesized information). All of these involve having multiple representations of the same object, which we have implemented in the spatial database, but not in the archaeological database (where, for example, we would need multiple entries for the same wall depending upon if it was the original or a reconstructed version).

To show multiple, differing segmentations of the same 3D model, it would make sense to move away from the segmentation method and instead apply attributes to portions of a mesh in order to distinguish between segments. This would better accommodate overlaying levels of certainty (a form of segmentation in itself) on a structural segmentation schema.

8.2 Adjusting the Data Structure to Move Towards Sustainability and Interoperability

Further steps have begun to be taken towards sustainability and interoperability to enable transfer of the MayaArch3D data to other aggregator databases (such as Arachne and Europeana). For example, some of the datasets have been placed in the DAI repositories, iDAI.gazetteer and iDAI.images (Arachne at arachne.uni-koeln.de/) where they receive URIs and to link our system to these data. We have also begun working with FORTH (www.forth.gr) and the ITN-DCH Project (www.itn-dch.org) to map the iDAI.field database to the CIDOC-Conceptual Reference Model (www.cidoc-crm.org/). Not only has this work enabled greater possibilities for interoperability with other cultural heritage data repositories, but it has provided us with deeper insight into how our data is structured and where to improve the data structure in the future. A next step will be to collaborate with Maya Dictionary Project (www.mayawoerterbuch.de/index_en.php) that is developing a new extension for the Getty Thesaurus for Maya Archaeology and include this in the data structure. Finally the CARARE (www.carare.eu) metadata schema should be assessed for its utility for adjusting the archaeological database to be more interoperable with other aggregator systems such as Europeana.

8.3   Adding or Linking to Better Data Management Functions and Capabilities

As for the 3D data, the 3D WebGIS is not set up either for uploading or updating models (this must be done manually) or long-term archival storage. These are features that would have to be added in the future as the system is further integrated into the DAI data management infrastructure, iDAI.world [37].

8.4   Representing Reconstruction Argumentation in More Detail

Finally, to improve our ability to represent archaeological arguments, the project has begun to collaborate with FORTH on the iconography data structure of the MayaArch3D iconography database in iDAI.field. The goal is to map it in CIDOC-CRM to more accurately model arguments for facade reconstruction, particularly those that are based upon patterns in iconography of the facades of Maya temples [38].

9   Conclusion: Structuring Complex Archaeological Data for Transparent and Interactive 3D Reconstructions or "Smart Models"

9.1   Summary

This paper has presented a real use-case of the methods and challenges of structuring 3D data and associated archaeological data for linkage in an online platform that offers interactive access to the models and data. This is important for reaching the goal of providing transparent 3D reconstructions of cultural heritage objects that offer high-quality information about the knowledge, uncertainties, and academic argumentation pertaining to them. An apt name for these would be "smart models". Providing such "smart models" is particularly crucial when these very same models will be used for further research, hypotheses development and analysis, such as in a 3D WebGIS.

The 3D WebGIS developed by the MayaArch3D Project is a prototype solution for web-based visualization and information systems to link 3D objects to other forms of information and make them traceable and accessible and available for further analysis on a multimedia level. Our pipeline for segmenting and structuring 3D data [16, 20] has already been published; we have followed this here and have explained the process and challenges of preparing our data for this pipeline. Two queryable models are presented in the system: a low-resolution city model of Copan, and a high resolution temple reconstruction. These demonstrate the system's potential for offering interactive access to knowledge about 3D reconstructions.

Like the MayaArch3D project, most projects will have existing datasets and databases that they want to link to their 3D models – and so they also will run into similar challenges mentioned in this paper. By defining and addressing these challenges in this research project, it has been possible to make recommendations for archaeologists with regard to file sizes and format, metadata standards, and ontologies and formats for structuring data to deliver online in a 3D WebGIS.

In conclusion, connecting digital 3D models with additional metadata is something not provided by current 3D formats, is a requirement for those working with cultural heritage, and is the topic of a great deal of current research in the digital humanities and cultural heritage fields The MayaArch3D prototype 3D WebGIS offers a step in this direction. It is a useful system to publish 3D reconstructions, as it offers a solution for the storage, visualization and querying of 3D models and the management and visualization of heterogeneous knowledge about the 3D models and 3D reconstructions. An ontology or generalized conceptual data structure for segmenting 3D models of archaeological structures and stone monuments has been developed that will be useful for others desiring to create "transparent" or "smart" models that support argumentation for a reconstruction. A data structuring pipeline for this system has been developed and tested, and offers a solution to the problem of transparency in 3D reconstructions by offering supporting data via clickable segments in a graphical user interface linked to an archaeological database, thereby allowing interactive and transparent 3D reconstructions.

Acknowledgements. This research has been funded by the German Federal Ministry of Education and Research (BMBF) in the funding program e-Humanities in a grant to the German Archaeological Institute and the University of Heidelberg from 2012–2015. Project coordinator, Markus Reindel, provided valuable guidance and collaboration. Special thanks go to the Honduran Institute of Anthropology and History for permission to work at Copan. Thanks to Reinhard Förtsch and Philipp Gerth for collaborative work and support with iDAI.field and other modules of iDAI.world. Heather Richards-Rissetto, Department of Anthropology and Center for Research in the Digital Humanities (CDRH) at the University of Nebraska-Lincoln kindly shared her Copan city model for the project and was involved with early discussions about ontologies and the importance of transparency and uncertainty. Fabio Remondino and Belen Jimenez Fernandez of the 3D Optical Metrology Unit, Bruno Kessler Foundation collected and processed much of the 3D data for the project, including the data for Structure 10L-18. Barbara Fash of Harvard University, and Karina Garci, and Reyna Flores in Copan kindly helped with access to the archival materials about Structure 10L-18 excavations. Elisabeth Wagner of the University of Bonn generously shared her theories on the original appearance of the structure. Martin Doerr and George Bruseker of FORTH, and Nicola Carboni of CNRS worked to map our database into CIDOC-CRM. Rossella Suma, University of Warwick assisted with post-processing.

References

1. Frischer, B., Dakouri-Hild, A.: Beyond illustration: 2D and 3D digital technologies as tools for discovery in archaeology. In: BAR International Series, 1805, p. xiii. Archaeo press, Oxford (1999)
2. Bentkowska-Kafel, A., Denard, H., Baker, D.: Paradata and Transparency in Virtual Heritage. Ashgate, Farnham, Surrey (2012)

3. von Schwerin, J., Richards-Rissetto, H., Remondino, F., Agugiaro, G., Girardi, G.: The MayaArch3D project: a 3D WebGIS for analyzing ancient architecture and landscapes. Literary and Linguistic Computing. Spec. Iss. Digital Humanit. 2012: Digital Divers. Cult. Lang. Methods **28**(4), 736–753 (2013)
4. Ahlfeldt, J.: On reconstructing and performing ancient maya architecture: structure 22. Copan Honduras (AD 715) UMI Microform 3128915, Columbia University (2004)
5. Pillsbury, J. (ed.): Past Presented at the History of Archaeological Illustration. Dumbarton Oaks, Washington, DC (2012)
6. Proskouriakoff, T.: An Album of Maya Architecture. Carnegie Institution of Washington, Washington, DC (1946)
7. Miller, P., Richards, J.: The good, the bad and the downright misleading: archaeological adoption of computer visualization. In: Huggett, J., Ryan, N. (eds.) CAA94 Proceedings of the 22nd CAA Conference, Tempus Reparatum, Oxford (1994)
8. Frankland, T., Graeme E.: Authority and authenticity in future archaeological visualisation. In: Proceedings of Ads-Vis2011: Making Visible the Invisible: Art, Design and Science in Data Visualisation, pp. 62–68. University of Huddersfield, London (2011)
9. IFVA (International Forum of Virtual Archaeology), Final Draft. The Seville Principles: International Principles of Virtual Archaeology). http://smartheritage.com/wp-content/uploads/2015/03/FINAL-DRAFT.pdf Accessed 05 Aug 2016
10. Lengyel, D., Schock-Werner, B., Toulouse, C.: Die Bauphasen des Kölner Domes und seiner Vorgängerbauten, Cologne Cathedral and Preceding Buildings. Verlag Kölner Dom e.V, Köln (2011)
11. Jansen, P., Paap, I.: Dzehkabtún 3D - leventamiento topográfico y reconstrucción virtual de un sitio maya. Los Investigadores de la Cultura Maya 23 (2014)
12. Forte, M., Pescarin, S., Pietroni, E.: The Appia antica project. In: Forte, M. (ed.) The reconstruction of archaeological landscapes through digital technologies. In: Proceedings of the 2nd Italy-United States Workshop, vol. 1379, pp. 79–91, Rome, Italy, 3–5 November 2003. BAR International Series, Berkeley, USA (2005)
13. Georgiou, R., Hermon, S.: A London Charter's visualization: the ancient hellenistic-roman theatre in Paphos. In: VAST: International Symposium on Virtual Reality, Archaeology and Intelligent Cultural Heritage-Short and Project Papers, pp. 53–56 (2011)
14. Manferdini, A., Remondino, F., Baldissini, S., Gaiani, M., Benedetti, B.: 3D modeling and semantic classification of archaeological finds for management and visualization in 3D archaeological databases. In: Proceedings of 14th VSMM Conference, Limassol, Cyprus (2008)
15. Manferdini, A.M., Remondino, F.: A review of reality- based 3D model generation, segmentation and web-based visualization methods. Int. J. Heritage Digital Era **1**(1), 103–123 (2012)
16. Agugiaro, G., Remondino, F., Girardi, G., von Schwerin, J., Richards-Rissetto, H., De Amicis, R.: QueryArch3D: querying and visualising three-dimensional archaeological models in a web-based interface. Geoinformatics, Faculty of Civil Engineering, Czech Technical University (2011)
17. de Luca, L.: 3D modelling and semantic enrichment in cultural heritage. In: Fritsch, D. (ed.) Photogrammetric Week 2013, pp. 323–333. University of Stuttgart, Institute for Photogrammetry (2013)
18. Kuroczyński, P.: Poster: digital 3D reconstructions in virtual research environments. The Portal: Palaces and Parks in former East Prussia. https://de.dariah.eu/documents/10180/472725/43_Poster_DIN-A0_HI_Kuroczynski.pdf/a90829a-07b3-4fe3-afb0-3e85c6d7f634. Accessed 26 July 2016

19. de Kleijn, M., de Hond, R., Martinez-Rubi, O.: Mapping the Via Appia. Poster: Computer Applications in Archaeology Meetings, Siena. http://mappingtheviaappia.nl/wp-content/uploads/2015/03/poster_mdk_rdh.pdf. Accessed 26 July 2016

20. Auer, M., Agugiaro, G., Billen, N., Loos, L., Zipf, A.: Web-based visualization and query of semantically segmented multiresolution 3D models in the field of cultural heritage. ISPRS Annals of the Photogrammetry, Remote Sensing and Spatial Information Sciences, II-5, pp. 33–39 (2014). doi:10.5194/isprsannals-II-5-33-2014,

21. Billen, N., Auer, M., Loos, L., Agugiaro, G., Zipf, A.: MayaArch3D: an integrative analytical platform for 3D archaeological data. In: Proceedings of the 4th Conference on Scientific Computing and Cultural Heritage (SCCH 2013), Heidelberg, Germany (2013)

22. Loos, L., Auer, M., Billen, N., Zipf, A.: MayaArch3D – a 3D webgis for archaeological research. In: Proceedings of Digital Geoarchaeology 2013, Heidelberg, Germany, p. 16 (2013)

23. Reindel, M., Isla, J., Otten, H., Gorbahn, H., von Schwerin, J.: Archäologische Forschungen in Peru und Honduras im Jahr 2013. Zeitschrift für Archäologie Außereuropäischer Kulturen 6, 289–308 (2014)

24. Reindel, M., Isla, J., Otten, H., Gorbahn, H., von Schwerin, J.: Archäologische Forschungen in Peru und Honduras. Zeitschrift für Archäologie Außereuropäischer Kulturen 5, 297–313 (2013)

25. von Schwerin, J., Reindel, M., Auer, M., Billen, N., Loos, L., Zipf, A.: Ein webbasiertes 3D-GIS zur Analyse der Archäologie von Copan, Honduras. In: Proceedings of the Digital Humanities Summit 2015, TextGrid – DARIAH.de, Berlin, 3–4 March 2015. https://de.dariah.eu/documents/10180/472725/45_DHSummitPosterFinal.pdf/c13b4541-663a-4239-af44-189580a32e5e. Accessed 26 July 2016

26. von Schwerin, J., Richards-Rissetto, H., Remondino, F., Grazia Spera, M., Auer, M., Billen, N., Loos, L., Stelson, L., Reindel, M.: Airborne LiDAR acquisition, post-processing and accuracy-checking for a 3D WebGIS of Copan, Honduras. J. Archaeol. Res. Rep. 5, 85–104 (2016). doi:10.1016/j.jasrep.2015.11.005

27. Fash, W.: Scribes, Warriors, and Kings: The City of Copan and the Ancient Maya. Thames and Hudson, London (2001)

28. Webster, D., Freter, A., Gonlin, N.: Copan: The Rise and Fall of an Ancient Maya Center. Harcourt Brace, Fort Worth (2002)

29. Baudez, C.-F.: Introducción a la Arqueología de Copán, Honduras. Proyecto Arqueológico Copán, Secretaria de Estado en el Despacho de Cultura y Turismo, Tegucigalpa, DC, pp. 108–134 (1983)

30. Richards-Rissetto, H.: From mounds to maps to models: visualizing ancient architecture across landscapes. In: Proceedings of Digital Heritage International Congress, Marseille, France, 28 October–1 November 2013

31. Becker, M.J., Cheek, C.D.: La Estructura 10L-18. In: Baudez, C.-F. (ed) Proyecto Arqueológico Copán, Secretaria de Estado en el Despacho de Cultura y Turismo, Tegucigalpa, DC, pp. 382–500 (1983)

32. Hohmann, H., Vogrin, A.: The Architecture of Copan (Honduras), Measurements, Plans, Investigation of Structural Elements and Spatial Concepts (in German). Akademische Druck u.- Verlagsanstalt, Graz/Austria (1982)

33. Remondino, F., Gruen, A., von Schwerin, J., Eisenbeiss, H., Rizzi, A., Girardi, S., Sauerbier, M., Richards, H.: Multi-sensor 3D Documentation of the Maya Site of Copan. XXII CIPA Symposium, Kyoto, Japan, 11–15 October 2009

34. Gerth, P.: iDAI.field - Archaeological field research database: a modular documentation system for field projects (2015) https://prezi.com/1gu7ak_w09g5/idaifield/. Accessed 24 June 2015

35. Loten, S.H., Pendergast, D.M.: A Lexicon for Maya Architecture. Royal Ontario Museum, Toronto (1984)
36. Schilling, A., Kolbe, T.H.: Draft for Candidate OpenGIS® Web 3D Service Interface Standard.- OGC Discussion Paper, Ref. No. OGC 09–104r1 (2010)
37. German Archaeological Institute. http://www.dainst.org/de/forschung/forschung-digital/idai. welt. Accessed 15 June 2015
38. Stelson, L., Bruseker, G., von Schwerin, J.: A public database and digital research tool for maya iconography. Unpublished Paper Presented at the European Association of Mayanists, Bonn, 13 December 2015

Enrichment and Preservation of Architectural Knowledge

Jakob Beetz[1(✉)], Ina Blümel[2], Stefan Dietze[3], Besnik Fetahui[3], Ujwal Gadiraju[3], Martin Hecher[5], Thomas Krijnen[1], Michelle Lindlar[2], Martin Tamke[6], Raoul Wessel[4], and Ran Yu[3]

[1] Eindhoven University of Technology, Eindhoven, The Netherlands
{j.beetz,t.krijnen}@tue.nl
[2] German National Library of Science and Technology, Hannover, Germany
{ina.bluemel,michelle.lindlar}@tib.eu
[3] L3S Research Center, Leibniz University, Hannover, Germany
{dietze,fetahu,gadirajul,yu}@l3s.de
[4] University of Bonn, Bonn, Germany
wesselr@cs.uni-bonn.de
[5] Fraunhofer Austria, Graz, Austria
martin.hecher@vc.fraunhofer.at
[6] CITA Copenhagen Institute of Technology and Architecture, Copenhagen, Denmark
martin.tamke@kadk.dk

Abstract. In the context of the EU FP7 DURAARK project (2013–2016), interdisciplinary methods, technologies and tools have been researched and developed, that support the Long Term Preservation of semantically enriched digital representations of built structures. The results of the research efforts include approaches of semi-automatically deriving building models from point cloud data sets acquired from laser scans and the integration and overlay of such representations with explicit Building Information Models (BIM). We introduce novel ways for the further semantic enrichment of such hybrid building models with contextual data and vocabularies from external resources using Linked Data (LD) and the recognition relevant features and building components. A special focus of the research reported here lies on strategies and policies for their long term archival, information retrieval based on rich semantic metadata and the use of such archival systems in research and commercial scenarios. We introduce a set of prototypical, open-source tools implementing these features that have been integrated into a modular preservation framework called the "DURAARK Workbench".

Keywords: Digital preservation · Semantic enrichment · Building Information Model · Linked data · Point clouds

1 Introduction

Digital reconstruction of cultural heritage employs methods and models from the fields of architecture, construction and Building Information Models (BIM) [12] in order to collect, extract and preserve knowledge about cultural heritage structures [38]. This requires a highly interdisciplinary approach which considers the historical perspective

© Springer International Publishing AG 2016
S. Münster et al. (Eds.): 3D Research Challenges II, LNCS 10025, pp. 231–255, 2016.
DOI: 10.1007/978-3-319-47647-6_11

alongside the state of the art in architecture, engineering and construction (AEC). It also involves the wider fields of knowledge and data representation, including the preservation of Linked Data (LD) which is distributed among heterogeneous, dynamic resources. In this chapter, we provide insights into the modeling and preservation of architectural knowledge in the DURAARK project.[1]

Interpreting and understanding data and models about buildings, architectural and cultural heritage artifacts, requires consideration of the context in which they exist. A context can be comprised of a building's geography, its specific legal setting, the environmental or infrastructural setting, its role or use and perception by the wider public. Gathering information about such contextual dimensions is essential to make this work accessible to architects, cultural heritage experts, urban planners or the general public.

The existence of a context is especially important for historical and archaeological artefacts and building structures. A BIM can concentrate and organize the many different types of information, including contextual information, in a single knowledge base that acts as an electronic reference dossier of the object during the entire process of investigation and conservation [31, 32]. Currently, this knowledge is spread among different disciplines and restricted to several disparate "knowledge islands" resulting in issues regarding partiality and data duplication [38]. Among these partial domain models, mere geometric representations such as point cloud models are particularly lacking in context information. In the recent past, it has become technologically feasible to acquire high precision geometric data, for example from laser scans, which is an important means of capturing and reconstructing the built environment. This geometric data also carries little context information, similarly to traditional computer-aided design (CAD) models, which only consist of mesh geometry without additional semantic information. One step towards creating a context to these models is the attachment of metadata. Shape recognition and geometric enrichment of these low-level models can be used as an automated extraction of structured metadata. Such metadata is naturally focused on the geometric data. The internet is a natural resource for connecting disperse information on historical artefacts and mining complementary information about a structure's context. Highly relevant structured data is increasingly accessible online, specifically in the form of LD [7] or microdata/schema.org annotations. Data about geoinformation,[2] building-related policies,[3] materials[4] or environmental and traffic statistics[5] is available in semi-structured formats such as RDF, and can be exploited through a large variety of publicly available tools. In addition, the social web provides a range of valuable indicators and clues which can be mined to shape a better understanding about the public perception, acceptance and use of structures [16].

---

[1] http://duraark.eu Accessed 26 Jul 2016.
[2] Examples include http://www.geonames.org/ Accessed 26 Jul 2016. or https://geoda-center.asu.edu/datalist/ Accessed 26 Jul 2016.
[3] Energy efficiency guidelines at http://www.gbpn.org/databases-tools/building-energy-rating-policies Accessed 28 Jul 2016.
[4] http://semantic.eurobau.com/ Accessed 26 Jul 2016.
[5] A wide range of traffic and transport-related data sets at http://data.gov.uk Accessed 26 Jul 2016.

Such information is usually spread across a multitude of sources and hidden in unstructured or semi-structured documents and data sets. State-of-the-art web mining and information extraction techniques, however, have the potential to significantly lower the costs to practitioners and researchers of gathering and analyzing data to enrich and further enhance existing low-level models. To achieve this, specific requirements have to be met. Buildings, specifically cultural heritage structures, exist and evolve over sustained periods of time, requiring the adoption of long-term preservation mechanisms. Furthermore, models and data evolve in a very dynamic fashion. This involves both low-level models, such as point clouds or CAD models, and structured contextual knowledge and data. Therefore scalable means for enriching, linking and preserving architectural models and relevant contextual knowledge are required to capture the evolution of models, data and the actual physical assets, and to ensure consistency over time.

The main focus of this chapter is on introducing the DURAARK project, which aims to tackle the challenges described above in an inherently inter-disciplinary manner. The PROBADO project was a precursor of DURAARK. It is briefly introduced in the following section along with some general preliminaries. The next section describes the continuation and further developments of this work in the context of the DURAARK project. This is structured around the three main focus areas of the project, which are geometric enrichment, semantic enrichment and preservation of architectural data. Each of these areas is discussed in a separate section. The chapter concludes with a discussion and summary.

2 Preliminaries: PROBADO

PROBADO was funded by the German Research Foundation from 2006 to 2011. One key goal of the project was to integrate 3D models from the architectural domain into the librarian process chain, starting with acquisition through indexing up to presentation and delivery. The main focus was on methods for content-based search and indexing [5].

Although the projects' main use-case scenarios were modern architectural 3D building and object models, methods and tools can be adapted for other applications in cultural heritage. PROBADO provides different techniques for (semi)automatic indexing architectural 3D data, elaborated user interfaces for searching and browsing and a rich metadata information scheme [8].

2.1 Content

The PROBADO repository is populated with architecture models, mainly building and interior models like furniture, but also context objects such as fences. The models were collected from university architecture departments or 3D portals like the Great Buildings collection.[6] Examples of 3D models from the cultural heritage domain in PROBADO are shown in Fig. 1.

---

[6] http://www.greatbuildings.com/ Accessed 26 Jul 2016.

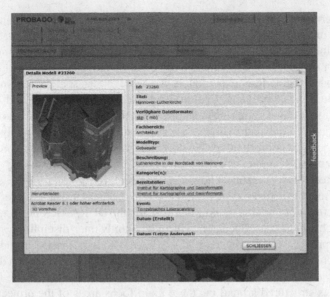

Fig. 1. 3D model in the PROBADO reference archive from the cultural heritage domain

2.2 Indexing

Content-based search relies on domain-specific indexing services which generate descriptors of the building models during an offline indexing stage. The predominant 3D CAD models at the time of the PROBADO project were mere geometric representations rather than semantic definitions of articulate structures such as walls, spaces and room functions. To be able to support indexing and searching, PROBADO focuses on whole building structures and supports an automatic content-based analysis stage in which semantic information is extracted. The descriptors include both global shape properties and connecivity information inside buildings. Specifically, an algorithm which is capable of extracting room structures from purely geometrical representations of buildings in the form of CAD models [43] was devised and developed further in DURAARK (see Sect. 4.3 below). The basic approach is to analyze the models and identify room-bounding elements such as floors and walls. Afterwards, rooms are identified as basic building elements and finally the room connection structure is derived by identifying linking elements such as doors or windows. The algorithm accepts polygon meshes without specific consistency requirements as input. The derived information about rooms and their connectivity is stored along with the 3D models, serving as the basis for user searches.

2.3 Search and Retrieval

For searching within content-based indexes, specific interfaces were developed to graphically formulate queries for similar content [6]. PROBADO supports searching in both metadata and content-based space in 3D architectural data, comprising models of buildings, interior and exterior elements. PROBADO user interfaces for queries and result visualization are realized using rich Internet application technology. Examples of the PROBADO 3D search interface are shown in Fig. 2.

(a) browsing

(b) details page

(c) search by location

(d) 2D result view

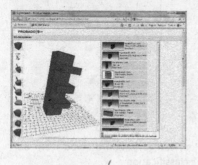

(e) search by 3D sketch

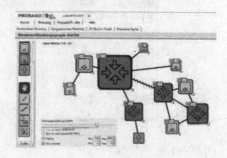

(f) search by room connections

Fig. 2. Examples of the PROBADO search interface

Querying for similar global shape: Queries about the shape of models can be supported by sketching 3D volumes, for example using the modeling capabilities of SketchUp.[7]

Querying for room configurations: The configuration of rooms inside a building is an important aspect of the design process, and can be considered as one functional criterion. In the PROBADO search interface, a graph editor enables editing of an abstract specification of the room connectivity structure. A plan-based interface enables editing of sketches of connectivity graphs, as illustrated in Fig. 2. Combining queries with space use functions can help architects or historians search for patterns in floor plan layouts.

Browsing functions and presentation of results: PROBADO supports browsing for collections, providers, file formats and categories. Depending on the type of query, PROBADO offers different presentations of the results. For all search and browsing options the results are displayed as a simple list. For content-based search elements the result set can be arranged in 2D, with similar results as clusters. A PDF-based 3D preview with embedded 3D content is integrated alongside the "classic" presentation of results using thumbnails. If a request is made by room connections, a results graph visualizes the request within the 2D floor plan of the building.

2.4 Classification

PROBADO also aimed at automatically classifying 3D models. As classification results are probabilistic, the PROBADO category browsing only considered class labels that had at least a 80 % confidence in assignment with other objects showing up on result pages. Examples from the PROBADO 3D category browsing interface are shown in Fig. 3.

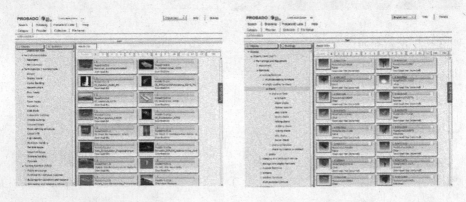

(a) browsing building categories

(b) object categorization derived from automatic classification

Fig. 3. 3D models in PROBADO are classified according to object and building categories based on the Getty Art and Architecture Thesaurus (AAT) (http://www.getty.edu/research/tools/vocabularies/aat/ Accessed 26 May 2016)

---

[7] http://www.sketchup.com/ Accessed 26 Jul 2016.

3   The DURAARK Approach

The importance and challenges of long-term digital preservation (LDP) in the fields of AEC and facility management (AEC/FM) have been recognized for many years. The life cycle of buildings from their design to construction, use and demolition typically spans several decades, but can reach centuries and occasionally even millennia. During this life cycle, changes in occupancy, floor plan layout, technical equipment and renovations occur frequently. The ability to plan, execute and control these changes depends largely on the quality of the documentation of a wide range of aspects covering many engineering disciplines. From the 15th century onwards, technical drawings have been used to capture the spatial composition of building elements and some of their properties in rather unambiguous semantic encodings, in the form of orthographic projections of exceptional buildings. Their widespread use for common residential and commercial buildings only dates back some 150 years, however, and the paper-based documents have often been lost along the way. In addition to the sparsity of documentation, the lack of as-built information is challenging in many regards: The as-planned state, which captures the design intent of architects and engineers, often differs significantly from the real physical state of the building. Changes from the original plans are often made ad hoc on the construction site and are seldom documented to their full extent.

With the advent of digital means of planning in contemporary AEC/FM, additional challenges surfaced. The lack of interoperability between the large variety of domain-specific computer applications used in building projects is one well-known problem [18]. In an industry with fast iterations of release cycles for CAD and BIM software packages, reliable preservation policies have to cover hundreds of proprietary data formats. These formats are quickly outdated, often not backward compatible and have their own complex underlying information models. This particular problem has been identified in earlier work on digital preservation of building information like PROBADO (see Sect. 2) and FACADE [35]. The use of vendor-neutral, interoperable, and self-documenting data models has also been employed in other areas of LDP engineering such as automotive and aerospace projects [9]. Accommodating established practices and workflows in the AEC community, DURAARK focuses on two types of primary architectural data: Semantically rich BIM models and point cloud representation generated by an appropriate acquisition device. While the former are especially used to plan, construct and maintain buildings, the latter have become the method of choice for documenting the current state of existing architecture, whether newly built or historical monuments. They also serve as a starting point for generating floor plans of older buildings for which no digital 2D or 3D data exists. This brings them into the focus of the cultural heritage community. These two representations constitute opposite extremes along the axes of semantic richness and geometric compactness which pose major challenges in terms of LDP. BIM models, on the one hand, include a compact description of explicit geometry, often conveying design intent, and attributions and classifications of elements like doors or walls. They also contain vast amounts of textual metadata which facilitates interpreting, navigating and browsing the data. In point clouds, on the other hand, geometry is represented by a huge set of unstructured, possibly colored points with virtually no additional semantics. In order to support many common use cases in the digital preservation of buildings, these two opposed forms of representation have to be mapped and transferred to enable a comprehensive overview of the physical artifact. This mapping can be thought of as a movement along the semantic richness and geometric compactness axis which form the fundamental building blocks of the DURAARK project. *Geometric enrichment* describes the effort of adding geometric details to existing as-built models or deriving explicit geometries from measured data. *Semantic enrichment* describes the contextualization and attribution of the underlying models from various resources including LD. Synchronizing both representations by bridging the semantic and geometric gap enables the seamless preservation of heterogeneous architectural data. Technically, the DURAARK project focuses on two open information models and file formats: Industry Foundation Classes (IFC) [2] provide a standardized data model for buildings based on ISO 10303 which is used across a large number of engineering domains [33] and the e57 file format to capture point cloud data structures [22]. For an in-depth look at the suitability of IFC as an archival format, we refer the reader to [25]. In the following sections we introduce the main aspects of geometric and semantic enrichment and their significance for LDP.

4   Geometric Enrichment

In the context of the DURAARK project, the concept geometric enrichment refers to various methods of connecting vast amounts of unstructured point cloud data representing measurements of real-world artifacts to semantically rich building information models.

4.1   Synchronizing BIM Models and Point Clouds

During its life cycle, built architecture usually undergoes changes caused by retrofitting and renovation efforts, weathering and other deliberate or unforeseen mechanical influences. As a consequence, digital building descriptions must be adapted to the new circumstances, which results either in additional point cloud measurements or in updates to the original BIM plan. Simply ingesting this new data into an existing long-term archive would result in isolated data graves which are of little use to stakeholders in the AEC community. DURAARK addresses this problem by providing latent Dirichlet allocation (LDA) tools to synchronize and link the descriptions as they evolve over time to provide users with seamless, coherent documentation.

Geometric Synchronization: One of the challenges of geometrically synchronizing point clouds with respective BIM models is that both representations are most likely given in different coordinate systems and usually only partially overlap. Additionally, the scale and the level of detail of both representations may vary. DURAARK's geometric enrichment components therefore provide a data ingestor with tools to (semi)automatically align different representations of the building. An example is shown in Fig. 4. After successful alignment and blending of the different representations as shown in (c), users of the long-term archive are able to view differences in the temporal changes of representations, see (d). Specialist commercial tools to synchronize point clouds and BIM models and to visualize differences have become available since the project started. Therefore we added this functionality to the rest of our framework, to allow curators to ingest the data into the digital archive smoothly and easily.

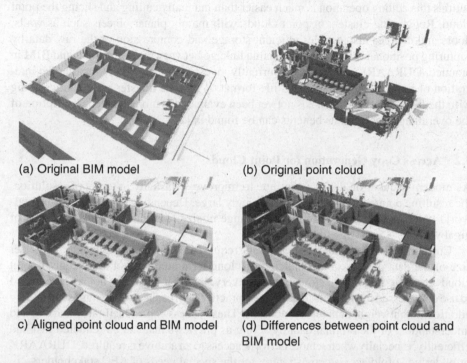

(a) Original BIM model

(b) Original point cloud

c) Aligned point cloud and BIM model

(d) Differences between point cloud and BIM model

Fig. 4. Synchronization of point cloud and BIM model. (a) and (b) show the original unaligned BIM model and point cloud, respectively. Note that both representations only partially overlap. The point cloud in (b) additionally shows clutter that does not correspond to the actual structures but probably originates from objects that were measured through windows. (c) shows the two representations after spatial alignment. (d) visualizes the differences between the two representations. The blue structures are present in the point cloud but not in the BIM model, e.g., most of the furniture. Red structures are only present in the BIM model, e.g., the outer walls in the upper section of the figure. The data shown represents the Risløkka Trafikkstasjon in Oslo, Norway. The point cloud consists of 23 single scans and contains a total of 80,625,944 points.

Transfer of Semantics: With the alignment of the two representations at hand it is possible to transfer high-level semantics from the BIM model to the point cloud. To this end, points are associated with the spatially closest geometric entity in the BIM model, if present in a certain neighborhood. The entity-to-point linkage makes navigating the point cloud much easier for the user. For example, the identification of points not linked to the model's entities makes it possible to hide scan clutter, for example from laser rays cast through windows. Using the same technique, furniture inside the building can be hidden easily. Furthermore, the linkage enables direct navigation to a specific part of the building, for instance by typing in the name of a BIM class element. It also allows for virtual tours of the point cloud which follow a sequence of neighboring rooms or stories. Apart from navigation, it also becomes easier to edit and trim the point cloud. For example, it might be useful for an architect or engineer to only store a particular part of the building for further processing. By identifying points within certain BIM room entities this editing operation is much easier than manually cutting and slicing the point cloud. Registering clusters of point clouds with mainly planar objects such as walls, floors and ceilings also enables efficient storage and compression of the raw data by capturing positional differences. To enable linkage between the point cloud and BIM in practice, DURAARK's partners are currently investigating and implementing the integration of point clouds into the IFC file format. While the transfer of semantics along with the file format extension has not yet been evaluated, a more detailed description of the overall approach and its benefits can be found in [24].

4.2   Access Copy Generation for Point Clouds

As modern acquisition devices continue to improve, especially in terms of resolution, the resulting point clouds become increasingly large. Depending on the size of the real-world building, a point cloud can easily range in size from hundreds to thousands of gigabytes.

Currently this trend of increasing storage requirements seems unstoppable. The sheer size of the data poses several challenges to long-term archiving of architectural point cloud data in terms of both storage and delivery. While it is usually not recommended to use compressed file formats in LDP, best-practice approaches today suggest providing additional lightweight data representations. These access copies facilitate handling and understanding of the original data by acting as previews that can be rendered fast and efficiently, especially when remote network access to an archive is required. DURAARK provides a twofold access copy strategy for the special needs of AEC stakeholders.

Abstract Access Copies: DURAARK enables the generation of volumetric and parametric boundary representations from the underlying point cloud. These only include the overall structure of the building and omit details like furniture, so the representations can be rendered efficiently. Though similar to polygon meshes, these representations are far more intelligent, as the resulting surface polygons are grouped into semantic entities representing the floor, ceiling, walls, doors, and windows. This allows users to intelligently edit the model, for example by removing several walls in order to simulate a retrofitting effort planned for the future. Additionally, access copies are mostly free of scan clutter, such as trees surrounding the building. An example of such an access copy can be found in Fig. 5. As a detailed description of the underlying method is beyond the scope of this article, we refer you to [29, 30, 42] for more comprehensive information.

Starting with a decomposition of the point cloud into vertical planes (see [37]) which correspond to wall surfaces, we project all planes to the ground, and extend the resulting 2D lines towards infinity. The latter step is performed to increase the robustness of the wall surface detection, as point clouds often contain holes caused by scan shadows. We then compute all line intersections. The resulting arrangement now consists of a large

(a) Original point cloud   (b) Abstracted polygonal representation

Fig. 5. Abstract access copy. The left image shows the original point cloud scan of the Hamar Bispegaard Museum (courtesy of Statsbyg Norway) including 6,811,285 points, which results in a file size of around 78 MB. The right image shows the generated abstract polygonal access copy, which only hints on the overall structure without providing details such as furniture. Its file size is around 26 KB.

number of 2D segments. A subset of those segments is extracted using an energy-minimization approach and is finally combined and extruded to wall entities. Additionally, windows and doors are detected using a supervised learning approach. Note that the resulting access copy is at most an abstraction of the original point cloud data rather than a "geometrically thinned" version, as it only contains the overall structure of the building, not the details.

Lower-Quality Access Copies: In case the stakeholder is not only interested in a lightweight structural abstraction of the original data, but in the real point cloud itself, DURAARK components offer representations of a lower quality in terms of the precision of the points localization. The underlying lossy compression techniques exploit the hidden structure arising from man-made geometric forms to reduce the amount of necessary storage space. They allow compression rates of very few bits per point while the induced loss in point localization precision is only in the range of very few millimeters. For a more detailed evaluation, see [20] and [19].

4.3 Improvement of Point Cloud Browsing and Navigation

No sophisticated 3D BIM plan exists for most of the huge legacy building stock. The necessary tools had not been developed until some decades ago, and even then the AEC community was slow to adapt to the new workflow. The segmentation methods to improve browsing, navigation, searching, and interaction from high-level BIM data described in Sect. 4.1 cannot be applied to scans of legacy buildings. To overcome this drawback, DURAARK provides powerful tools that (semi)automatically enrich point clouds with the information most relevant to the AEC community. Some examples of this augmentation process follow below. For further details and additional results, please refer to [28, 30, 42].

Automated Point Cloud Segmentation: To enable intelligent navigation of huge point cloud data, it is necessary to segment it into meaningful parts. In the context of architectural models this means detecting the stories and rooms. While most data sets are already divided into stories manually, room segmentation poses a difficult challenge, especially in the presence of scan clutter generated by furniture, plants, or people. Over the course of the DURAARK project, powerful algorithms have been developed to tackle this problem. An early result is shown in Fig. 6, where the original complex point cloud in (a) was automatically segmented into rooms in (b).

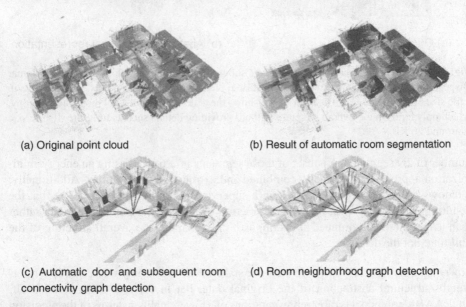

(a) Original point cloud   (b) Result of automatic room segmentation

(c) Automatic door and subsequent room   (d) Room neighborhood graph detection
connectivity graph detection

Fig. 6.   Point cloud augmentation. Starting with the unstructured point cloud shown in (a). we first detect room boundaries and subsequently segment the point cloud. The localization of doors gives rise to the extraction of room connectivity graphs in (c). Additionally, room neighborhood graphs can be extracted to serve as content-based indexing structures, see (d).

Object Recognition and Structural Enrichment: AEC users need to locate doors and windows or identify the configuration of rooms. These properties help to understand the current or former purpose and function of a building and are also of great importance for renovation or retrofitting.

The extraction of room connectivity graphs [43] (see 6c) or room neighborhood graphs (see 6d) can be used as a starting point for graph-based searches for certain room configurations [44].

5   Semantic Enrichment

While geometric enrichment focuses on the generation of metadata about a building's shape and structure, semantic enrichment aims at providing additional contextual data about a building and its models.

5.1 Semantic Enrichment Overview

As part of model preprocessing, DURAARK developed tools to ingest and preserve building information models. An essential component of these facilitates the semantic enrichment (see [11]), annotation and extraction of relevant metadata. Semantic enrichment exploits both expert-curated domain models and heterogeneous Internet data sources, in particular LD, to gradually enrich a BIM model with related information. Key targets are:

Vocabulary linking: improving interoperability at the schema/vocabulary level by linking existing data to established vocabularies on the Internet.

Entity interlinking and enrichment: enriching existing building and model metadata with related information about a building's context, such as its historical, geographic, environmental or legal setting and the evolution of these aspects over time.

During the creation and modification of initial BIM models, individual objects in the building are enriched by architects and engineers. For example, general functional requirement specifications of a particular door set in the early stages of the design (the door must be 1.01 m wide and have a fire resistance of 30 min according to the local building regulation) are gradually refined with the product specification of an individual manufacturer (product type A of vendor B, catalogue number C, serial number D in configuration E3 with components X, Y, Z). While a number of such common requirements and product parameters can be specified using entities and facets of established schemas and vocabularies such as the IFCs, a great deal of information is currently modeled in a formally weak and ad hoc manner. To address this, a number of structured vocabularies have been proposed in the past. Unfortunately, these have not been adopted widely due to their limited exposure via standard interfaces. They include the buildingSMART Data Dictionary (bsDD)[8] [23], which explains several tens of thousands of concepts. The DURAARK project is currently limited to custom simple object access protocol (SOAP) and representational state transfer (REST) web services, but the plan is to preserve this information as 5 star LD within the Semantic Digital Archive (SDA).

Automated and semi-automated interlinking and correlation with related web data includes enrichment and interlinking at the entity level. Architectural BIM models are enriched with related information prevalent on the web, including the geolocation, surrounding traffic, transport and infrastructure, usage and perception by the general public. Previous work on entity linking [27], data consolidation and correlation for digital archives [36] has been used to develop dedicated algorithms for the architectural domain. These can be tailored to detect data relating to specific geospatial areas or architecturally relevant resource types. The user can define the parameters for semi-automated enrichment of the data as it is ingested for archiving. This can be useful for librarians, archivists and the staff of municipalities, construction companies and architectural offices.

The SDA serves as central storage for all semantic and geometric metadata within DURAARK. It thus contains a continuously growing knowledge graph of buildings,

---

[8] http://bsdd.buildingsmart.org/ Accessed 26 Jul 2016.

their digital models and their context. The latter includes both geometric and semantic information, for instance about the geographic, historic or legal context. Data within the SDA can be roughly assigned to the following three categories:

1. Primary metadata of digital objects and physical assets: the SDA serves as a repository of metadata describing physical assets (buildings) and their context as well as the data object representing them. As such, it is an index and catalogue providing information about the buildings preserved in the DURAARK system as a LD set.
2. Geometric metadata: the SDA contains some baseline geometric information about the shapes and structures captured by the described digital assets, as provided by the geometric enrichment components defined in the previous section.
3. Semantic enrichments: targeted crawls retrieve background knowledge from the LD graph about data captured in the SDA. This specifically includes more details of the geographic, environmental or structural context of the captured physical assets. Cross-domain reference graphs such as DBpedia[9] and Freebase are used together with more focused data sets with a clear temporal or regional focus.

Each of the categories described above adheres to a different schema. The first category (base metadata for digital and physical assets) is expressed using a well- defined vocabulary, namely the BuildM schema.[10] The semantic enrichments, i.e. crawled context graphs, follow arbitrary vocabularies as these are used in their source data sets, for instance, the DBpedia ontology[11] or the GeoNames ontology.[12]

The BuildM schema,[13] a central vocabulary for annotating digital models and physical structures, primarily describes the concepts DigitalObject[14] and PhysicalAsset,[15] while suitable terms are derived from a number of existing vocabularies. As such, the population of BuildM instances defines the core of the SDA and serves as central registry of buildings and their digital models, further enriched with contextual background knowledge. The overall combination of a set of BuildM instances describing a particular asset and their corresponding context graphs (crawls) is referred to as BuildM+.

5.2 Vocabulary Mapping and Interlinking

At present, the use of meaningful, unambiguous semantically rich vocabularies to classify buildings and their components is limited to local classification systems such as Uniclass, OmniClass or the German DIN 276. Such semantic tagging is mostly done to comply with local regulations demanding legally binding specifications of certain components (see also 5.1). Vendor-neutral vocabularies to classify buildings, components and products such as the bSDD, Bau Data Web [34] and Getty AAT [40] are

---

[9] http://dbpedia.org Accessed 26 Jul 2016.
[10] http://duraark.eu/wp-content/uploads/2015/02/DURAARKD6.2.pdf Accessed 26 Jul 2016.
[11] http://dbpedia.org/ontology/ Accessed 26 Jul 2016.
[12] http://www.geonames.org/ontology. Accessed 26 Jul 2016.
[13] http://data.duraark.eu/vocab/buildm/ Accessed 26 Jul 2016.
[14] http://data.duraark.eu/vocab/buildm/DigitalObject Accessed 26 Jul 2016.
[15] http://data.duraark.eu/vocab/buildm/PhysicalAsset Accessed 26 Jul 2016.

becoming more widely available, however. These allow for greater machine-readable semantic richness than traditional attributions intended only for consumption by human readers. These traditional and purely text based attributions are prone to ambiguity, spelling mistakes and locale restrictions [4]. The DURAARK project aims to map and align these large and rich vocabularies using automated alignment technologies validated and enhanced by crowdsourcing to cope with the sheer volume of information they contain.

5.3 Entity Interlinking and Enrichment

Entity interlinking enables the enrichment of architectural data within the SDA with related information from the Internet, specifically the Web of Data, and is a prerequisite for efficient retrieval [14] and more user-oriented semantic search. The graph-based yet distributed nature of LD has serious implications for enriching digital archives with references to external data sets. Distributed data sets (schemas, vocabularies and actual data) evolve continuously, and these changes have to be reflected in the archival and preservation strategy. Enrichment and preservation must be considered together in archival efforts, but all too often this is not done in an integrated fashion. Generally, in theory all data sets (and RDF statements) in an LD graph are somehow connected. LD archiving strategies are increasingly complex and have to strike a balance between correctness and completeness on the one hand, and scalability on the other. These decisions are highly dependent on the domain and characteristics of each individual data set, as each poses different preservation challenges. The dynamics in which data sets evolve, or the frequency of changes made, can vary widely. In some fairly static data sets, changes occur only under exceptional circumstances (e.g., 2008 Road Traffic Collisions in Northern Ireland from data.gov.uk[16]). Other data sets are meant to change with high frequency (e.g., Twitter feeds or Highways Agency Live Traffic Data[17]). In the majority of data sets changes occur moderately frequently (i.e., on a weekly, monthly or annual basis) as is the case for Bau Data Web[18] or DBpedia. We are exploring Internet data preservation strategies according to the specific requirements, nature and dynamics of individual data sets. These strategies include (a) non-recurring capture of URI references to external entities as is common practice within the LD community, (b) non-recurring archiving of subgraphs or the entire graph of external data sets and (c) periodic crawling and archiving of external data sets.

5.4 Focused Crawling of Linked Data

Previous work [13] on preserving structured data aimed at providing generic crawlers for LD sets. Given the scale required, more targeted approaches are now being developed

---

[16] https://data.gov.uk/dataset/2008_injury_road_traffic_collisions_in_northern_ireland Accessed 26 Jul 2016.

[17] http://www.data.gov.uk/dataset/live-traffic-information-from-the-highways- agency- road-network Accessed 26 Jul 2016.

[18] http://semantic.eurobau.com/ Accessed 26 Jul 2016.

to provide scalable and efficient enrichment of building metadata. Earlier experiments have shown that a 2-hop crawl of a given seed lists results in 38,295 entities on average. Therefore, the relevance of entities is computed as part of the crawling process and determines the seeds for the following hops [45].

While the overall LD graph might contain highly relevant information about the semantics of a specific entity, identifying the relevant paths and entities, or the semantic neighborhood of a given entity or set of seed entities, is a challenge. We define *focused crawling* of LD as follows.

Given a specific seed list of entities $S = \{e1, ..., en\}$, the aim is to crawl and rank relevant candidate entities $C = \{el, ..., el\}$. Though seeds could commonly be represented through terms which require a disambiguation step, for simplification purposes we assume that seed entities are represented by entity URIs, for instance, referring to instances within the DBpedia graph.

In order to tackle the challenges of focused crawling, we adopt the following steps: (i) seed list analysis, (ii) breadth-first search crawl (BFS) for candidates, (iii) seed list specific candidate entity ranking. The last two steps are embedded into a crawling cycle using the relevant entities selected from step (iii) as the next hop crawling queue for step (ii). An attrition factor of each seed entity is considered to reflect the crawl intent during the focused crawling process, as explained below. This is based on the assumption that entities within a seed list are of varying importance for the crawl intent, and hence, their individual impact on the ideal result set differs.

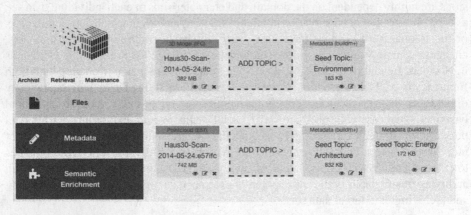

Fig. 7. Integration of the focused crawler into the DURAARK prototype.

A focused crawling configuration is an implementation of a specific crawling algorithm, dependent on specific attributes of the candidate crawling process and seed list analysis, such as depth for candidate crawling and attrition factor of seed entities in a seed list. Crawls are either based on (a) manually defined seed lists, for instance, to retrieve relevant LD subgraphs about the geographic, historical or infrastructural context of buildings and their model or (b) automatically extracted seeds, directly derived from existing BuildM instances. Based on experimentally defined crawl configurations, we introduce an efficient means to crawl LD relevant to the specific instances in the SDA.

The focused crawler is shown as a generic REST API and already integrated into the DURAARK prototype[19] and workflows (Fig. 7).[20]

5.5   Case Study: Extracting Architectural Patterns from the Web of Data

One aspect of urban planning and architecture is the need to assess the popularity or perception of built structures (and their evolution) over time. This aids in understanding the impact of a structure, identifying the needs for restructuring or drawing conclusions useful for the entire field, for instance about successful architectural patterns and features. Knowing what people think about a building could also prove invaluable for cultural heritage preservation experts, building operators, and policy makers. In this section, we introduce some work [15] on how the aforementioned technologies can be used for detecting a successful architectural pattern.

Research originally focused on a combination of the aesthetic and functional aspects of the perception of architecture [39, 41]. It is easy to see how appearance plays a vital role in the emotions induced by, for example, churches. In the case of airports or railway stations, however, functional aspects such as efficiency or accessibility may be more important. This suggests that the same factors have a significantly different impact depending on the type of building.

As part of the semantic enrichment research we identified influence factors for a predefined set of architectural structures. We aligned these factors with structured data from DBpedia. This work is a first step towards semantic enhancement of the architectural domain, which can support semantic classification, analysis, and ranking.

We used crowdsourcing to determine influence factors for more aesthetic and more functional building types. For bridges, churches, skyscrapers and halls, these were: History, surroundings, materials, size and personal experiences. For airports, these were ease of access, efficiency, appearance, choice/availability, facilities, and size. We followed guidelines and recommendations for designing the crowdsourcing tasks, to ensure the reliability of responses and quality of the results [17].

Based on these influence factors we acquired perception scores for the buildings on a Likert scale, again through crowdsourcing. By aggregating these scores, we arrived at a ranked list of buildings of each type within our data set.

In order to determine patterns in the perception of well-received structures (as for the building rankings), we correlated the influence factors with concrete properties and values from DBpedia.

Table 1 depicts some of the properties extracted from the DBpedia knowledge graph in order to correlate the influence factors corresponding to each structure with specific values. This makes it possible to analyze well-perceived patterns for architectural structures at a finer level of granularity, in terms of explicit properties. In order to extract relevant data from DBpedia for each structure in our data set, we first collected a pool of properties that correspond to the influence factors for each building type (see

---

[19] https://github.com/DURAARK/duraark-system Accessed 26 Jul 2016.

[20] The DURAARK deliverables D2.5 and D3.6, available from http://duraark.eu/deliverables/ Accessed 26 Jul 2016, describe the crawler and its API in more detail.

Table 1). In the next step, traversing the DBpedia knowledge graph which leads to each structure in our data set, we sought to extract corresponding values for each of the identified properties. Only those properties available on DBpedia were used, but these properties were not the same for all structures of a particular type. Therefore, although all the identified values accurately correspond to the structure, the coverage itself is restricted to the data available on DBpedia.

Table 1. DBpedia properties used to correlate influence factors.

Airports	Bridges	Churches	Halls	Skyscrapers
dbpedia-owl:runwaySurface, dbpedia-owl:runwayLength, dbprop:cityServed, dbpedia-owl:locatedInArea, dbprop:direction	dbprop:architect, dbpedia-owl:constructionMaterial, dbprop:material, dbpedia-owl:length, dbpedia-owl:width, dbpedia-owl:mainspan	dbprop:architectureStyle, dbprop:consecrationYear, dbprop:materials, dbprop:domeHeightOute dbprop:length, dbprop:width, dbprop:area, dbpedia-owl:location, dbprop:district	dbpedia-owl:yearOfConstruction, dbprop:built, rd, bprop:architect, dbprop:area, dbprop:seatingCapacity, dbpedia-owl:location	dbprop:startDate, dbprop:completionDate, dbpedia-owl:architect, dbpedia-owl:floorCount

By correlating the influence factors to specific DBpedia properties, we can identify patterns for well-perceived architectural structures. To illustrate how this information can be used within the limited scope of this article, we chose to showcase just one influence factor: Size of the structure.

We observed that for each airport we can extract indicators of size using the DBpedia property dbpedia-owl:runwayLength. Similarly, for bridges size can be represented using the DBpedia properties dbpedia-owl:length, dbpedia-owl:width and dbpedia-owl:mainspan. We can use the properties dbprop:area and dbprop:seatingCapacity for halls, and dbpedia-owl:floorCount and dbprop:height for skyscrapers. The corresponding property values for each structure in our data set[21] were extracted using the DBpedia knowledge graph.

We discovered that halls with a seating capacity of one to four thousand are well-perceived with the positive perception varying between 0.1 and 1. By leveraging the rankings and correlating with the property dbpedia-owl:architecturalStyle we found that the most well-received styles of churches in Germany are (i) Gothic Revival, (ii) Romanesque, and (iii) Gothic. This is shown in Fig. 8.

In this section we demonstrated that by correlating building characteristics with extracted data from DBpedia, as retrieved through the focused crawler, it is possible to compute and analyze architectural structures quantitatively. Based on this, we plan to develop algorithms to provide multi-dimensional architectural patterns such as

---

[21] Our data set and building rankings: http://data-observatory.org/building-perception Accessed 26 Jul 2016.

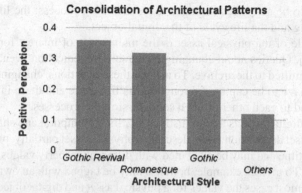

Fig. 8. Best perceived architectural patterns for churches, in terms of their *architectural styles*, by correlating top ranked churches with their DBpedia property.

"skyscrapers with x size, y uniqueness, and z materials used are best perceived". This will be useful to architects and urban planners in the future.

6 Preservation

State-of-the-art approaches to digital preservation are based on a number of processes as described in de-facto standards such as the OAIS Reference Model ISO 14721:2012 [1], the Producer-Archive Interface Methodology Standard ISO 20652:2006 [3], or the Lifecycle Model of the Digital Curation Centre (DCC) [21]. Following these guidelines, the key processes of a holistic preservation approach are built on technical and procedural factors. Technical specifications are addressed along the three levels of a digital object – namely, the bit-stream, logical and semantic levels. Procedural requirements are met by lifecycle implications in a producer, consumer, and archive context. While the basic underlying processes hold true for any form of digital object, regardless of complexity or domain, they need to be adapted for every information type. The following section sheds light on three areas for which the DURAARK project has developed methods and tools in line with preservation processes.

6.1 Meeting Requirements of Building and Object Life Cycles in an Archive

Archives do not categorize digital objects on a solitary file level, but consider them to be embedded in an archival unit, frequently referred to as the Intellectual Entity (IE). The term IE was framed in the context of the preservation metadata standard PREMIS, which defines an IE as a distinct intellectual or artistic creation that is considered relevant to a designated community in the context of digital preservation: for example, a particular book, map, photograph, database, hardware or software [10]. Each IE can be described through various levels of metadata, whether descriptive, technical, administrative, or structural. When mapping IE to building information, two distinct life cycles exist and need to be supported throughout the archiving process: the life cycle of the physical building and the life cycle of the digital object.

The life cycle of the physical asset is the main focus of interest for the AEC/FM domain [25, 26]. Queries about changing ownership, rededication events or structural changes are submitted to the archive. To answer these questions, changing properties of physical asset have to be captured throughout its life cycle and these information sets need to be linked to each other through solid versioning processes.

In contrast, digital objects have a distinct relation to temporal and spatial aspects of their physical asset description. They describe a physical asset partially, or in its entirety, at a set point in time and may be attributed with different property values than the physical asset itself. To give an example, both IEs may be tagged with an owner and creator property, but in most cases the values for a physical asset and digital object are different. The life cycle of the digital object is completely detached from that of the physical asset, as it is determined by technological changes and the constantly evolving access requirements of the designated community. Preservation planning and action are major building blocks of a digital object's life cycle.

The detached life cycles of the physical asset and digital object need to be adequately supported within an archive of building information. The DURAARK project has proposed a nested IE structure in which the physical asset and digital object can be linked, but remain independent of each other within lifecycle actions such as representation versioning, information updates and file format migration. This process is supported by the descriptive metadata schema, buildM, which clearly differentiates between the two types of information.

6.2 Characterizing the Digital Object with Technical Metadata

Digital preservation at the logical encoding level is supported through automatic characterization of the digital object. This includes a file format identification based on a signature pattern. Such a pattern describes the object at the level of the schema or the file format through a unique identifier (e.g., those assigned by PRONOM[22]) and the extraction of technical metadata from the object. With no technical metadata schemas previously available for 3D objects, the DURAARK project has advanced the digital preservation processes for BIM and 3D point cloud scans by identifying suitable candidates for characterization. These are mapped and described in the technical metadata schemas buildM and e57m. Extractors which can be embedded in digital preservation workflows are one public result of the project. The technical metadata schemas describe the object according to three basic categories: Creation process, parametric information, and content extent.

Information related to the creation process includes the technical provenance of the digital object, such as the scanner make and model for e57 point clouds or the modeling software and export routine for IFC BIM objects. Knowledge of the digital object's

---

[22] http://www.nationalarchives.gov.uk/PRONOM Accessed 26 Jul 2016.

genesis is important for archives to combat software or hardware bugs during a preservation action such as migration. It also helps interpret data correctly, such as in the case of missing weather data in an e57 object due to limitations of the creating software.

Parametric information properties give insight into systems within which a digital object's data should be interpreted. Examples include the coordinate system in which the points of a scan are described or the unit systems applied to measurements such as length, width and height in building information models. In an archival context this information is useful for re-engineering file formats, and provides prerequisites for target formats in preservation actions via migration.

The content extent describes the breadth and depth of information contained in the digital object, such as the total number of points in a scan or number of entities in a plan. In an archival context they are typically used as object-related input for significant properties in preservation planning. Significant properties contain characteristics of an object which the archive wants to preserve, for example color information assigned to points in a scan. The RGB color values can then be automatically extracted from the object, described in technical metadata (e57 m) and monitored over the course of a preservation action.

6.3   From Semantic Enrichment to Semantic Preservation

The DURAARK approach facilities a higher semantic depth of building information objects through enrichment with linked open data sources. While the enriched information is stored in metadata which can easily be queried by the user, one-time enrichment only provides the information available as-is at a given point in time. Moving from semantic enrichment to semantic preservation, the DURAARK system architecture includes an observatory and an archive level for the semantic enrichment sources. The data sets exploited for enrichment are harvested into an intermediate archive layer (SDA), while the Internet source of the data is monitored regularly for changes. Trigger events for re-harvesting may be defined by the archive, such as fixed intervals or certain thresholds of changing source properties. The different harvests of the source graph are time stamped to maintain information about the versioning. While re-harvesting facilitates a history of property updates in the source material itself, the archive needs to define a policy which leverages versioning of the metadata associated with the enriched objects themselves. The SDA is an intermediate archive, which stores and versions the harvests and metadata, but does not fully preserve it. The data in the SDA needs to be passed to an OAIS compliant digital preservation system on an on-going basis. Again, the interval in which this happens needs to be defined in policies and may depend on various organizational factors, such as the as number or relevance of changes occurring since the last snapshot.

7   Conclusions and Outlook

This chapter has introduced the work of the PROBADO and DURAARK projects on long-term digital preservation of buildings important for cultural heritage. This coordinated interdisciplinary effort has focused on three main aspects of archiving, namely geometric and semantic enrichment, and preservation strategies suitable for the volatile nature of buildings.

Geometric enrichment of building models can be achieved using semi-automated tools and models. To cope with large quantities of data acquired in the form of bulk point cloud data sets, explicit Building Information Models can be generated, or registered and superimposed on manually crafted existing models. This makes it possible to track changes in buildings over long periods of time on a high level of detail. Further improvements in the automated classification and clustering of meaningful structures in point clouds will allow fine grained searches in large archives in the future. Intertwining BIM and point cloud data sets in heterogeneous ways, including different levels of detail, enables incremental refinements of data access for various uses. Challenges include addressing the large quantities of data beyond the terabyte frontier in more efficient ways.

Semantic enrichment improves descriptions of buildings through contextualization and interlinking with further information resources in the form of Linked Data. These include dedicated vocabularies, other data sets capturing environmental conditions and urban context, and the perception of the general public in social media or the news.

Preservation strategies pose new challenges for archiving cultural heritage. "Living" artifacts like buildings are subject to frequent changes. Volatile Linked Data referred to during the semantic enrichment processes and within BIMs is also not easy to preserve. The tools and models demonstrated here will help to meet these preservation challenges in the future.

Acknowledgements. The work presented in this chapter has been funded by the German Research Foundation (DFG) and the European Community in the 7th Framework Program on Grant No. 600908.

References

1. 14721:2012, ISO 14721:2012 Reference Model for an Open Archival Platform Specification (IFC2x Platform) (2012)
2. 16739:2013, ISO 16739:2013 Industry Foundation Classes, Release 2x, Platform Specification (IFC2x Platform) (2013)
3. 20652:2006, ISO 20652:2006 Producer-archive Interface - Methodology Abstract Standard (2006)
4. Beetz, J.: A scalable network of concept libraries using distributed graph databases. In: Proceedings of Joint ICCCBE 2014 and the 2014 CIB W078 Conferences, Florida, USA (2014)
5. Berndt, R., et al.: The PROBADO project - approach and lessons learned in building a digital library system for heterogeneous non-textual documents. In: Fuhr, N., Kovács, L., Risse, T., Nejdl, W. (eds.) TPDL 2016. LNCS, vol. 9819, pp. 376–383. Springer, Heidelberg (2010). doi:10.1007/978-3-642-15464-5_37
6. Bernd, R., Blümel, I., Krottmaier, H., Wessel, R., Schreck, T.: Demonstration of user interfaces for querying in 3D architectural content in PROBADO3D. In: Agosti, M., Borbinha, J., Kapidakis, S., Papatheodorou, C., Tsakonas, G. (eds.) ECDL 2009. LNCS, vol. 5714, pp. 491–492. Springer, Heidelberg (2009)

7. Bizer, C., Heath, T., Berners-Lee, T.: Linked data - the story so far. Int. J. Semant. Internet Inf. Syst. **5**(3), 122 (2009)
8. Blümel, I.: Model, content, context (2013). http://www.semantic-media-Internet.de/downloads/files
9. Brunsmann, J., Wilkes, W., Schlageter, G., Hemmje, M.: State- of-the-art of long-term preservation in product lifecycle management. Int. J. Digit. Lib. 1–13 (2012) http://www.springerlink.com/content/931pt3302k9v546w/abstract/. Accessed 26 July 2016
10. PREMIS Editorial Committee: PREMIS Data Dictionary for Preservation Metadata v3.0 (2015)
11. Dietze, S., Beetz, J., Gadiraju, U., Katsimpras, G., Wessel, R., Berndt, R.: Towards preservation of semantically enriched architectural knowledge. In: 3rd International Workshop on Semantic Digital Archives (SDA 2013), September 2013
12. Eastman, C., Teicholz, P., Sacks, R., Liston, K.: BIM Handbook: A Guide to Building Information Modeling for Owners, Managers, Designers, Engineers and Contractors. Wiley, Hoboken (2011)
13. Fetahu, B., Gadiraju, U., Dietze, S.: Crawl me maybe: iterative linked data set preservation. In: Horridge, M., Rospocher, M., van Ossenbruggen, J. (eds.) International Semantic Internet Conference (Posters and Demos), CEUR Workshop Proceedings, vol. 1272, pp. 433–436. CEUR-WS.org (2014). http://dblp.uni-trier.de/db/conf/semInternet/iswc2014p.html. Accessed 26 July 2016
14. Fetahu, B., Gadiraju, U., Dietze, S.: Improving entity retrieval on structured data. In: Arenas, M., et al. (eds.) ISWC 2015, Part I. LNCS, vol. 9366, pp. 474–491. Springer, Heidelberg (2015)
15. Gadiraju, U., Dietze, S., Diaz-Aviles, E.: Ranking buildings and mining the internet for popular architectural patterns. In: Proceedings of ACM Internet Science 2015 (Internet - Sci2015) (2015)
16. Gadiraju, U., Kawase, R., Dietze, S.: Extracting architectural patterns from internet data. In: Proceedings of ISWC 2014 Posters & Demonstrations Track a Track Within the 13th International Semantic Internet Conference, ISWC2014, pp. 461–464, October 2014
17. Gadiraju, U., Kawase, R., Dietze, S., Demartini, G.: Understanding malicious behavior in crowdsourcing platforms: the case of online surveys. In: Proceedings of 33rd Annual ACM Conference on Human Factors in Computing Systems, CHI 2015, pp. 1631–1640. ACM, New York (2015). http://doi.acm.org/10.1145/2702123.2702443
18. Gallaher, M.P., O'Connor, A.C., Dettbarn, J.L., Gilday, L.T.: Cost Analysis of Inadequate Interoperability in the U.S. Capital Facilities Industry, August 2004. http://fire.nist.gov/bfrlpubs/build04/art022.html
19. Golla, T., Klein, R.: Real-time point cloud compression. In: IEEE/RSJ International Conference on Intelligent Robots and Systems (IROS) (2015, to appear)
20. Golla, T., Schwartz, C., Klein, R.: Towards efficient online compression of incrementally acquired point clouds. In: Vision, Modeling & Visualization. The Eurographics Association, October 2014
21. Higgins, S.: The DCC curation lifecycle model. Int. J. Digit. Curation **3**(1), 134–140 (2008)
22. Huber, D.: The ASTM E57 file format for 3D imaging data exchange. In: IS&T/SPIE Electronic Imaging, p. 78640A. International Society for Optics and Photonics (2011)
23. ISO12006-3: Building construction organization of information about construction works Part 3: framework for object-oriented information (2006)
24. Krijnen, T., Beetz, J., Ochmann, S., Vock, R.: Extending IFC with point cloud data. In: 22nd International Workshop on Intelligent Computing in Engineering 2015, July 2015

25. Lindlar, M.: Building information modeling – a game changer for interoperability and a chance for digital preservation of architectural data? In: Proceedings of 11th International Conference on Digital Preservation, iPRES Proceedings, vol. 11, pp. 204–209. State Library of Victoria, State Library of Victoria, Melbourne, Australia (2014)

26. Lindlar, M., Tamke, M.: A domain-driven approach to digital curation and preservation of 3D architectural data: stakeholder identification and alignment in the duraark project. In: Archiving 2014 Final Program and Proceedings, Archiving: Conference Proceedings, vol. 11, pp. 204–209. Society for Imaging Science and Technology, Society for Imaging Science and Technology, Springfield, VA, USA, May 2014

27. Pereira Nunes, B., Dietze, S., Casanova, M.A., Kawase, R., Fetahu, B., Nejdl, W.: Combining a co-occurrence-based and a semantic measure for entity linking. In: Cimiano, P., Corcho, O., Presutti, V., Hollink, L., Rudolph, S. (eds.) ESWC 2013. LNCS, vol. 7882, pp. 548–562. Springer, Heidelberg (2013). doi:10.1007/978-3-642-38288-8_37

28. Ochmann, S., Vock, R., Wessel, R., Klein, R.: Towards the extraction of hierarchical building descriptions from 3D indoor scans. In: EUROGRAPHICS Workshop on 3D Object Retrieval (3DOR 2014), April 2014

29. Ochmann, S., Vock, R., Wessel, R., Klein, R.: Automatic reconstruction of parametric building models from indoor point clouds. Comput. Graph. **54**, 94–103 (2016). http://www.sciencedirect.com/science/article/pii/S0097849315001119

30. Ochmann, S., Vock, R., Wessel, R., Tamke, M., Klein, R.: Automatic generation of structural building descriptions from 3D point cloud scans. In: GRAPP 2014 - International Conference on Computer Graphics Theory and Applications, SCITEPRESS, January 2014

31. Pauwels, P., Verstaeten, R., De Meyer, R., Van Campenhout, J.: Architectural information modelling for virtual heritage application. In: Proceedings of 14th International Conference on Virtual Systems and Multimedia, Lymassol, Cyprus, pp. 18–23 (2008)

32. Penttil, H., Rajala, M., Freese, S.: Building information modelling of modern historic building. In: Predicting the Future - 25th eCAADe Conference Proceedings, Delft, Netherlands, vol. 1, pp. 607–613 (2007)

33. Pratt, M.J.: Introduction to ISO 10303 the STEP Standard for Product Data Exchange. J. Comput. Inf. Sci. Eng. **1**(1), 102–103 (2001). doi:10.1115/1.1354995

34. Radinger, A., Rodriguez-Castro, B., Stolz, A., Hepp, M.: BauDataInternet: the Austrian building and construction materials market as linked data. In: Proceedings of 9th International Conference on Semantic Systems. pp. 25–32. ACM (2013). http://dl.acm.org/citation.cfm?id=2506186

35. Reilly, W.: Crossing the curatorial Chasm-lessons from the FACADE project. In: 4th International Conference on Open Repositories, May 2009. https://smartech.gatech.edu/handle/1853/28505

36. Risse, T., Demidova, E., Dietze, S., Peters, W., Papailiou, N., Doka, K., Stavrakas, Y., Plachouras, V., Senellart, P., Carpentier, F., Mantrach, A., Cautis, B., Siehndel, P., Spiliotopoulos, D.: The ARCOMEM architecture for social- and semantic-driven internet archiving. Future Internet **6**(4), 688–716 (2014). doi:10.3390/fi6040688

37. Schnabel, R., Wahl, R., Klein, R.: Efficient RANSAC for point-cloud shape detection. Comput. Graph. Forum **26**(2), 214–226 (2007)

38. Simeone, D., Cursi, S., Toldo, I., Carrara, G.: B (H) IM - built heritage information modelling - extending BIM approach to historical and archaeological heritage representation. In: Fusion - Proceedings of 32nd eCAADe Conference, vol. 1, pp. 613–622 (2014)

39. Sitte, C.: City Planning According to Artistic Principles. Rizzoli, New York (1986)

40. Soergel, D.: The art and architecture thesaurus (AAT): a critical appraisal. Vis. Resour. **10**(4), 369–400 (1995). doi:10.1080/01973762658306

41. Sullivan, L.H.: The Autobiography of an Idea, vol. 281. Courier Dover Publications, New York (1956)
42. Tamke, M., Blümel, I., Ochmann, S., Vock, R., Wessel, R.: From point clouds to definitions of architectural space. In: Fusion - 32nd International Conference on Education and Research in Computer Aided Architectural Design in Europe. eCAADe: Conferences, vol. 2, pp. 557–566. Northumbria University, Newcastle upon Tyne, UK, September 2014
43. Wessel, R., Blümel, I., Klein, R.: The room connectivity graph: shape retrieval in the architectural domain. In: Proceedings of International Conference in Central Europe on Computer Graphics, Visualization and Computer Vision (2008)
44. Wessel, R., Ochmann, S., Vock, R., Blümel, I., Klein, R.: Efficient retrieval of 3D building models using embeddings of attributed subgraphs. In: 20th ACM Conference on Information and Knowledge Management (CIKM 2011), Posters, October 2011
45. Yu, R., Gadiraju, U., Fetahu, B., Dietze, S.: Adaptive focused crawling of linked data. In: Wang, J., Cellary, W., Wang, D., Wang, H., Chen, S.-C., Li, T., Zhang, Y. (eds.) WISE 2015. LNCS, vol. 9418, pp. 554–569. Springer, Heidelberg (2015). doi:10.1007/978-3-319-26190-4_37

Simplifying Documentation of Digital Reconstruction Processes

Introducing an Interactive Documentation System

Jonas Bruschke[✉] and Markus Wacker

University of Applied Sciences, Dresden, Germany
jbruschke@htw-dresden.de, wacker@informatik.htw-dresden.de

Abstract. Digital reconstruction is becoming ever more common in archaeology, architecture and other disciplines. Lost, but also present structures are being visualized to enhance the understanding of a reconstructed object and point out historical and constructional relationships of the objects under consideration. Furthermore, the process of reconstruction leads to an aggregation of knowledge, becoming a substantial part of historical research. However, such projects usually lack a proper, traceable, rigorously applied – therefore valuable – documentation practice. In the final reconstruction of the object the references to its sources may only be known to the experts involved in the project. Those not involved in the reconstruction project may not be able to understand this relationship. Research into documentation practice has until now typically concentrated on theoretical approaches; effective tools are still missing. The authors propose a documentation tool for use in 3D reconstruction projects to support frequent tasks in digital reconstruction processes. The tool aims mainly to facilitate documentation and development processes in such a way that the input of data becomes simple and intuitive. The benefit of this work becomes apparent to all stakeholders. The proposed tool aims to be both, a collaboration platform and a research environment, complying with metadata standards and guidelines, such as the London Charter principles. Drawing on the authors' experience of applying the tool to reconstruction of historic buildings, abstract concepts for a wider range of reconstruction tools are presented.

Keywords: Documentation · Digital reconstruction · Graph database · CIDOC CRM · WebGL · Web application

1 Introduction

Digital reconstruction, especially of individual buildings and architectural complexes, is becoming ever more common in archaeology and historical architectural studies. They visualize lost, but also present structures and can broaden the understanding of the reconstructed object. Historical and constructional relationships, which are hard to determine from plan material and other sources, can be presented much better in 3D models. Different interpretations of the source material and hypotheses can be quite easily run through by different versions of the 3D model and make contribution to the

© Springer International Publishing AG 2016
S. Münster et al. (Eds.): 3D Research Challenges II, LNCS 10025, pp. 256–271, 2016.
DOI: 10.1007/978-3-319-47647-6_12

aggregation of knowledge. Therefore, the 3D model is not just a visualization object, but becomes also an object of research. Besides tangible sources, such as plans and photographs, also intangible sources, such as decisions from experts (paradata) play an important role in the course of research into the object. The reconstruction process becomes transparent and traceable if the decision process, and the sources taken into consideration during this process, have been documented and visualized in an appropriate manner. In practice, it is often the case that the resulting visualizations do not reference the sources used. Someone, who has not been involved in the construction of the model, may find it difficult to assess whether the reconstruction was based on reliable facts or hypotheses, or both. Comprehensive documentation of the underlying reconstruction is therefore essential for a correct understanding of a digital model. The documentation should preferably cover all aspects that have led to the results and any new knowledge. To achieve this objective, the documentation should also include a record of the decisions made and problems encountered during the reconstruction process, with appropriate explanation. The quality of a model can better be judged by taking its development into account.

However, an examination of multiple reconstruction projects in [1, 2] showed that documentation either was missing completely or was only done insufficiently. Instead, often only the end product is presented, where much effort is made and much attention is paid to the quality of presentation. The important fact, that the visualization is a result of intensive research and how it was achieved, falls behind. Occasionally, the source material and approaches are exemplarily presented, but a direct link between objects and documents is missing. Even during the project's active phase the creative and cognitive processes are only scarcely documented; the storage and maintenance of the data are not done appropriately. Some key intellectual content may remain intelligible to those persons who were involved in the project. If eventually, they are not accessible anymore, the hardly gained knowledge is often lost or may fade easily with time, also in the head of project members and experts.

Such a comprehensive and well-structured documentation as desired, and postulated above, is often a time consuming task. It is often considered as a necessary evil that can be neglected. To make matters worse, projects often lack financial and human resources for such tasks. Many projects even have difficulties to achieve their main goals (cf. [2, p. 209]). Resources for a proper documentation may even not be taken into consideration. Post documentation of paradata, i.e. the documentation of a process after is has been completed, is a well-known practice. It may be dangerous, because a distant view may not permit to reconstruct some of the decision made in detail anymore, even by the project participants. Records are therefore recapitulated and summarized. In [2] is postulated, and practically proved in many research projects, that the documentation should rather be done just during the reconstruction or review processes. Of course, such a forceful execution demands a high level of discipline of the participants which may not always be possible.

Thus, the authors propose that reconstruction projects should be assisted, if possible, by an appropriate software tool, so that documentation is done automatically. This means as little additional effort as possible. Standards should be defined and supported, or even forced, by the software. It is believed that in this manner, documentation becomes transparent, understandable and a useful tool for project communication.

2   Related Work

The issue of lacking documentation practices in digital reconstruction projects is as old as digital reconstructions themselves. First definitions about what to record and ideas on how to enrich virtual reconstructions with metadata have been presented in the late 1990s [3]. These considerations continued within the EPOCH Research Agenda (2004 – 2008) and finally led to the definition of the London Charter for the Computer-based Visualisation of Cultural Heritage [4]. The defined principles relate to the intellectual integrity, reliability, transparency, documentation, standards, sustainability, and access. The principles concerning the documentation aspects are most substantial. Not just the source material should be documented and archived, but almost every aspect and piece of information, including the methodology, the paradata, the formats and standards used, and the dependency relationships between all this information. The outcomes and the documentation need to be preserved for future (sustainability) and made accessible for further research. The Seville Charter was the first of implementation guidelines recommended by the London Charter for individual communities of visualization practice, for the specific use in virtual archaeology [5]. Since both charters aim to define general principles for a broad range of applications and not to prescribe specific methods, they do not provide any advice or strategies how to practically comply with them. A guide to best practice is missing.

The EPOCH Research Agenda also considered the question of how to document digital objects to effectively support processes such as the 3D acquisition of 3D objects and their documentation in digital libraries, and the visualization of the history of a reconstruction [6]. An outcome of EPOCH is a tool for managing the interpretation process [7, 8], aiming to record how the available sources have led to the 3D visualization. The tool is web-based. It builds upon wiki technology, thus consists of interlinked pages. The pages are primarily structured into source sheets, recording the provenance, context, quality, and interpretation of a source; the source correlation sheets, documenting matching features and differences of multiple sources; the hypothesis sheets, discussing a set of possibilities in a tree-like structure; and the 3D/4D visualization sheets, containing the actual reconstruction results. The online approach enables the collaboration of multiple experts contributing their knowledge. However, the tool could not be practically evaluated. Given that only little information could be found, it seems that this tool has remained a prototype.

Pfarr [1] proposes a different, theoretical approach. She proposes four levels of documentation. The first level pertains to background information to the project, the second describes the historical context of the project, and the third explains the system, methodology and chronology of the reconstruction and documentation. The relationships between sources, models and processes are listed in the catalogs of sources and methods, representing the fourth level. Decision making is explained in text documents with reference to used material. Pfarr focuses on the principles and norms of technical documentation and uses prescribed vocabulary for classification of source material and models. She also proposes to disseminate documentation online for accessibility. The four-level structure is supposed to lead the user from general to more detailed information.

Both approaches presented above propose web-based solutions to ensure the (literally) worldwide access to the documentation. However, both are static solutions and do not adhere to any metadata standard.

Other projects that conform to several metadata standards include 3D-COFORM [9] and 3D-ICONS [10]; both arose from the EPOCH project. However, they aim to digitize artifacts, enriching them with information about the acquisition, provenance, context etc. They supply digitized objects to digital libraries, mainly Europeana. The digital artifacts are presented as 3D PDFs or within a simple WebGL viewer. Digital reconstruction involving complex interpretation processes are not addressed.

3   An Interactive Documentation System

The authors believe that no tools are available yet that would meet the specific demands of digital reconstruction projects. Here, the authors' approach comes into play. The main objective of the presented tool is to ease and partly automate the documentation process during reconstruction projects; so the project team may concentrate on the main tasks and content. The tool needs to assist the project in every matter, from archiving the sources and subsequent phases of the model, to communication within the team and the organization of the projects tasks. Moreover, it should be possible to explore the information recorded in the database. On the one hand the tool supports the project work as a collaborative platform, on the other, it serves as a research environment. The application has been designed as an online tool to ensure a wide accessibility. The 3D model, being the main goal in the reconstruction process, plays a central role in visualizing information and being an object of interaction.

A clearly laid out user interface is another aspect of the tool that should not be neglected. Only if the usage is quickly comprehensible and consistent in its use, the tool can be really a help and will be accepted by the team and the community. To this end, principles of human-centered design are applied comprising the processes of usability engineering into the whole development process.

In order to design such a tool it is important to understand the behaviors of the users, so the tool may be adapted to their working practices, so they are likely to adopt the tool [11]. Our tool is based on the findings and observation of Sander Münster [2]. Münster researched several projects and interviewed their respective participants to identify the workflows and strategies that proved to be significant for the project. His work provides some major insights into and guidelines for a successful reconstruction project.

3.1   Tasks and Roles

The identification and assignment of roles within a reconstruction project (i.e. connected to (read/write) access rights to certain data like import of new sources or editing of protocols) are important, as the user should be provided with a tool that meets the specific requirements of his or her tasks. In a reconstruction process several roles can be identified. First, there are the historic data providers, for example, historians and archaeologists. They gather and prepare the source material available and provide it together with metadata for the application. During the active reconstruction phase they also verify the intermediate reconstruction done by the modelers. They may request amendments to the model. If the sources are ambiguous or findings of historical research are unclear, their important task is to propose hypotheses and to take decisions with respect to the development of the model. They are the link to the professional community. Their decisions are decisive for the final results.

Second, there are the modelers and computer scientists. They use the supplied source material to construct the model. They upload their models to the system. They need to comment the changes and link the model to the used sources. Hence, they establish the reconstruction and decision process.

In addition to these basic roles, the third role of the project coordinator is to be mentioned, having organizational and administrative tasks. He or she manages the project, invites participants, oversees a work schedule, including milestones and deadlines, and assigns tasks. Finally, the proposed tool offer general functionalities for all users. These functionalities include access to and research into the data; the ability to comment on the model and the documents; the insight into the project development and the open tasks and issues.

At the end there is even a fourth role: the project observer or visitor. The general kind of user may only use the navigation and search functions for locating information in the database. Within a project, or task, a user may have multiple roles, if necessary.

3.2 Features and Concepts

A reconstruction project involves different tasks. These tasks are listed below with a subsequent discussion of their realization in an interactive application. Many of the concepts are based strategies recommended by Sander Münster [2]. Some proposed solutions are adapted from other tools for handling similar tasks, since familiar operations do not need to be learned anew.

Project Management. For the overview of the tasks, their duration, milestones and deadlines, a Gantt chart visualization has proved to be suited in the context under consideration (Fig. 1). The chart illustrates the activities in relation to a timeline. The activities and tasks are presented as bars reaching from start to finish dates. In such a way the volume of a task can be easily estimated. The dependencies between the tasks can be displayed, signalizing that a task can only be started when another one has finished. Additionally, the tasks can be hierarchically structured. With this tool the project members gain a good overview of the workload. There are many, mostly commercial project management tools on the market, from which workflows and operability can be adopted.

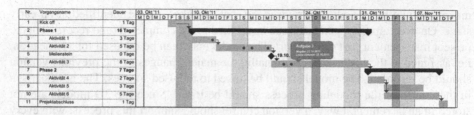

Fig. 1. Draft Gantt chart of task management

Data Acquisition. One of the first tasks of the historian is to acquire the source material and provide it to the modelers. This step should be completed before the modeling process starts to prevent major changes later on. The most relevant sources might be plans and photographs, but also literature or references to similar buildings of the same period may apply.

To this end a window for displaying the sources for reconstruction is proposed. In the corresponding window the respective first element is reserved for new entries (Fig. 2). The new sources can be inserted by drag and drop on the field or by clicking on the field. A new form opens up to provide specific information on the added source. Also in this form, the historian enriches the sources with metadata, e.g. type, title, author, and creation date. It may be necessary for some documents to be prepared (e.g. rectifying plans) for the prospective modeling process. Since some of the source material consists of scanned book pages, there is the option to convert them into searchable and editable text by optical character recognition. Prioritization of the primary sources for modeling should be possible. The database can be searched through a browser. The resulting sources are listed, offering further sorting and filtering modes (Fig. 2).

Fig. 2. Prototype of a source browser

Modeling. The modeling is usually done by computer scientists. For the modeling process often highly complex software products are applied. Such complex applications need to be learned. Every modeler has his or her own preference for modeling software. As each application has its own quirks, it would be disadvantageous to force the modeler to use a specific piece of software. An unfamiliar environment reduces the productivity. The proposed tool is therefore strictly separate from the actual modeling process. Instead, the application offers different exchange formats (e.g. COLLADA, OBJ) for import.

Usually, the modelers provide a first primitive model to the application on which the discussions and the iterative process of analysis, theory and reconstruction can start. The models should be periodically revised, so that mistakes can be identified at an early stage. On every update open tasks can be marked off as completed (and recorded in the project management part of the tool). The model may then be released for verification, i.e. assigned to the historian. Additionally, the major changes to the previous version should be recorded. The model should be linked to the used sources. The issues arisen in the course of the modeling process should be listed. Since the 3D models are not stored in an incremental way, a version control should support this process: with every update the model may be compared with its previous version and the changes highlighted. An appropriate presentation enables an overview and access to the different versions of the model (Fig. 3). Each version can be downloaded for further modeling or rendering within the modeling software.

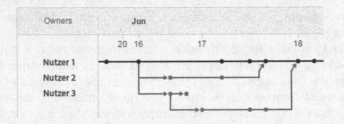

Fig. 3. Draft visualization of the model development, inspired by *GitHub*

In projects involving several modelers, the model is split into sections. Each modeler is in charge of one section. Hence, it is important to develop an appropriate model structure that is followed by everyone. Models of buildings often get separated into several components. It is recommended to name the objects after those component and constructional entities (e.g. floor, pillar, and stairs). Experience shows that the modeling starts without having any idea of structuring the model. Later into a project and with increasing complexity, a structured approach becomes essential. The application should provide advice and guide the modelers how to structure the model from the beginning of the project.

The separation of the model into several sections has to ensure that all the sections fit together. Thus, master plans should be provided with all relevant information. The modelers should start with an initial file containing the master plan and references for altitudes, so they can construct the model using the same dimensions and coordinates. Several parallel versions of the models should be developed, to be joined at the end. An object library may be useful to exchange recurring elements, such as capitals, statues and balustrades. The reusable elements should be identified in advance.

Visualization and Quality Management. By linking the objects to advanced information new queries and visualizations are possible. This includes spatial, temporal and functional aspects or even multiple levels of uncertainty. The objects can be highlighted and color-coded, depending on their assigned categories. For the visualization of temporal information, a timeline may be suited to specify the query (Fig. 4).

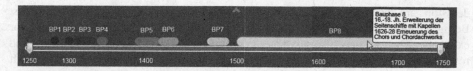

Fig. 4. Draft timeline for the visualization of construction phases, by Katrin Lütt

During reconstruction projects there are two types of quality control: technical and historical accuracy. The first concerns the quality and integrity of the model, and the level of detail to ensure uniform appearance. The specification and standards should be defined in advance and observed by all contributors. To control the compliance with the agreed quality standards it is recommended to appoint a quality manager.

However, the historical accuracy is more important. A major task of the historian is to validate the model by comparing it with the source material and against his or her expert knowledge of the subject (cf. Sect. 3.1. Tasks and Roles). For this verification visual comparisons are substantial. In order to support this task, the application enables the user to view plans and photographs together with the interactive model (Fig. 5). A measure and slice tools, and diverse display and projection modes, offer a better view of contours and inner structures. It is also recommended to consult perspective renderings, which should be supplied by the modelers. Some details can be evaluated much better by realistic computation of light.

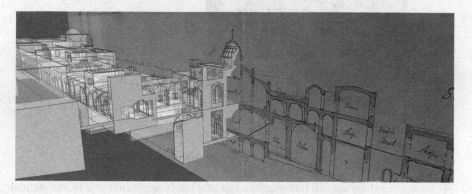

Fig. 5. Sliced model and integrated plan

For the historical rigor it is important to assign different levels of uncertainty or to mark the model as hypothetical. To this end, comments and certainty levels may be introduced to parts of the model.

Communication. Communication is essential for the success and the progress of a project. Usually, the project contributors reside at different places, so face-to-face meetings with the necessary regularity may not be possible. Email correspondence or conference calls offer an alternative. Consequently, the information is scattered and not recorded comprehensively. Sander Münster [2] points out that archiving all communication in the course of a project is important for its development. Within these archives decisions are documented and contribute to transparency of the reconstruction process. Being a central repository for all project data, the proposed tool is a medium for exchange. The tool may also serve as a communication platform during meetings and revision phases, to ease the documentation of occurring problems and decisions. It proved to be helpful to enhance textual comments with pictures and drawings, to describe the problem in multiple ways and to prevent misunderstandings due to different or missing specialist terminology. Beyond that, a picture can very precisely address the region of interest. To this end, the tool offers functionality to make screenshots of the model or document/comment particular regions of interest. Markers can be set on the screenshots (Fig. 6). They can be drawn on with a digital pen and annotated. Consequently, the discussion elements (snapshots, comments, drawings) are connected to the model and the documents. They can also be inspected commented upon by others. This way decision processes are established and recorded. They may be evaluated in a later phase of the project or after the reconstruction has been completed. The comments are linked to the model: they are visually pinned to a specific region of interest. Thus, the information is spatially localized, enabling the user to locate a problem or discussion. Simple 3D annotation capabilities are already implemented in other tools, e.g., *Autodesk A360 Viewer* and *Sketchfab*.

Fig. 6. Screenshot of prototype collaborative annotation tools

Personal meetings are still important and should not be neglected. It is recommended to provide a list of problems to be solved in advance of the meeting. The list of open tasks, or other questions to be discussed, can be generated using the protocol function. The application may also prove useful during the meeting. The models can be presented interactively and commented upon immediately. However, the verbal communication should still be recorded. Using the protocol function of the application a list of new tasks can be generated on the spot.

To prevent misunderstandings due to missing specialist terminology the tool includes a glossary, or wiki, of all relevant architectural and archaeological terms with definitions. IT terms are also included. The glossary can be accessed and enhanced by all users.

3.3 Graphical User Interface and Operability

The integration of a wide range of functionality into the graphical user interface without taxing the user is a challenge. A thorough, iterative layout, informed by the results of considerable user evaluation, will lead to an intuitive user interface. An interface with a double split screen layout, with four windows (Fig. 7) is being proposed as suitable. Since the proposed tool concentrates on virtual reconstruction, the main window in the upper left shows the 3D model. It can be chosen from, or searched in a list in the upper right. Additional options and functions concerning the appearance and manipulation of the 3D model (e.g. measure and slice tools) can be shown. The upper right window also contains the comments and discussion, including screenshots and drawings. The lower left window is for the sources. Sources can be imported here. One can select, search through and filter the available sources; some can be viewed in 3D. The lower right window contains navigation and workflow guidance. Alternatively, this space can be used to extend the upper right or lower left panel.

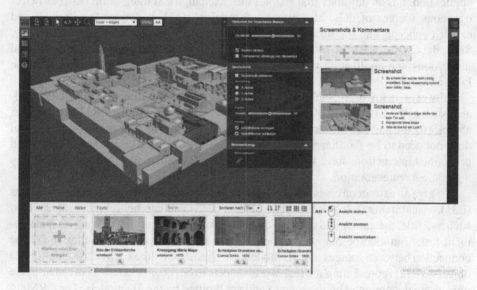

Fig. 7. Prototype graphical user interface

Many 3d viewers are just for displaying the 3d content and camera navigation in the 3d scene. They usually provide the user with simple navigation (rotate, pan, zoom). Handling the 3d model gets more complex, when advanced functionality is available; e.g. how to operate the slice and measure tools. First user tests revealed that some people, especially the elderly who are not used to interactive 3D content, had difficulties even with simple navigation. Others, who have advanced skills in operating with 3D models, had no difficulties. The two main target groups (historians and modelers) have different computing skills and know-how. The tool should accommodate the different needs of both these groups.

4 Data Storage and Processing

As the project progresses using the proposed tool, a lot of data is generated that need to be stored in a proper way. An effective and sustainable design for the structuring and formalization of the data, for implementation in a suitable database, is needed to store and retrieve the data. This design should be well elaborated to prevent later changes, when the data and queries may no longer be compatible; in particular, the variety of the data and the manifold relationships between them should be considered. It is possible to develop a proprietary concept, or structure, to store data in a database, but such a concept may not be sustainable. The adherence to standards is recommended.

4.1 CIDOC CRM and Extensions

The CIDOC Conceptual Reference Model (CRM) meets the demands of the proposed application. It is an ontology that enables the "exchange and integration between heterogeneous sources of cultural heritage information" [12]. It defines the implicit and explicit concepts and the semantic relationships that are used within cultural heritage. Since the CIDOC CRM is a standard (ISO 21127:2006) and has been applied by several institutions, the application complies with the sustainability principle defined in the London Charter.

However, many users, including the modelers, are not familiar with metadata standards such as the CIDOC CRM. Some classes and relationships of the CRM have a rather abstract nature and can be very confusing to non-experts. The user of the proposed tool does not need to be familiar with CIDOC classes or relationships as all the inputs and predefined interactions have been mapped to the CRM internally. Access is solved by a graphical representation.

To give an extract on class-level: source material is usually in the form of documents (E31), visual items (E36) or linguistic objects (E33) and can be linked to information such as a title, the author and creation date. Information concerning the project management tasks can also be mapped to the CRM as specific types of activities (E7). The connection between sources and 3D models is established by the CRM class "man-made objects" (E22) representing the real-world objects to be reconstructed. These man-made objects are documented by the sources and are typified by the 3D models. The CRMdig is becoming a valuable extension of CIDOC CRM for digital objects. It describes the steps and methods for digitization of artifacts. It has been applied to the projects 3D-COFORM and 3D-ICONS. The digitization process is primarily composed of events relying on digital optical measurement, e.g. laser scanning, and software execution. Manually constructed digital 3D models are not considered. For the specific needs of digital reconstructions resulting from an interpretation process, the CIDOC CRM might need to be extended in this matter.

4.2 Implementation in Databases

With the CIDOC CRM defining the basic data structure, an appropriate type of database needs to be chosen. The use of a relational database would be a traditional approach, while more recent types of databases offer new potentials.

Relational Databases. Relational databases have been used since the 1970s and are most common. Since all the data are stored in tables, no direct connection between datasets in different tables exists. To establish such connections, relationships are stored in so-called JOIN tables as sets of two IDs. However, those relationships are not available on the user's request. The IDs of the datasets need to be compared and matched at runtime. A JOIN creates a Cartesian product of all potential combinations of rows, and then filters out those that are matching the WHERE clause. To gain the required datasets all relevant tables have to be processed, but in average 99 % of the datasets are discarded [13, 14]. Additionally, the more data content in those tables is stored the more calculation load for processor and memory is produced. Dealing with cultural heritage data, and the CIDOC CRM, often implicates connected data. Usually, the queries are compositions of several relationships, so there would be lots of JOIN clauses within one query. Handling several thousands of datasets may then result in a severe decrease of performance.

Graph Databases. Graph databases are just one representative of NoSQL (Not only SQL, or non-relational) databases and are especially suited for highly connected data. They consist of nodes and relationships (Fig. 8), where the relationships are directed and properties can be stored on each node and relationship [14]. An ontology, the CIDOC CRM, is basically a graph and so the CRM matches exactly the structure of a graph database. The logical conclusion is to use such a graph database for storing and querying cultural heritage data based on the CIDOC CRM.

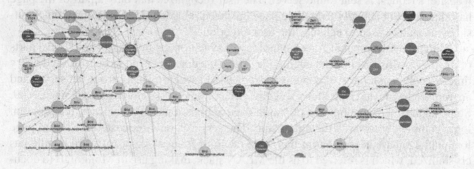

Fig. 8. Excerpt from a graph database

In contrast to relational databases, graph databases do not have the above mentioned JOIN performance issue as the relationships are stored directly within the database. The query starts from a node and then navigates along the relationships to the next nodes (i.e. traversing a graph). Only local operations on each node have to be performed, regardless of the total count of nodes and relationships [13]. Further benefits are the new types of queries. To understand the relation of two nodes, the shortest path between these nodes can be determined. Other queries are sub-tree matching or breadth-first search. In relational databases such queries are rather difficult as the table names have to be explicitly declared and there are no recursive JOIN statements. The Neo4j is a widespread used graph database.

NoSQL databases have replaced relational databases in some fields of application. However, the chosen database should always fit the purpose and data structure, hence relational databases still remain the most applied type of database. Although many projects have implemented the CIDOC CRM in relational databases successfully [15], the authors see the huge potential of graph databases in combination with the CRM. The ability to export the data to the RDF standard, for the use in the context of Linked Open Data, is the next objective.

5   Technical Implementation

5.1   LAMP vs. MEAN

The tool has been designed as a web application. Thus, it can serve as a collaborative platform, enabling simultaneous access to the data (c.f. London Charter). For implementation, available software and already existing tools, that could be re-used and integrated, had to be researched. Many websites apply a content management system (CMS), which is generally used for publishing edited content, shopping and marketing. They implement rights management and other common features. Most CMSs require the traditional LAMP stack, a commonly used software combination in web technology, composed of Linux (or Windows) as operating system, Apache as web server, MySQL as representative of relational databases, and PHP/Perl/Python that are server-side scripting languages responsible for the program logic. When the user interacts with the website, a request is sent to the server. The user recognizes that only a part of the page has changed, but actually the whole page has been reloaded [16]. JavaScript on client-side was mainly used to enhance the user experience.

With the evolvement of Ajax technology (Asynchronous JavaScript and XML) parts of the logic shifts towards the client-side. The page does not need to be refreshed every time, as only small parts of content are requested asynchronously from the server and are replaced by JavaScript. Many new JavaScript frameworks have emerged since 2009. Some address the development of single-page applications (SPA) shifting the program logic completely towards the client-side. The server is only requested for initial page load and database access. From this wide range of frameworks a software bundle has crystallized, which is referred to as the MEAN stack, making use of MongoDB (a document-oriented database), Express.js (a server framework for Node.js), AngularJS (a single-page application framework), and Node.js (a server-side JavaScript runtime environment). A widespread use and an active community are good indicators whether a framework or project will still be active in the next years. First CMS, building on the SPA approach, is available, but not established yet.

Since the 3D content forms a vital part, it would be counterproductive, when user interactions result in a page reload. The 3D content would reload each time as well.

Hence, the implementation of the tool follows the SPA approach. The proposed tool does not fall in the field of application of common CMS. Adopting a specific CMS would require predefined structures and could be restrictive. Considering the specialist requirements, the tool is built from scratch, but using existing technologies, frameworks and modules (AngularJS, Node.js, Express.js, and Neo4j).

5.2 Integration of Existing Tools

Since the introduction of HTML5 and WebGL it has been possible to display 3D content within the web browser without the use of third-party plugins. The accessibility has improved. In the proposed tool, the 3D viewport forms a central part with a variety of interactions. The viewport and the rest of the webpage need to communicate effectively with each other. Thus, the integration of one of the ready-to-use 3D viewers is not an option. Instead, an all-purpose WebGL framework (three.js) is used. This allows the implementation of custom features, rendering options, and real-time manipulation of the models, as it suits the needs of the application.

There are already version control systems for texts, code and even images. However, the control and differentiation of 3D models is more difficult. The 3D Repo seems a promising solution. It is a 3D version control system supporting distributed editing and visual differencing and merging of 3D models [17]. Only an alpha version was available at the time of writing (2016). It needs to be researched in detail how it can be integrated and adopted within this application.

Further tools that were integrated are Tesseract OCR for translating scanned book pages into editable and searchable text and Swish-e for indexing documents for better full-text search. All these tools and frameworks are open source and free to use.

5.3 Limitations

The 3D models of digital reconstructions can rapidly grow to millions of polygons, depending on the size of the reconstructed object and the level of detail. Since they can engross several hundreds of megabytes, it can take rather long to load and display the 3D models in the browser. Thus, the 3D models are converted into a compression file format (OpenCTM [18]) reducing the file size by over 90 %. For example, a COLLADA DAE file with size of 175 MB is compressed to just 10 MB. It is a lossy compression, meaning that some decimals of vertex positions and normals are shortened; it is sufficient for display purposes.

The number of polygons to render is, however, still the same. Depending on the computing power of the client, the framerate starts to drop at about 1 million polygons. User experience slowly decreases at about 2 million polygons and more. To support complex models, further optimizations are necessary. It should be noted that computing power tends to increase continuously.

6 Conclusion

Often in projects a severe lack of documentation and documentation discipline can be observed. Many theoretical approaches claim to address this problem, but practical solutions are still missing. The presented software proposes a package of tools to improve and simplify the documentation practice of digital reconstruction. It helps to ease this important part of the finding process. It should rise to an indispensable part of reconstruction work. With the help of the proposed tool, it will be possible to understand the development of the 3D model to final state, at the end of a project, by reviewing used sources and made decisions. Furthermore, it provides a method to present the gained knowledge to specialists, as well as to a broader public, for subsequent research and presentation. It complies with the principles of the London Charter and integrates the CIDOC CRM as metadata standard and backbone of the underlying data structure. Designed as an online tool, it makes use of latest technologies with new potentials.

The tool is still in early development and the mentioned features are only partly implemented. Detailed user evaluations still need to be carried out. The tool accompanies some active projects within the authors' research group and strives for broader acceptance within the community. Some aspects mentioned are in a conceptual state and need to be elaborated in detail.

References

1. Pfarr, M.: Dokumentationssystem für Digitale Rekonstruktionen am Beispiel der Grabanlage Zhaoling, Provinz Saanxi, China. Dissertation, TU Darmstadt (2010)
2. Münster, S.: Interdisziplinäre Kooperation bei der Erstellung virtueller geschichtswissenschaftlicher 3D-Rekonstruktionen. Dissertation, TU Dresden (2014)
3. Ryan, N.: Documenting and validating virtual Archaeology. In: Archeologia e Calcolatori, vol. 12, pp. 245–273. All'Insegna del Giglio, Florence (2001)
4. Denard, H. (ed.): The London Charter for the Computer-based Visualisation of Cultural Heritage. London (2009). http://www.londoncharter.org. Accessed 26 Jul 2016
5. Spanish Society of Virtual Archaeology: The Seville Charter. International Principles of Virtual Archeology. Seville. (2012). http://www.arqueologiavirtual.com
6. Arnold, D., Geser, G.: EPOCH Research Agenda – Final Report. Brighton (2008)
7. Pletinckx, D.: Interpretation management: how to make sustainable visualisations of the past. In: EPOCH Conference on Open Digital Heritage Systems, Rome (2008)
8. Pletinckx, D.: How to make sustainable visualizations of the past. An EPOCH common infrastructure tool for interpretation management. In: Bentkowska-Kafel, A., Denard, H., Baker, D. (eds.) Paradata and Transparency in Virtual Heritage, pp. 203–244. Ashgate, Farnham (2012)
9. 3D-COFORM. http://www.3dcoform.eu/. Accessed 27 Jan 2016
10. 3D-ICONS. http://www.3dicons-project.eu/eng. Accessed 27 Jan 2016
11. Warwick, C.: Studying users in digital humanities. In: Warwick, C., Terras, M., Nyhan, J. (eds.) Digital Humanities in Practice, pp. 1–21. Facet Publishing, London (2012)
12. ICOM/CIDOC CRM Special Interest Group: Definition of the CIDOC Conceptual Reference Model. Version 5.0.4 (2011)
13. Partner, J., Vukotic, A., Watt, N.: Neo4j in Action. Manning Publications, New York (2013)
14. Robinson, I., Webber, J., Eifrem, E.: Graph Databases. O'Reilly Media, Sebastopol (2013)

15. Hiebel, G., Hanke, K., Hayek, I.: A relational database structure and user interface for the CIDOC CRM with GIS integration. In: 22nd CIDOC CRM SIG Meeting, Nuremberg (2010)
16. Fink, G., Flatow, I.: Pro Single Page Application Development. Apress, New York (2014)
17. Doboš, J.: Management and Visualisation of Non-linear History of Polygonal 3D Models. Dissertation, University College London (2015)
18. Geelnard, M.: OpenCTM. http://openctm.sourceforge.net/. Accessed 08 Jun 2015

Cultural Heritage in a Spatial Context – Towards an Integrative, Interoperable, and Participatory Data and Information Management

Nikolas Prechtel[1(✉)] and Sander Münster[2]

[1] Institute of Cartography, Dresden University of Technology, 1062 Dresden, Germany
nikolas.prechtel@tu-dresden.de
[2] Media Centre, Dresden University of Technology, 1062 Dresden, Germany
sander.muenster@tu-dresden.de

Abstract. The authors discuss a concept for a comprehensive three dimensional cultural heritage (CH) information architecture including a time component that takes geographic space as the dominant organizing, presentation and exploration principle. Activities concerning a complex, decentralized information architecture with a cooperative component have only recently gained full relevance since they rely on new achievements. We name three such achievements: fast and user-friendly 3D reconstruction technologies, web-based 3D visualization within standard browsers, and emerging maturity and usage of volunteered geo-content, which is built from vector data, photo collections and 3D models. Achieving more than academic ephemera requires overcoming key problems associated with interoperation, spatial disparities of knowledge, object referencing, data volumes, abstraction, or object lifetime, to name only a few. Reliable and comprehensive solutions will perform well as upcoming business models. Full accounts of the state of the art of all mentioned key issues cannot be given (each of them justifies its own paper). Nor can fully developed solutions or approaches be offered in all cases. At least, a structured compilation of ideas on versatile and practical CH management architecture may provide incentives for future developments.

Keywords: Cultural heritage · Information management concept · Data integration · Virtual globe · Geo-data visualization · User-generated content · Time handling

1 Introduction

It has frequently been stated that present day access to data is unprecedented and the volume of available information is constantly growing [1]. In contrast, there is currently comparatively poor access to *structured information* stemming from skilled data organization, analysis and dissemination. This is despite the fact that structured information would obviously contribute more strongly to cognizance and – on a more general level – to knowledge when compared to uncontrolled data streams [2]. This statement applies pretty well to the informational context of cultural heritage (CH) sites and objects.

© Springer International Publishing AG 2016
S. Münster et al. (Eds.): 3D Research Challenges II, LNCS 10025, pp. 272–288, 2016.
DOI: 10.1007/978-3-319-47647-6_13

Awareness and cognition related to CH may be seen in the cultural context where *virtual geographic space* progressively forms a gateway to a wide range of spatial [3], and (indirectly) non-spatial information (i.e. *geobrowsing*). This goes along with a pictorial turn [4], a tendency to augment or even replace lingual knowledge representation by *visual models*. There can be little doubt that virtual 3D landscapes will assume a central role in many affairs related to CH [5], be it with a scientific, an educational, an administrative or a marketing background.

The last decade has shown that sustainable information architecture has to be dynamic and open for volunteered contributions and shared content. Herein, volunteered geographic information (VGI) is one major component. The online community Historypin can be named as a showpiece of a crowd-sourced, digital multi-media collection, which allows geographic query and content retrieval [6]. The most popular volunteered geographic data source, OpenStreetMap (OSM), has established CH offshoots, too, as documented by close to 500,000 objects with the data tag "historic" [7] and a specialized "historic place" subproject [8]. Explicit authorities will continue to be important players but may also be faced with the task of filtering, evaluating and approving external input of various types. If one agrees that spatial context matters, then geo-information – including paradata and metadata [9] – can and should be widely exchanged and integrated into digital CH documentation whilst avoiding redundancy and consistency problems.

This article takes up findings, ideas, and open questions that have emerged within application projects guided by the authors: (1) The Turkic name *Uch Enmek* (which is also the project name) relates to a mountain in the Russian Altai Mountains, which overlooks an important archaeological site of primarily Scythian origin. In cooperation with archaeologists from Ghent University, a prototype of an interactive landscape model was created and presented based on the OpenWebGlobe framework [10]. This imbeds archaeological information into the rural 3D environment of an archaeological conservation area [11]. (2) A second project is called GEPAM, an acronym formed from German and Czech words for commemoration [12]. Dedicated to a virtual memorial, the web application comprehensively introduces places of Jewish persecution during the "Third Reich" within the towns of Dresden and Terezin in a perceivable spatial context. Both a historical and a present representation of each urban space have been included [13] along with detailed context information referring to places of interest (POI), the focal points of Jewish history from 1933–1945. The application was based on Google Earth technology. (3) A third project focuses on combined 3D reconstruction and textual treatment of the historically important elements of Freiberg Cathedral (Saxony, Germany). The main practical outcome of this cross-disciplinary educational project is a smartphone app that serves as an interactive church guide [14].

Moreover, we imbed theory extracted from studies dealing with principal issues of research cooperation and scientific structures. This type of research primarily uses methods from scientometrics, management studies and social sciences [15, 16].

This article continues with a brief look at some integral parts of a technical environment relevant for digital information management (Sect. 2). Section 3 proposes a geo-centered integrative concept as one possible solution in the CH context. This has consequences for modes of data structuring, analysis, and visual presentation. If on-demand (geo-)integration of indexed and authored model components can be developed,

3D models and context information will improve significantly. Section 4 sheds some light on selected key issues related to the establishment of comprehensive CH information handling. Due to space limitations, this article will concentrate on highlighting important concepts and promising facets of an integrative solution.

2   Key Achievements as the Necessary Basis

Both tangible and intangible CH can certainly profit from virtual counterparts. The latter can support internal and external conservation tasks, and also facilitate analysis, dissemination and scientific dialogue, mainly by connecting CH models to web facilities. By focusing on CH assets in their spatial context, we are fortunately able to build upon recent generic achievements.

One major breakthrough was the introduction of user-friendly *3D reconstruction technologies* delivering metric results. Quick and accurate 3D content is appreciated as for its superior analytic potential and attractiveness in comparison to 2D sketches and photographs. Vergauwen and van Gool [17] published a modular concept, implementation strategies and results of a CH-related photogrammetric 3D reconstruction web service nearly 10 years ago. With greatly increased computing power, typically distributed via a cloud, 3D reconstruction services have meanwhile become a well-staffed service (e.g., Pix4D). Terrestrial laser scanners (TLS) have been known as a strong alternative model source for more than ten years [18]. The complementary use of dense matching and TLS is possible and has been tested [19]. Vrubel et al. [20] describe the transformation of range and color images into accurate textured 3D models in detail. Roosevelt et al. [21] recently published on synergetic digital recording in archaeology and cite reference projects dealing with the "third dimension in archaeological recording" (p. 326f.). Processing techniques influence geometric reliability, especially in photogrammetric solutions, whilst equipment type and costs are more critical with TLS. Skill and experience remain crucial factors in any case.

A second trigger for the development of three-dimensional virtualization is a *standardized visualization technology*. Originating from proprietary specialized software and data formats, 3D visualization is becoming a more ubiquitous experience almost regardless of the operating system, specific software or hardware. Increasing developer response to Web3D consortium standards, in particular WebGL and HTML5, makes it possible to show and manipulate 3D models without any difference between desktop and web applications, with a JavaScript code running in the browser window [22]. Greater simplicity in provision (interoperable 3D assets) and interaction with 3D models will drive 3D applications in the CH context. The VR (virtual reality) model of Siena Cathedral makes a persuasive case. This complex model generation dates back 15 years [23], but can now be explored by everyone using advanced web and browser technology [24].

Another influence originates from new players in geo-data capture and distribution. The result has been termed *volunteered geoinformation*. The starting point is the general spatial context in the sense of topographic references. In this domain OpenStreetMap (OSM) has gained spatial coverage [25] and a level of detail that has even attracted numerous commercial users. Especially in first world urban environments, active OSM communities provide data upon which detailed 3D townscape/landscape models can be built [26]. Schemes have been published to even extend them to interior spaces [27]. At least a rough landscape context of a CH site can be modeled with moderate effort in most cases. Categorized geo-data as OSM can further be augmented by free pictorial content from photo collections like Flickr® and Panoramio®. Their potential may be demonstrated by a figure taken from Pippig et al. [28]: 32,984 geo-tagged photos have been found and extracted for the town center of Dresden alone. Even missing localization can be mitigated within a web community: Historypin aims to reference pictorial information to places [6]. Alternative web-based geotagging activities can, for instance, be taken from Bourn [29]. Localized images assist interpretation and manual modeling, or – in combination with powerful cloud-based photogrammetry – even feed automated workflows for extensive 3D model creation. Concepts and related technology can be examined on the BigSFM project website [30]. The last category of relevant user-generated content consists of digital 3D models. There is no easy accessible information on volume and typical quality, but their general potential and modes of future incorporation are worth considering.

We agree with Chiabrando and Spano that "an integration of [...] models into Web-GIS for a global management of spatial information concerning built heritage is under great attention" [31, p. 67]. As more and more heterogeneous sources become available (including survey results, digital archive and user-generated data) integration becomes the bottleneck. The OGC's (Open Geospatial Consortium) efforts towards *interoperable geo-data* have been successful, but the present situation is still not ideal. The assumption may hold that primarily geographic content from GIS-like environments can potentially semantically and spatially cooperate, the latter through coordinates and unambiguously defined spatial reference systems. Yet this will not work in the short term with user-generated 3D content, since common 3D data (X3D, COLLADA, etc.) do not feature semantic or absolute positional information [32]. In a model assembly process drawing on numerous web resources, manageable models are impossible to achieve without major human effort in controlling, editing, harmonizing and streamlining (e.g., downsizing) assets, a challenge that is discussed further below.

3   Challenges

3.1   An Integrative Access to Relevant Content

Modeling and presenting individual CH objects in various selections, scales, and details have become easier and more effective, and further progress is still to come. Comparable advance could be achieved by a concerted effort to concentrate on the best-possible use and dissemination of these achievements and their digital results. We understand use in a broad sense which encompasses the documentation, exploration, scientific transformation and analysis, maintenance, surveillance, reconstruction, presentation and marketing of CH. The CARARE project is one related and impressive European initiative. All collected CH content bears an explicit spatial reference. Thus, 2D references provide information about "what is where" as shown on a web map. Methods of access to 3D/VR content still need to be studied and formalized [33].

3D is still mostly "ad hoc, redundant, not efficient, and not exploiting its full potential" [34, p. 14]. Thus, new effort might be directed into a convenient and strongly *computer-assisted integration of numerous object- or profession-centered information components* under one umbrella. Ideally, requests could be served by a single architecture which relies on decentralized cooperative resources. The allegory of an umbrella is used for a flexibly shaped and scaled information architecture, with some degree of standardization and well-designed workflows (offline or as services). Standards foster interoperability and stimulate software development, but acceptance criteria should not be overly restrictive. *Minimum standard compliancy* is a prerequisite to smooth support of elementary processes such as data query and evaluation, editorial selection and content structuring including hyper-linking resources, geographic integration and joint visualization from multiple sources, interchange of addressable contents for scientific and administrative use, and smooth front end presentation.

3.2   Geo-Access as a Versatile, Integrative Solution

Such an umbrella could flexibly span geographic space as the proposed primary access mode. Without excluding different organization principles, geo-centered access is suitable for the vast majority of sites and artefacts tagged as CH. A 2D case can already be realized with the help of well-established IT components like Content Management Systems, WebGIS, and dynamic HTML technology. The success of the geo-approach in information retrieval is documented by ubiquitous and every-day products like Google Maps, Google Earth, Bing Maps, or MapQuest. This type of product (*virtual globes*) is part of the average person's information environment, and usability is therefore highly facilitated by existing experience. This also seems to address the *ludic drive* of human beings; it has become a prerequisite of commercial success for many types of computer games to present a well-made and interesting landscape (typically a 3D representation) to the gamer community. A third emerging geo-application is a branch of *augmented reality* (AR), where a known viewpoint and view direction reported by a mobile device can be used to blend a physically existing section of the environment with further digital context in various presentation and interaction modes (pictorial, textual, audible, etc.). Web-based interaction with 2D worlds is nowadays operational.

Upgrading to versatile digital 3D portrayal of CH in a geo-context suggests itself. At the composite level the concept seems fresh but various ideas and technical solutions have a longer history, as illustrated by selected references from archaeology in the next section.

3.3   Selected Contributions to Geo-Access and Integration

Digital 3D visualization was already being evaluated in the late 1980s for archaeological purpose [35]. A demand for improved *spatial analytics* comprising 3D topology and queries, which amount to a 3D GIS ("what is next to", "what surrounds", "what is above, below, to the side of", "what is the value of the object at this location", and "what are the relationships between this feature to surrounding features", [36, p. 309]) dates back to the 1990s, but this is still not sufficiently supported by standard software. As the context extends from site to landscape level and computing power increases, 3D reconstructions in a wider geographic context emerge. The Appia Antica Project [37] may serve as an example. A high degree of *immersion* (VR) is seen as research stimulant, since an "impartial observer becomes an active participant" [38]. The most immersive technical environment may, however, not automatically perform better at problem solving compared to more abstract depictions [39]. *Integrative 3D visualization* imbeds 3D CH content into a landscape representation and uses a browser as the front end [40], whilst implementations relying on open source software components are preferred [41].

Integration of decentralized 2D and 3D content on demand through web-based services, meaning without tedious manual model augmentation and harmonization, is obviously a key factor. It may determine the future success and dispersion of such context-oriented concepts, which presents a big challenge. On one hand, this relates to *ontology*. A wide spatial and, even more so, thematic integration greatly complicates the taxonomies, which are typically developed in parallel, each serving a specific professional domain [42]. An all-encompassing Cultural Heritage Markup Language – CHML - has been proposed [43], but this is neither fully elaborated nor accepted. On the other hand, domain-specific 3D components have to be technically assembled [44] for a joint visualization, once the relevant assets have been identified. 3D interoperation standards, especially CityGML [45], are seen as one promising solution [46]. A CityGML adaption to CH, however, cannot follow a predetermined path; its provenance as a model of functionally defined topographic reference objects [47] calls for amendments prior to utilization, for example in an archaeological site. Moreover, a plethora of non-standard-compliant models cannot be toughened for full cooperation without major interactive modification. Therefore, a more straight-forward 3D model fusion, disregarding all complex relations in terms of attribute space and topology, might still coexist in the medium term. Structured geo-database storage of 3D objects and on-demand export to a X3D representation for subsequent exploration in a browser without plug-ins has been tested prototypically for a UNESCO heritage site [48]. In developing user-driven 3D assemblies further, we can fortunately rely on strong technical progress in client-based 3D rendering. The X3DOM framework, a JavaScript library, has proved capable of handling massive models if applied in connection with recent HTML and browser technology [49].

The uses of CH 3D landscapes are also worth a closer look. Recent projects have also shown virtual 3D environments as a stage for (educative and entertaining) storytelling [50]. This will most often imply adapting the model to various temporal states. The MayaArch3D Project [51] already bundles and implements many of the ideas cited in this section. The theme of the project is Maya architecture in Copan, Honduras [52]. Using the technical tool QueryArch3D [53], 2D and 3D landscape objects have been integrated by means of a geo-database to allow individual geographic navigation and exploration of architectural objects along with context information. In interfacing software from different domains QueryArch3D tries to connect the visual and explorative capabilities of 3D scenes and the analytical capacities of 2D GIS.

4 Identified Core Aspects

4.1 Object Identifiers

Three-dimensional reconstruction projects accumulate digital entities such as digital objects, part or even full-scale models, metadata and paradata. Identification, exchange and referencing would be facilitated by a comprehensive declaration scheme. Europeana projects have addressed the problem, for example through classification, linking and long-term availability strategies [54]. An alternative can be found in the digital object identifier (DOI) scheme [55]. It identifies and guides the handling of digital objects, and is already established for digital publications. The Uniform Resource Identifiers (URI) system provides identifiers for worldwide use including a database hosting basic metadata on classification and external references. No central repositories are needed, and providers can define access conditions. Along with auxiliary technologies [56] it provides registration and checks for the uniqueness of both entities and identifier.

4.2 Scale Restrictions

Scale and scope adjustments in an interaction with a model have been described as non-linear processes essentially connected to the individual appropriation of a modeled reality and to creative work on and revision of the model. This has been stated for the field of architecture [57], but seems equally applicable to 3D CH models in other disciplines. Scale and scope are opposites. Since, in any pragmatic solution, the spatial contextualization of CH may impact on the dominant research questions and identified causal chains, the extent of the phenomena involved may steer scope and scale as well.

It is, however, questionable whether data and model integration can seriously aim at the full range of spatial dimension, from a global view to extreme close-ups. The provenience may require tracing on a global or continental level, whilst conservation of a particular artefact may concentrate on structures in the millimeter range. The wider a possible scale range is defined, the more complicated class hierarchies and class relations will become. The same goes for visibilities and LOD (Level of Detail) representations. A composite (graphic) model may only jointly exhibit data that share comparable properties in terms of reliability and granularity. Otherwise, fidelity will be lost. A conceptual zoom limit is reached when cognition becomes too scattered or selective to form a complete image. "A researcher must assess how far the uncertainties in analytical results are due to the information loss associated with the data [...] or the model employed (Goodchild 2011)." [58, p. 11].

Consequently, a preliminary *scale restriction* makes sense: At maximum zoom we find a historic site including all exterior components, and at the wide angle end we arrive at a highly generalized, wide geographic scope. Frequently, some inconsistency in the level of (known) detail or scale will be inevitable. In these cases, different graphic levels of abstraction (compare 4.4 below) can help in avoiding misinterpretations. If indoor, underground environments and much of the inventory (e.g., of a museum) are realistically beyond the scope of the concept, sensible interface nodes for the detail level should nevertheless be provided.

4.3   Cultural Heritage Within Different Thematic Spaces

Geospatial context can potentially free CH objects and domains from a museum-like (more or less displaced) arrangement. Geographic space in holistic terms, including history, perception and scale, may even be the proper focus of CH research, as in landscape archaeology: "The Historic Landscape Character method of landscape archaeology is distinguished by a concern for how the past and its remains contribute to people's contemporary perception of landscape at a variety of scales and to a variety of degrees (depending on knowledge, understanding and interest of the individual beholder)." [59, p. 137]. Also in cases where research is centered on precisely localized CH objects and sites, a major range of associated topics will relate to a much broader context. The postulated geospatial anchor point of information retrieval and presentation can be exemplified by some geospatial units associated with CH. These units will come with more or less clearly defined outlines and with a wide range of geographical and time scales.

In zooming out, we may encounter units such as an ethnic or cultural space, a stylistic space (e.g., the spread of perpendicular architecture from the Île-de-France over a certain time), a space spanned by trade links, or a political space (territorial division at a certain time). In zooming in, we can eventually delineate a space from which the building material originates. A detectable geomorphic setting may then reflect strategic importance or determine the spiritual meaning of a site (e.g., pre-historic burial sites). At even closer quarters, the internal layout and all patterns of the material components of a site can be explored.

As each theme occupies its own geographic space, comprehension requires specific fields of view and presentations, which react within the technical and perceptive limits associated with scale. Whenever a broad spatial context has to be shown, "full" 3D is not essential. Systematic considerations regarding the visual interplay of the dimension of the geo-reference and the corresponding thematic content [60] provide initial orientation in a choice of visualization options. Such options, including dimensionality and LOD, can be further optimized by evaluating the diverse interrelations between geographic setting and all the themes portrayed.

While it is clear that not all desirable thematic content can be made accessible, and some of it not even in the medium term, a concept should nevertheless provide structures for these spaces and the context information.

4.4   Abstraction in 3D Presentations

An interactive model of the geographic environment has to adapt to the user's field of view and the associated scale variation. The field of view controls the number of visible objects. Total data volume restrictions and acceptable rendering times now demand strict rules on object visibility and suitable LOD. Three-dimensional content is anyway only justified once a shape can be perceived as a 3D object. Below this level a 2D overlay suffices.

An elaborate concept of abstraction goes far beyond LOD and scale-dependent visibility. It includes *schematization* "to maximize task-adequacy while minimizing nonfunctional detail" [61, p. 301]. Schematic 3D content can improve 3D visualization (compare [47]). Like prototype objects and textures, it does not claim to copy reality as photo-textures do. The idea that photography is an accurate representation has been challenged for a long time. Gombrich's 1960 book *Art and Illusion* "shows how heavily abstracted a photograph actually is through exposing the many artifices employed: the micro-instant frozen forever, the limited angle of view, and the arbitrariness of photographic processing" [62, p. 29]. Photography can only get close to historical reality as it captures a visual appearance determined by momentary environmental factors (e.g. illumination), when the data is taken, that is, in the past. Excluding photographic portrayal frees a complex model from unwanted content, and will divert the user's attention less. If combined with a series of digital graphic techniques (e.g., edge enhancement, reduced color spaces), non-photorealistic (NPR) depictions [63] can be even more expressive, and thus convey specific contents more efficiently than photographic ones. For the geo-context, Semmo et al. [64] have presented inspiring NPR solutions, using an object context to decide on a level of abstraction. By applying multiple texturing techniques, this approach even circumvents a hard choice between realism and abstraction.

Schematic content is directly creatable from standard geo-data sources through automated workflows, whereas a categorical class is - in combination with visually relevant properties - translated into a prototype object. This strategy has been tested already and, as Fanini and Ferdani state, the biggest challenge has been in the "different typologies [...] needed to reproduce a reliable virtual copy" [65, p. 111]. A schematic model requires less storage space. It also improves rendering performance, due to less different geometric and textural content. Furthermore, prototype contents facilitate scale transformation (zoom); transitions between prototypes can be stored explicitly (e.g., objects of type A, B, C will be amalgamated to a new object of type D), and surface properties can be optimized for smooth transitions. Defined graphic parameters make visual transitions predictable, instead of necessitating a switch between different images.

Despite these advantages, users might criticize that such models express a professional, filtered view, since all objects are solely shaped by the underlying conceptual data model and prototype design. If only instances of a limited number of primary objects exist, some degree of unrealistic uniformity might be bemoaned. This can be mitigated, but not eliminated, for instance by applying random modifiers to graphic parameters.

Reflections on realism versus schematization in 3D models also matter in an educational context. Visual experience, high authenticity, simple feedback between model and real world are arguments for the first option, whilst a stronger visual focus and higher demand for reflected perception favor the second. Preferences in one or the other direction can only be substantiated if a usage scenario is given [66]. A compromise between purist solutions could often achieve the best effect. To give one simple example, high realism (photorealism) through detailed explicit 3D modeling including photo-textured exterior shapes might be reserved for the focus objects which are obviously located within the CH sites and contain their prominent objects. The other parts of the environment could then be depicted in a more abstract, schematic way as outlined above.

4.5   The Role of Time

Undisputedly temporal relations are highly critical in the field of CH. The tension between time and space is currently a matter of intense debate and was the theme of the Computer Applications and Quantitative Methods in Archaeology (CAA) Conference 2013: "Across Space and Time". The key issues in time handling are discussed below.

Time-related question types were compiled and discussed back in 2007 by Constantinidis [67, p. 409]: "[…] a spatio-temporal GIS could respond to the following queries: Where and when did change occur? What types of change occurred? What is the rate of change? What is the periodicity of change?" Time as an independent dimension has not been introduced to complement standard GIS entities since 2007. It is true that time stamps can be assigned, and a pair of them can indicate a lifetime. In general, however, the lifetime of a geometric entity is very unlikely to be prime concept for use in CH. Take the example of a building. How does a standard model express a situation after a fire, where one part has been fully reconstructed, another demolished, and a third rebuilt on the remaining ground floor, whereas extensive reuse of building material has taken place? *Transformations*, a very common historical process, do not fit into a standard GIS concept, even less so if this process is lingering, like the gradual decay of a disused structure. Toughening up historical geo-data for the limited potential of current models would not only require shaping entities according to structural, functional or other thematic criteria, but also subdividing them into smaller entities thought to have a homogeneous transformation history. This seems impractical.

A second issue is *imperfect knowledge*. The further we go back in time, the more imprecise time references will normally become; time stamps have to be supplemented by uncertainty measures. A further related theme concerns relative time assessments, or models allowing for time relations to external events. A further complicated problem is missing synchronicity of knowledge about a geographic space, in particular an issue when CH is linked to a landscape context. Whilst prominent objects (e.g. a mansion) are often reasonably well documented, average objects (e.g., a farmstead) have sparser and very different reported timelines, if any are available at all. Promising proposals have been made for reassessing time in GIS. These include introducing a triangular time space model (time versus duration) along with the rough set theory, which nicely accounts for imperfect knowledge in defining temporal memberships as "definitely in", "definitely not in", and "possibly in" [68]. Such features are by no means part of standard software, however.

On the user side, dynamic landscape model visualizations will hardly ever allow a free choice of time, but only offer predetermined pseudo-snapshots along a limited timeline. Consequently, there is an urgent need for graphic coding of vagueness, which should be associative and reduce the risk of drawing false conclusions due to unquestioned perception.

4.6   Handling User-Generated Content

Volunteered (geo-)information has been tremendously successful, making it necessary to open up an integrative architecture to this sort of input. Sylaiou et al. [69] name examples of VGI input to CH research: Besides their established role in data collection, volunteers may also act as research assistants in scanning and interpreting large open data sets (e.g., archaeological site detection).

A data-oriented scheme may show the following modes of volunteered contribution:

1. Comments and corrections on an existing published status of information;
2. New links to or submission of recent and historic textual documents;
3. New links to or submission of recent and historic pictorial documents.
4. Contribution of prefab 3D content (SketchUp's 3D Warehouse, the most popular source, calls itself the world's biggest model repository [70]).

Whilst the first three contributions might be treated like internal documents, a 3D model merge (4) involves much more than drag and drop. Either complete geo-coordinates plus spatial reference complement a model, or – more likely – an anchor point plus inner orientation directs an initial geometric integration. Especially in dealing with a multitude of models, transformations and modifications prior to integration will be necessary. On a very generic level, the *object formation* inherent to a model has to be questioned and eventually modified. Other researchers have suggested that 3D (re-)constructions might become self-evident subjects of expert discourse and academic negotiations [71]. Consequently, addressing objects will only be possible if a minimum set of mandatory *object classes* reliably exists, which has to be proved. It is also doubtful that a broad integration of geometries will not generate conflicts (e.g., by overlaps or gaps). Three-dimensional topology testing is demanding [72], and requires automation, which links back to defined object classes. Beyond geometry, *object appearance,* that is its surface and environment properties, will definitely not match well if set by different model providers. As in the case of geometry, modifications may be inevitable. With respect to OpenStreetMap, rigid modeling guidelines might be omitted for the sake of greater attractiveness within the community of contributors, but ambiguities and redundancies have to be tackled by those in charge of the integration. If the right software resources are available, subject to the condition that fine front end applications might eventually gain popularity, it is likely that even complete 3D models can be composed from volunteered sources.

4.7 Remarks on the Database

The above discussion makes it clear that the key components of successful data information management are a well-designed database model and a powerful management system. The following subtasks must be performed to support this, although the list is far from being complete:

1. Ingestions or linking of primary documents;
2. Ingestion of documents to be published (authorized documents);
3. Geospatial hierarchies and their visual representations;
4. Administration of authorship;
5. Handling of temporal events;
6. Tagging of uncertainty levels;

7. Identification of missing constituents (in relation to output to be published);
8. Versioning;
9. Links between documents and associated formats and standards.

These subtasks have already been largely incorporated into published database schemes. Other sources refer to metadata [73], database architectures [74], usage schemes and their practical application [54].

5 Summary

If integration is a priority, standards are essential right from the beginning. It seems sensible to identify practical rules that can serve as a *broker* between various modeling standards associated with potential input. The integration initiatives applied to official European topographic references are a good example. A 3D modeling standard, CityGML [45], has been developed to meet the challenge of interoperation. It has already catered for various circumstances: It is flexible for semantic augmentations, different LODs, and visual properties. It is best suited to a GIS modeler, however, and not necessarily to the volunteer offering a fully textured stand-alone 3D asset. Tedious efforts to transform heterogeneous input into *one uniform binding standard* are best avoided, but then metadata has to show what part of the information relevant for integration exists and what is missing. Even if complete harmonization remains impossible in the short and medium term, multi-source model assemblies might work at a higher generalization level.

We propose directing research efforts into an *open framework*. The goal would be integrative, interoperable, and participatory geospatial information transfer related to CH. In the context of the present application, CH will be reduced to extant or historic built structures, whilst the geospatial context will rely on a comprehensive concept of the associated landscape, augmented with information on territorial patterns, trade links, sites of major historical events, and so on. Both experts and the interested public will have access to information, including modes of participation. Visibility management, transparent authorship, and versioning can prevent unintended seepage of internal or uncertified information components. Geospatial objects will carry scale-dependent 3D and 2D representations to allow them to cooperate within different spatial configurations (from continental to local). Cooperation between individual objects within a 3D scene depends on numerous prerequisites. Crucial parameters include the quality of the modeling reference, LOD, compliance to standards, geometric consistency, and unambiguous spatial referencing. For shared and distributed resources to work, a catalogue system must allow for searching, querying and identifying geospatial contents. Therefore we propose that the DOI approach be extended to the class of 3D geospatial objects.

Clearly, interoperability and smooth support by automated workflows are key factors in a framework becoming widely accepted and practically used. Neither the practitioners within the field of CH management nor the majority of exterior participants will have an in-depth expertise in geo-informatics or database management systems. Workflow development has to identify flaws and bottlenecks in close cooperation with users. Existing bottlenecks have already been located here: They include quality control of geospatial objects, the automation of 2D-3D upgrade of landscape data, clever data volume reduction as a prerequisite of a manageable cooperation, handling time, topological model adaption reacting on new elements, the categorization and systematization of new geo-objects, and the management of volunteered contributions, including requests for augmentation or corrections.

References

1. Gantz, J., Reinsel, D.: The digital universe in 2020: big data, bigger digital shadows, and biggest growth in the far east. In: IDC iView, December 2012. http://www.emc.com/collateral/analyst-reports/idc-the-digital-universe-in-2020.pdf. Accessed 30 Sept 2016
2. Hasler Roumois, U.: Studienbuch Wissensmanagement: Grundlagen der Wissensarbeit in Wirtschafts-, Non-profit- und Public-Organisationen. Orell Füssli, Zürich (2007)
3. Blower, J.D., Gemmell, A.L., Haines, K., Kirsch, P., Cunningham, N., Fleming, A., Lowry, R.: Sharing and visualizing environmental data using virtual globes. In: UK e-Science All Hands Meeting 2007, 10–13 September 2007, Nottingham, UK, pp. 102–109 (2007)
4. Mitchell, W.J.T.: Picture Theory. University Press, Chicago (1994)
5. Brovelli, M.A., Hogan, P., Minghini, M., Zamboni, G.: The power of virtual globes for valorising cultural heritage and enabling sustainable tourism: NASA world wind applications. In: International Archives of the Photogrammetry, Remote Sensing and Spatial Information Science, vol. XL-4/W2, pp. 115–120 (2013)
6. Historypin. http://www.historypin.org. Accessed 30 Sept 2015
7. Taginfo. http://taginfo.openstreetmap.org/. Accessed 30 Sept 2015
8. Historic Place. http://gk.historic.place/. Accessed 30 Sept 2015
9. Bentkowska-Kafel, A., Denard, H., Baker, D.: Paradata and Transparency in Virtual Heritage. Ashgate, Farnham (2012)
10. Loesch, B., Christen, M., Nebiker, S.: OpenWebGlobe – Ein quelloffenes Software Development Kit zur Entwicklung virtueller Globen auf Basis von HTML5 und WebGL. In: Seifert, E. (ed.) Erdblicke – Perspektiven für die Geowissenschaften, Publ. der DGPF 21, pp. 275–283. DGPF, Potsdam (2012)
11. Prechtel, N., Münster, S., Kröber, C., Schubert, C., Sebastian, S.: Presenting cultural heritage landscapes – from GIS via 3D models to interactive presentation frameworks. In: ISPRS Annals of the Photogrammetry, Remote Sensing and Spatial Information Sciences (XXIV International CIPA Symposium), vol. XL-5/W2, pp. 253–258 (2013)
12. Brödner, J., Kröber, C.: GEPAM – Eine interaktive Informationsplattform zur "Landschaft des Gedenkens". In: Koch, M., Butz, A., Schlichter, J. (eds.) Mensch & Computer 2014 – Workshopband Fachübergreifende Konferenz für Interaktive und Kooperative Medien – Interaktiv unterwegs – Freiräume gestalten, vol. 14, pp. 21–23. De Gruyter Oldenburg, Berlin (2014)
13. Jedlička, K., Čada, V., Fiala, R., Hájek, P., Janečka, K., Ježek, J., Strejcová, J., Vichrová, M., Roubínek, J.: Techniques used for optimizing 3D geovisualization of terezín memorial. In: Digital Proceedings of ICC 2013, "Cartography from Pole to Pole", paper 281 (2013). http://icaci.org/files/documents/ICC_proceedings/ICC2013/_extendedAbstract/281_proceeding.pdf. Accessed 15 June 2016
14. Kröber, C., Münster, S.: An app for the cathedral in Freiberg – an interdisciplinary project seminar. In: Sampson, D.G., Spector, J.M., Ifenthaler, D., Isaias, P. (eds.) Proceedings of the 11th International Conference on Cognition and Exploratory Learning in Digital Age 2014 (CELDA), pp. 270–274 (2014)

15. Münster, S.: Researching scientific structures via joint authorships – the case of virtual 3D modelling in humanities. In: International Conference on Infrastructures and Cooperation in E-Science and E-Humanities (forthcoming)

16. Münster, S.: workflows and the role of images for a virtual 3D reconstruction of no longer extant historic objects. In: ISPRS Annals of Photogrammetry, Remote Sensing Spatial Information Science, vol. II-5/W1, pp. 197–202 (2013)

17. Vergauwen, M., Van Gool, L.: Web-based 3D reconstruction service. Mach. Vis. Appl. **17**, 411–426 (2006)

18. Boehler, W., Heinz, G., Marbs, A.: The potential of non-contact close range laser scanners for cultural heritage recording. In: Albertz, J. (ed.) Surveying and Documentation of Historic Buildings – Monuments – Sites. Traditional and Modern Methods. Proceedings of the XVIII. International Symposium CIPA 2001, pp. 430–436. CIPA, Berlin (2001)

19. Bastonero, P., Donadio, E., Chiabrando, F., Spanò, A.: Fusion of 3D models derived from TLS and image-based techniques for CH enhanced documentation. ISPRS Ann. Photogramm. Remote Sens. Spat. Inf. Sci. **II-5**, 73–80 (2014)

20. Vrubel, A., Bellon, O., Silva, L.: A 3D reconstruction pipeline for digital preservation. In: IEEE Conference on Computer Vision and Pattern Recognition 2009, pp. 2687–2694 (2009)

21. Roosevelt, C.H., Cobb, P., Moss, E., Olson, B.R., Ünlüsoy, S.: Excavation is digitization: advances in archaeological practice. J. Field Archaeol. **40**(3), 325–346 (2015)

22. Sawicki, B., Chaber, B.: Efficient visualization of 3D models by web browser. Computing **95**(8), 661–673 (2013)

23. Behr, J., Fröhlich, T., Knöpfle, C., Kresse, W., Lutz, B., Reiners, D., Schöffel, F.: The digital Cathedral of Siena – innovative concepts for interactive and immersive presentation of cultural heritage sites. In: Bearman, D. (ed.) ICHIM 2001, International Cultural Heritage Informatics Meeting. Full papers, Cultural Heritage and Technologies in the Third Millennium, vol. 1, pp. 57–71. ICHIM, Milan (2001)

24. Web3D Consortium: X3D - large model high quality rendering: Cathedral at Siena, Italy. Example provided by Fraunhofer, IGD, VCST (2014) http://examples.x3dom.org/Demos/Siena/siena.html. Accessed 15 June 2016

25. Neis, P., Zielstra, D., Zipf, A.: Comparison of volunteered geographic information data contributions and community development for selected world regions. Future Internet **5**(2), 282–300 (2013)

26. OSM2World, http://osm2world.org/. Accessed 30 Sept 2015

27. Goetz, M.: Towards generating highly detailed 3D CityGML models from OpenStreetMap. Int. J. Geograph. Inf. Sci. **27**, 845–865 (2013)

28. Pippig, K., Burghardt, D., Prechtel, N.: Semantic similarity analysis of user-generated content for theme-based route planning. J. Location Based Serv. **7**, 223–245 (2013)

29. Bourn, D.: Geotagging: Using Maps to Organize Historic Images. http://usingsfhistory.com/2011/09/17/using-maps-to-organize-historic-images/. Accessed 30 Sept 2015

30. BigSFM: Reconstructing the World from Internet Photos. http://www.cs.cornell.edu/projects/bigsfm/. Accessed 15 Sept 2016

31. Chiabrando, F., Spanò, A.: Points clouds generation using TLS and dense-matching techniques. A test on approachable accuracies of different tools. ISPRS Ann. Photogram. Remote Sens. Spat. Inf. Sci. **II-5/W1**, 67–72 (2013)

32. Zlatanova, S., Stoter, J., Isikdag, U.: Standards for exchange and storage of 3D information: challenges and opportunities for emergency response. In: Bandrova, T., Konecny, M., Zhelezov, G. (eds.) 4th International Conference on Cartography and GIS, vol. 2, pp. 17–28. Bulgarian Cartographic Association, Sofia (2012)

33. Fernie, K.: CARARE – D1.8 – Final Report, http://www.carare.eu/eng/content/download/8733/74310/file/D1_8%20Final%20Report.pdf

34. Stoter, J.: 3D Modelling in the Netherlands. Presentation Slides at Geospatial World Forum, 5 May 2012. http://www.geospatialworldforum.org/2012/gwf_PDF/Jantien.pdf

35. Harris, T.M.: Digital terrain modelling and three-dimensional surface graphics for landscape and site analysis in archaeology and regional planning. In: Ruggles, C., Rahtz, S. (eds.) CAA 87. Computer and Quantitative Methods in Archaeology 1987. BAR International Series, vol. 393, pp. 160–170. B.A.R, Oxford (1988)

36. Harris, T.M., Lock, G.R.: Multi-dimensional GIS: exploratory approaches to spatial and temporal relationships within archaeological stratigraphy. In: Kamermans, H., Fennema, K. (eds.) Interfacing the Past. Computer Applications and Quantitative Methods in Archaeology CAA95, vol. II. Analecta Praehistorica Leidensia, vol. 28, pp. 307–316. Institute of Prehistory, University of Leiden, Leiden (1996)

37. Forte, M., Pescarin, S., Pietroni, E.: The Appia Antica Project. In: Forte, M. (ed.) The Reconstruction of Archaeological Landscapes Through Digital Technologies. Proceedings of the 2nd Italy-United States Workshop. BAR International Series, vol. 1379, pp. 79–95. Archaeopress, Oxford (2005)

38. Rouse, J.: You had to be there: landscape archaeology using GIS and VR (1994). http://www.wvgis.wvu.edu/Conference2004/ppt/session4/rouse.ppt. Accessed 30 Sept 2015

39. Bennett, R., Zielinski, D.J., Kopper, R.: Comparison of interactive environments for the archaeological exploration of 3D landscape data. In: 3DVis (3DVis), IEEE International Workshop on 3DVis (3DVis), pp. 67–71. IEEE, Piscataway (2014)

40. Pescarin, S., Calori, L., Camporesi, C., Forte, M.: Interactive landscapes reconstruction: a web 2D and 3D opensource solution. In: Mudge, M., Ryan, N., Scopigno, N. (eds.) The 6th International Symposium on Virtual Reality, Archaeology and Cultural Heritage VAST Short Presentations, pp. 33–38. Ed. Star, Pisa (2005)

41. Scianna, A., Ammoscato, A.: 3D GIS data model using open source software. In: International Archives of the Photogrammery, Remote Sensing and Spatial Information Sciences. Part 4-8-2-W9, vol. 38, pp. 120–125 (2010)

42. Bittner, T., Donnelly, M., Winter, S.: Ontology and semantic interoperability. In: Prosperi, D., Zlatanova, S. (eds.) Large-Scale 3D Data Integration: Problems and Challenges, pp. 139–160. CRCpress (2005)

43. Kuroczinsky, P.: Digital reconstruction and virtual research environments – a question of documentation standards. In: Access and Understanding – Networking in the Digital Era, Proceedings of the Annual Conference of CIDOC, Dresden, Germany (2014)

44. Nebiker, S., Schütz, S., Wüst, T.: Geo-roaming: model-driven content management for web-based 3D geoinformation services. In: XXII International Cartographic Conference (ICC2005), La Coruna, Spain (2005)

45. Gröger, G., Kolbe, T.H., Nagel, C., Häfele, K.-H. (eds): OGC City Geography Markup Language (CityGML) Encoding Standard. Version 2.0.0, OGC Doc No. 12 019, Open Geospatial Consortium, published 04 April 2012, 344 p. (2012)

46. D'Andrea, A., Lorenzini, M., Milanese, M.: A novel approach to 3D documentation and description of archaeological features. In: Contreras, F., Melero, J. (eds.) CAA'2010 Fusion of Cultures – Proceedings of the 38th Conference on Computer Applications and Quantitative Methods in Archaeology (2010)

47. Prechtel, N.: On strategies and automation in upgrading 2D to 3D landscape representations. CaGIS **42**(3), 244–258 (2015)

48. Hanitzsch, J.: Konzeption, Datenhaltung und – synthese für die 3D-Präsentation der Wörlitzer Anlagen. Diploma thesis TU Dresden, Inst. f. Cartography, 115 p. (2014)

49. Stein, C., Limper, M., Kuijper, A.: Spatial data structures for accelerated 3D visibility computation to enable large model visualization on the web. In: Web3D 2014 – Proceedings of the 19th International ACM Conference on 3D Web Technologies. ACM, New York, pp. 53–61 (2014)

50. Liestøl, G.: Along the appian way. storytelling and memory across time and space in mobile augmented reality. In: Ioannides, M., Magnenat-Thalmann, N., Fink, E., Žarnić, R., Yen, A.-Y., Quak, E. (eds.) EuroMed 2014. LNCS, vol. 8740, pp. 248–257. Springer, Heidelberg (2014). doi:10.1007/978-3-319-13695-0_24

51. MayaArch3D. http://www.mayaarch3d.org/language/en/sample-page/. Accessed 30 Sept 2015

52. von Schwerin, J., Richards-Rissetto, H., Agugiaro, R.F.G.: The MayaArch3D project: a 3D WebGIS for analyzing ancient architecture and landscapes. Literary Linguist. Comput. **28**(4), 736–753 (2013). The MayaArch3D Project: A 3D WebGIS for Analyzing Ancient Architecture and Landscapes

53. Agugiaro, G., Remondino, F., Girardi, G., von Schwerin, J., Richards-Rissetto, H., de Amicis, R.: QueryArch3D: querying and visualising 3D models of a maya archaeological site in a web-based interface. Geoinf. FCE CTU **6**(2011), 10–17 (2011)

54. Pletinckx, D.: Europeana and 3D. In: ISPRS Archives vol. XXXVIII-5/W16, pp. 483–490 (2011)

55. International DOI Foundation Inc.: The DOI Handbook (2005)

56. Reilly, S., Tupelo-Schneck, R.: Digital object repository server: a component of the digital object architecture. D-Lib Mag. **16**(1/2), 8 (2010)

57. Yaneva, A.: Scaling up and down. extraction trials in architectural design. Soc. Stud. Sci. **35**, 867–894 (2005)

58. Lloyd, C.D.: Exploring Spatial Scale in Geography. Wiley, Hoboken (2014). 272 p.

59. Turner, S., Fairclough, G.: Common culture: the archaeology of landscape character in Europe. In: Hicks, D., McAtackney, L., Fairclough, G. (eds.) Envisioning Landscape: Situations and Standpoints in Archaeology and Heritage. One World Archaeology, 52, Left Coast Press, vol. 52, pp. 120–145 (2007)

60. Dubel, S., Rohlig, M., Schumann, H., Trapp, M.: 2D and 3D presentation of spatial data: a systematic review. In: 3DVis (3DVis), IEEE International Workshop on 3DVis (3DVis), pp. 11–18 (2014)

61. Mackaness, W., Reimer, A.: Generalisation in the context of schematised maps. In: Burghardt, D., Duchêne, C., Mackaness, W. (eds.) Abstracting Geographic Information in a Data Rich World, pp. 299–328. Springer, Cham (2014)

62. Landsdown, J., Schofield, S.: Expressive rendering: a review of nonphotorealistic techniques. IEEE Comput. Graph. Appl. **1995**, 29–37 (1995)

63. Sayeed, R., Howard, T.: State of the art non-photorealistic rendering (NPR) techniques. In: McDerby, M., Lever, L. (eds.) EG UK Theory and Practice of Computer Graphics, pp. 1–10 (2006)

64. Semmo, A., Trapp, M., Kyprianidis, J.E., Döllner, J.: Interactive visualization of generalized virtual 3D city models using level-of-abstraction transitions. In: Eurographics Conference on Visualization (EuroVis) 2012, Computer Graphics Forum, vol. 31, pp. 885–894 (2012)

65. Fanini, F., Ferdani, D.: A new approach from 3D modelling and scanning of archaeological data to realtime online exploration. In: Zhou, M., Romanowska, I., Wu, Z., Xu, P., Verhagen, P. (eds.) Revive the Past. Computer Applications and Quantitative Methods in Archaeology (CAA). Proceedings of the 39th International Conference, Beijing, 12–16 April 2011, pp. 107–115. Pallas Publications, Amsterdam (2011)

66. Schwan, S., Buder, J.: Virtuelle Realität und E-Learning. Portalbereich Didaktisches Design, 20 p. (2006). http://www.e-teaching.org/didaktik/gestaltung/vr/vr.pdf. Accessed 15 Sept 2015

67. Constantinidis, D.: TIME to look for a temporal GIS. In: Figueiredo, A., Velho, G.L. (eds.) The World is in Your Eyes. CAA2005. Computer Applications and Quantitative Methods in Archaeology. Proceedings of the 33rd Conference, Tomar (Portugal), March 2005, pp. 407–411 (2007)

68. Qiang, Y., Delafontaine, M., Neutens, T., Stichelbaut, B., Tré, G., De Mayer, P., van de Weghe, N.: Analysing imperfect temporal information in GIS using the triangular model. Cartograph. J. **49**, 265–280 (2012)

69. Sylaiou, S., Basiouka, S., Patias, P., Stylianidis, E.: The volunteered geographic information in archaeology. IŞPRS Ann. Photogrammetry Remote Sensing Spat. Inf. Sci. **II-5/W1**, 301–306 (2013)

70. https://3dwarehouse.sketchup.com/. Accessed 26 Sept 2015

71. Münster, S., Prechtel, N.: Beyond software. Design implications for virtual libraries and platforms for cultural heritage from practical findings. In: Ioannides, M., Magnenat-Thalmann, N., Fink, E., Žarnić, R., Yen, A.-Y., Quak, E. (eds.) EuroMed 2014. LNCS, vol. 8740, pp. 131–145. Springer, Heidelberg (2014). doi:10.1007/978-3-319-13695-0_13

72. Xu, D., Zlatanova, S.: An approach to develop 3D Geo-DBMS topological operators by re-using existing 2D operators. In: ISPRS Annals on the Photogrammery, Remote Sensing and Spatial Information Sciences II-2/W1, 8th 3DGeoInfo Conference & WGII/2 Workshop, 27 – 29 November 2013, Istanbul (Turkey), pp. 291–297 (2013)

73. Ronzino, P., Amico, N., Niccolucci, F.: Assessment and comparison of metadata schemas for architectural heritage. In: XXIII CIPA Symposium – Proceedings (2011)

74. Märker, M., Uleberg, E.: Databases on cultural heritage and their geographic visualization. Session at CAA 2013 conference. http://caa2013.org/drupal/sessions. Accessed 30 Sept 2014

Author Index

Printed in the United States
By Bookmasters